A STATE OF BLOOD

The Inside Story of
IDI AMIN

by Henry Kyemba

with a Foreword by Godfrey Lule,
former Minister of Justice and
Solicitor General of Uganda

ace books
A Division of Charter Communications Inc.
A GROSSET & DUNLAP COMPANY
1120 Avenue of the Americas
New York, New York 10036

To all Ugandans: The history of Amin's rule will be an oral one. For this book I have drawn largely on my own memories. It is no more than a beginning. The memories of all Ugandans must contribute to a deeper understanding of our country's agony. I beg all those with experiences of Amin's terror to write them down and send them to me c/o Ace Books, 1120 Avenue of the Americas, New York, N.Y. 10036.—HENRY KYEMBA.

ISBN: 0-441-78524-4

An ACE Book by arrangement
with Paddington Press, Ltd.
Designed by Richard Johnson

Cover photo by Patrick Chauvel-SYGMA
First Ace printing: August 1977
Published simultaneously in Canada.

Printed in U.S.A.

Contents

Acknowledgment

Many people have helped make this book possible—so many that I cannot name them all.

I am most deeply indebted to my family—Teresa, Elizabeth, Susan and Henry. Their courage and confidence during these very difficult days has been a great source of strength to me.

My special thanks go to John Man, who initiated this book and helped me to put it together in its present form. I will always value his friendship.

My gratitude also extends to Elspeth Purchase for her kindnesses and her editorial assistance; to the Purchase and Man families for their fortitude during an arduous month; to Peter and Alan, who encouraged me to speak out; to the *Sunday Times*, in particular Harold Evans and Russell Miller; to Sylvia Richards and Nicole Graves for all their commitment and typing help; John and Janet Marqusee of Paddington Press for their support and guidance; to Harriet McDougal of Ace Books for her professional help; and to Alan Burgess and Dorothy Schock of University College, Oxford. My thanks are also due to David Chipp, Susan Goldblatt, Helen Dunman and Rhodes House, Oxford.

Finally, I want to thank the community of Oxford. Following my escape from Uganda, Oxford provided a calm and secure haven in which I was able to write this book. It removed me from a constant sense of personal danger. Most important, it created an environment consistent with my pursuit of truth and justice.

Foreword

by Godfrey Lule

As Uganda's former Attorney General and Minister of Justice, I welcome this book by Henry Kyemba. It is the first extended, detailed, and authoritative statement revealing the true nature of Idi Amin's regime.

I have special reason to welcome it because I know, perhaps more than anybody, the humiliation of being asked to defend Amin's murderous acts before the world.

Four years ago, such a defense would not have seemed so unacceptable. Like other cabinet ministers, indeed, like the country as a whole, I at first gave Amin the benefit of the doubt. He had no formal education, we told each other, and he should be given time to learn. Perhaps he did not know what was really going on in the country, or perhaps he was not able to control it. I, like the other ministers, was prepared to forgive, and was determined to influence events. Only recently did I fully realize that I would never be able to do so.

By early 1977, there had been two reports accusing Amin of complicity in murder—one by the International Commission of Jurists in 1973, and another, in 1975, by a Commission of Inquiry in Uganda itself.

The report of the International Commission of Jurists provided detailed evidence of murder of both officials and ordinary individuals. It included a letter from the exiled Foreign Minister, Wanume Kibedi, who estimated that Amin's rule of terror had resulted in at least 100,000 dead.

The Uganda Commission of Inquiry report concluded that although there was no hard evidence indicating Amin's direct involvement in any one murder, there was evidence in plenty showing that his various terror units had killed wantonly. It strongly implied, therefore, that Amin would be directly responsible for any future killings.

This Commission had been set up as a whitewash operation on Amin's orders, but Amin had not bothered to check the brief that defines their powers; hence their unexpectedly tough findings. As soon as I told him what was in it, he suppressed it.

In February 1977, the UN Human Rights Commission was due to meet in Geneva. As part of their agenda, discussed in private session, they heard the evidence submitted by the Uganda Commission of Inquiry. Amin called me in and ordered me to defend him against any charges. "You go and deny everything," he said. "Say you don't know anything about the accusations." I could not, of course, make such a statement. I would not have been taken seriously. Instead I told the UN Commission that more time should be given for consideration of the report's allegations. This action was a great embarrassment to me; I avoided the press assiduously; I did not know how I could continue to serve Amin.

While I was in Geneva, I had two horrifying telephone conversations with Amin which clinched my decision to flee.

He called first to tell me of the deaths of Archbishop Janan Luwuum and two Cabinet ministers, Erinayo Oryema and Charles Oboth-Ofumbi. He said they had been arrested and killed "in a motor accident." I knew this could not be true; it was too ridiculous.

Then he laughed, smugly and conspiratorially, and said, "God has punished them."

In a second conversation, I mentioned to him that I understood I had been implicated in the "plot" with the archbishop. I told him this was nonsense. He agreed, and then said that he had seen another report accusing me of disloyalty, but had not believed it: "If I really thought you were plotting against me," he said, "you would not be in Geneva now; you would be dead."

He obviously made this assertion of faith in my loyalty to win my confidence. Not surprisingly, it only served to show me that if I returned I would be at the mercy of his arbitrary judgments. I feel sure I would never had gotten out of the Entebbe Airport lounge as a free man.

That was the turning point. I left a message with my family to leave Uganda; I flew to London and there, joined later by my family, retired into private life.

To my mind, those two phone calls came from a very evil man.

Henry Kyemba's book is most important because it reveals the full story of Amin's regime and personality. It is vital that the world understand clearly the true nature of the man who rules Uganda. For too long Amin has been considered a clown. Indeed, he is a clown, when he chooses. Face to face, he is relaxed, simple and charming—he seems incapable of wrongdoing or of sanctioning any crime. But this is no more than a façade. He is at heart a manipulator—charm and generosity are his two greatest weapons. He will say anything to win the affection of the person he is with—but thinks nothing of saying exactly the opposite to his next visitor. He kills rationally and coolly.

The system Amin has built up reflects his own background and peculiar talents. He comes from the far northwestern part of Uganda. He is a member of the Kakwa tribe, which is based only in part in Uganda. There are Kakwa in far larger numbers in Zaire and in Southern Sudan. The basis of his power lies with the Southern Sudanese, who are recruited in large numbers to staff his police force and army. Many of these Southern Sudanese have lived in Uganda itself for several generations, forming a community known as Nubians.

The Nubians and the newly recruited Sudanese have no interest in Uganda's people or the future of the country. They owe personal loyalty only to Amin, a loyalty bought with imported luxury goods and the loot of their victims. They exercise a foreign tyranny more vicious than anything dreamed of by European imperialists or modern white minority governments in Africa. The system is, in the long term, self-defeating.

Eventually, there will be no more money to finance imports. The weapons and the vehicles will no longer be available, and, most important of all, the luxury goods that keep Amin's troops loyal will vanish.

Idi Amin's regime must end. It must be toppled as soon as possible. The decision is in large measure in the hands of other nations. As Henry Kyemba shows, Amin is largely supported by trade with foreign powers. This trade must be cut off.

It may be argued that to take such a drastic step would be to work against the interests of Uganda's trading partners and would injure the people of Uganda without harming the government. Neither of these arguments holds water.

To serve their economic interests best, Uganda's trading partners should ensure that Uganda's long-term economy is viable and that the trade is as varied and profitable as possible. It is thus in their own interests, as well as those of Uganda, that Uganda be allowed to develop its economy to its full potential. This will never happen under Amin.

Those who believe that to cut off trade will injure Uganda's population should understand that the people never receive the benefit of aid or imported goods. Incoming wealth of any kind never gets past the grasp of Amin's friends. The people of Uganda could not possibly be further injured by economic sanctions. They are living already at subsistence level. They can best be helped by a rapid end to Amin's rule.

Until recently, I, like Henry Kyemba, believed that Uganda's problems could and should be solved by Ugandans. Now, however, we see that—as in the case of Hilter—the issue has become an international one. Like the Nazis, Amin and his thugs have committed crimes against humanity, and continue to do so. There should be concerted international action against Amin. This book will aid that cause, and thus the cause of justice and humanity in Uganda.

A Dedication
In Memory of One Hundred Friends

*Below are the names of one hundred of the 150,000
who have died at Amin's hands. All I knew
personally. Most were prominent people. Each
represents the center of spreading, overlapping waves
of death and violence. This is the social and emotional
impact of Amin's rule: imagine my grief, and multiply
it by eleven million.*

R. L. Kisajja, *my brother, Personnel manager, Nyanza
   Textile Industries.*
Benedicto Kiwanuka, *The Chief Justice and former
   Prime Minister.*
Archbishop Janan Luwuum, *Anglican Church of Uganda.*
Lt. Col. Erinayo Oryema, *Minister of Land and
   Water Resources.*
Charles Oboth-Ofumbi, *Minister of Internal Affairs.*
Lt. Col. Michael Ondoga, *Minister of Foreign Affairs.*
Mr. Yekosfati Engur, *Minister of Culture and
   Community Development.*
Haji Shaban Nkutu, *Former Minister of Works.*
William Kalema, *Former Minister of Commerce.*
Basil Bataringaya, *Former Minister of Internal Affairs.*
Mrs. Edith Bataringaya
John Kakonge, *Former Minister of Agriculture.*
Joshua Wakholi, *Former Minister of Public Service.*
Alex Ojera, *Former Minister of Information.*
Haji Ali Kisekka, *Former Deputy Minister for the
   East African Community.*
James Ochola, *Former Minister of Local Government.*
Mr. Frank Kalimuzo, *Vice Chancellor of Makerere
   University.*
Mr. Joseph Mubiru, *Governor of the Central Bank.*
Professor V. Emiru, *eye consultant, Mulago Hospital.*

9

Mrs. Dora Bloch, British-Israeli hostage.

Brig. Charles Arube, *Chief of Staff.*

Brig. Hussein, *Second in Command, Ugandan Army.*

Brig. Smuts Guweddeko, *Air Force Commander.*

Lt. Col. Langoya, *School of Infantry, Jinja.*

Lt. Col. Ochima, *A.D.C. to Amin.*

Lt. Col Kakuhikire, *Army headquarters.*

Lt. Col. Ekiring, *Ugandan Army.*

Captain Avudria, *Ugandan Army.*

Captain Aswa, *Ugandan Army*

Captain Wolukusanga, *Ugandan Army.*

Captain Kayongo, *Ugandan Army (killed John Kakonge and was then killed himself in 1977.)*

Joseph Kiwanuka, *Long-time politician.*

Mr. Waisi, *Bugisu Coffee Union.*

Mr. Simbwa, *Engineer, Lugazi Sugar Works.*

Miss Nanziri, *Lecturer at Makerere University.*

Henry Kagoda, *Commissioner of Veterinary Services.*

Father Clement Kigundu, *Editor of Munno.*

Mohamed Hassan, *Head of Police, C.I.D. (Moslem).*

F. Wawuyo, *Deputy Head of Police, C.I.D.*

Father Mukasa (priest), *Masaka.*

Francis Walugembe, *Mayor and businessman of Masaka.*

George Kamba, *Ambassador to India and West Germany.*

Mr. Justice Michael Kagwa, *President, Industrial Court.*

Paul Bitature, *Businessman of Mbarara and former official of the East African Community.*

Dr. George Ebine, *Mulago Hospital.*

Dr. Sembeguya, *general practitioner, Kawempe.*

Ahmed Oduka, *Director of the Police Band.*

H. Kasigwa, *Town Treasurer, Jinja.*

Martin Okello, *M.P.*

Martin Rubanga, *Secretary for Defense.*

James Buwembo, *Pharmacist.*

Baron Kawaddwa, *Director of National Theater.*

Godfrey Kiggala, *Ministry of Foreign Affairs.*

Leonard Kigonya, *Commissioner of Prisons.*

Jimmy Parma, *photographer.*

K. Kasadha, *Makerere University.*

Mr. Kigundu, *businessman, Kampala.*

Mrs. Kay Amin, *wife of President Amin.*

Mr. Ogwal, *Nyanza Textiles.*

Mr. Sekitoleko, *businessman, Masaka.*

Haji Balunywa, *Administrative Secretary, Busoga.*

N.K. Banañuka, *Secretary General, Ankole.*

Mr. Sebanakitta, *old Buganda chief.*

Bulasio Kavuma, *old Buganda statesman.*

Dr. Edward Kizito, *dentist.*

D. Lubega, *Manager at the Nile Mansion.*

Mr. Nshekanabo, *Manager, Rock Hotel, Tororo.*

James Bwogi, *Ugandan television Personality.*

Augustine Kamya, *Kampala businessman.*

E.R.K. Mawagi, *Lawyer.*

M. Omuge, *Director of Ugandan television.*

Mr. Nakibinge, *former Mayor of Kampala.*

Mr. Ruhesi, *Town Engineer, Jinja.*

Samson Ddungu, *Ugandan Guide Post.*

Henry Berunga, *Director, East African Railways.*

Mr. Ocungi, *Police, C.I.D.*

Mr. Mulekezi, *District Commissioner, Bukedi.*

Patrick Ruhinda, *Barrister.*

Peter Oketta, *Assistant Commissioner of Prisons.*

Lt. Col. Toloko, *Ugandan Army, once in charge of
    killings at Tororo and Fort Portal.*

Albert Erikodi Masurubu, *State House driver.*

David Ocaya, *Secretary, Lint Marketing Board.*

J. Okech-Omara, *East African Railways employee.*

A. Owuor, *East African Railways employee.*

Mr. Tomusange, *East African Railways employee.*

Mrs. Ogwang, *businesswoman, Jinja.*

Stephen Epunau, *Barclays Bank, Kabale.*

Kaman Gitau, *Kenyan businessman.*

Miss Chesire, *Kenyan sudent at Makerere University.*

John Tidhamulala, *National Insurance Corp. Secretary.*

Anil Clerk, *Ugandan lawyer.*

Capt. Ausi, *Ugandan Army.*

Capt. Azo, *Ugandan Army.*

Mr. Wafula, *Senior Police officer.*

Major Ogwal, *Ugandan Army.*

Mr. Masembe, *Brooke Bond (OXO).*

Natolo Masaba, *Mbale politician.*

Mr. Okurut, *Lawyer in Soroti.*

Abdu Kato, *Engineer Uganda Hotels.*

Lt. Col. Abwola, *Ugandan Army.*

Prologue: Decision

I have been an insider in Ugandan affairs since 1962 and a Cabinet minister for five years. From a place of hope and optimism, a place where life was good and comfortable, I have seen Uganda collapse into near civil war, increasing chaos and finally a state of blood and random slaughter.

Since becoming one of Amin's senior officials in 1971, when he seized power, I have worked intimately with the man who gradually revealed himself to be Africa's most ruthless killer. My friends were killed—even my brother. I saw corpses by the hundred. I heard of horrendous massacres. I experienced the death throes of a whole nation as it spiraled down toward mere subsistence, its population cowed by thugs who were bribed with luxury goods and easy money to kill on Amin's orders.

I had, by 1976, considered escape many times, but I had always postponed a decision. I thought I had Amin's confidence and I did not fear for myself. Defection would make no real difference to the regime—or so I told myself. Besides, it was a minority regime, and ludicrously inefficient. It never seemed anything but temporary.

But in late 1976, I began to feel my time was running out. Two disquieting incidents, which seemed like omens, further undermined my dwindling confidence. A friend called me late at night from a remote part of the country to find out if I was still alive. Then even more touching and disquieting, in January 1977, I received a note, hastily written in an uneducated hand, that ran as follows:

Dear Sir, i have felt that i must warn you.
Recently as i was having dinner in the Speke
Hotel i over-heard two men, dressed quiet
smartly saying that Kyemba was next on the
list, on what list exactly i don't know.
Sir i felt it was my duty to warn you They
entered a car UVS 335 or (336) i couldn't really
see it.
So you may take this warning, and again you
may not, one of the men was mixing lusoga and
swahili They also said 'I hear Kyemba is
causing chaos for men,' The other one said, 'Is
that why they want him' that is all i managed to
hear

> *your faithfully*
> (signature deleted)

I knew from the registration letters that the car belonged to Amin's bodyguards, the notorious killers of the State Research Bureau.

But the real turning point for me came on February 16, 1977, with the arrest and martyrdom of the Anglican archbishop, Janan Luwuum, a man I respected for his bravery and honesty. Slaughtered with him were two Cabinet ministers whom I had known personally for many years, and who were good friends of Amin. I now knew that however friendly the President seemed I would never be safe.

I also had another of those ominous warnings. On February 22, an old man stopped me in the street and said, like some ancient prophet, "Beware, my son—you are the last one." He meant that I was the longest surviving member of Amin's government.

After these murders, I realized I had no choice. To

survive I had to flee. Moreover, I had a duty to leave. My experiences would allow me to speak with unique authority. I determined to tell the truth, as far as I knew it, about Amin's reign of terror. If I did not, Amin would continue to hide his brutalities behind any cause and any slogan that suited his purposes.

For too long the world has laughed Amin off, for too long the world has excused him. Too many exiles have been frightened into silence by the fear that he would wreak terrible revenge on friends and relatives remaining behind. I knew that by speaking out I would risk more lives, but I also knew that my silence would guarantee nobody's safety.

To end the injustice, the world has to be told the truth of how Amin came to power, the nature of his rule, his random viciousness, his wild unpredictability, his talent (for it is a talent) for manipulating colleagues into compliance. Someone has to speak out.

1
Roots of Evil

TO AN OUTSIDER, Amin's regime seems inexplicable. How could such a man gain and hold power? Although future historians will have the final say, I believe that the answer lies in Uganda's immediate past and the course of events that offered Amin opportunities to assert his remarkable personality. It is not a personality to be underrated. True, he is nearly illiterate; he is politically naïve; he is violently unpredictable; he is utterly ruthless. Yet he is also jovial and generous; and he has extraordinary talents—for practical short-term action, for turning apparent weaknesses to his own advantage, and for asserting his leadership among his gang of thugs. This maverick personality, its brutalities largely hidden in the early years, emerged with the erosion of democracy that has marked Uganda from Independence in 1962 to the present day.

Although my influence on Ugandan affairs was largely indirect—even as a Cabinet minister, I was a civilian in a system dominated by military men—I have, by chance, been an insider all my life. I was born with the tradition of government behind me. From my teens, I was familiar with the principal characters in the drama that has been played out over the years. I survived to serve longer than any other minister, and was able to escape, largely because I expressed little political ambition, and because I was able to maintain an outward detachment that never threatened Amin. What happened, and why it happened the way it did, forms a story in which public events and personal experiences have often been inextricably interwined.

I come from Bunya county of the Busoga tribal area in southeast Uganda, just north of Lake Victoria, not far from the source of the Nile. My grandfather and father were chiefs of our area, which, a hundred years ago, was one among many small, self-contained, independent fiefdoms that lay in the Central African highlands.

From some thirty of these tribal areas, the British forged Uganda in the late nineteenth century. Britain, the greatest imperial power, had a particular interest in Uganda, because the region controlled the source of the Nile, which controlled Egypt, which controlled the Suez Canal, which controlled the most direct route to India, the jewel in Britain's imperial crown. Because Uganda was important to the British for its own reasons, the borders were set without much thought for the people involved. Thus the borders did not coincide with tribal territories, which overlap neighboring Zaire, Sudan, Kenya, Tanzania and Rwanda.

Within the new Uganda, there were four long-established kingdoms: Buganda (the most powerful), Bunyoro, Ankole and Toro. Each had its king. The best-known king was the Kabaka of the dominant power, Buganda. In fact, it is from the root syllables of Buganda that Uganda takes its name. The four kingdoms dominated the southern, most fertile part of Uganda. The south also had a number of smaller tribes, including the Bakiga, Bagisu, Bakedi, and my own—the Basoga. Ethnically and linguistically, the southern tribes were all predominantly Bantu—the same stock as tribes like the Zulus to the south. To the north, in the sparser, more open countryside that fringes southern Sudan and northern Kenya, was a looser collection of mainly Nilotic tribes whose languages belonged chiefly to the Luo group. Although today the official language is English, there are still almost as many languages as tribes.

Uganda Radio used to broadcast news in twenty-four different languages. In one eastern area, Bukedi, there are fourteen small tribes, speaking several different languages.

When the British arrived in the late nineteenth century, they found that the southern areas, with their well-established social systems, were relatively easy to administer. These areas became provinces of the Empire, and their kings became in effect provincial governors. As long as they ruled in peace with the aid of British administrators, they were left largely alone. The Kabaka of Buganda remained in some ways a king among kings.

The more diverse and scattered northern tribes presented problems. Some, like the Kakwa, Amin's tribe, which spanned what is now the Uganda-Zaire border, were no more than village communities; some—like the Acholi and Langi—occupied much larger regions; some—like the Karamojong and Turkana of the northeast—roamed immense areas and have never taken to the idea of formal administration. They still pose problems for centralized government.

Throughout this diverse, fertile and beautiful area—Churchill called it the "Pearl of Africa"—there existed rivalries that have affected much of Uganda's recent history. For instance, the southern kingdoms of Bunyoro and Buganda were traditional enemies, and the northern Nilotic tribes were—and still are—suspicious of the more highly organized, better-educated Bantus.

When the Europeans came, three other elements were added to Ugandan society. One was European religion. The British brought their Anglicanism, and the French their Catholicism. These were more than a match for the Moslem faith brought by the Arab slave traders in the early nineteenth century. Today, only ten per cent of the population is Moslem, and the rest are about half-and-half Anglican and Catholic. The Europeans also established Christian schools. Since the Moslems did not do this, Islam soon came to be equated with a lack of education.

The British were also responsible for the introduction of Uganda's Asians. The Asians were originally brought to build the Kenya-Uganda railway, which was supposed to carry troops to protect the source of the Nile against the imperial ambitions of the French, Belgians and Germans. Long before it was finished in 1901, however, such strategic justifications seemed foolish—the railway was nicknamed the "Lunatic Line" by British MP's appalled at its soaring cost. The line never carried troops, but it did enable the Asians to develop trade; they became the middle class of Uganda, and indeed of all British East Africa.

A third element, and one of particularly tragic significance for Uganda today, was the community of Southern Sudanese brought in as mercenaries by the British to staff the lower ranks of the army and the police. In Uganda, indeed throughout East Africa, they became known as Nubians. They have retained their own identity, like the Asians. They are wholly Moslem, and still speak their own version of Arabic.

I was born in December 1939. My father's name was Suleiman Kisajja; his surname was handed on to only one of my brothers. (Until recently, children did not automatically inherit surnames from their father. None of my brothers or sisters are called Kyemba, although—in response to European practice and the dictates of modern bureaucracy—my children are.) Soon after I was born, my father, who was not a chief in the old sense, but more an established member of the Imperial civil service, was transferred to another part of Busoga, our tribal area.

I was my mother's seventh son; I also had four half-sisters, children of my father's second wife.

To Europeans and Americans, the idea of having several wives seems strange. There is such a vast cultural gulf between Africans and western nations that the practice is often condemned out of hand by westerners (as we condemn the western custom of extramarital affairs). But in Uganda—indeed in many parts of Africa—the system is long established, and still works well. In fact, I myself have two wives. Formerly, as in many warrior societies, there was usually an excess of women over men. Polygamy allowed—and still allows—single women to be readily absorbed into family life.

Moreover, large families, which confer status on the men, have always been regarded as a blessing. Uganda is on the equator, but it is also high—at an average of 5,000 feet above sea level—and never oppressively hot. The land is fertile and extra children cost nothing to feed.

Jealousy was—and is—seldom a serious problem. It is a foolish husband who allows his emotions to make a favorite of one wife. Marital sex is arranged on a rota system, as are the household duties. A senior wife often asks for a junior wife to help with the house and the children.

Traditionally, a man had to pay a price for his brides. In some areas, a bride costs a hundred head of cattle. In others—in Karamoja, for example—the price could be many times more. This encouraged cattle raiding, which led to local warfare and the loss of many lives.

Before 1971, the economic realities of living in an increasingly consumer-oriented, urbanized society tended to undermine these practices, although they were still quite common. Since 1971, however, more men have been killed than in the worst tribal wars, and the system has again become vital for some tribes. But there are already signs that the social strain imposed by Amin's slaughter is too great. Among the Acholi and Langi, for example, so many young men have been killed that for the first time ever there are single women without any social framework to support them.

I grew up mostly in government houses—colonial-style bungalows with a verandah and a surrounding hedge or fence. I soon became familiar with the business of government. My father had all the wide-ranging duties of a colonial officer of the time. He was a magistrate, tax administrator, agricultural adviser and community welfare officer.

My father was stern but loving. He used most of his salary to pay for our education. The family had no car when we were young—we all walked the mile or two to school, and he rode a bicycle until we were in secondary school. Although my elder brother and I were the only two to go to university, all the boys were educated well enough to make good careers.

While I was in primary school, I spent one year in Busesa where the local headmaster was Mr. Kibedi, Amin's future father-in-law and father of the future Foreign Minister (who has since fled). Then I went to Busoga College at Mwiri, where the first Prime Minister of independent Uganda, Milton Obote, was also at school.

Obote was several years senior to me and I had no contact with him, but I knew him by reputation as a Langi, one of the many different tribes brought together by the British headmaster, Reverend F. G. Coates. Busoga College was to become a breeding ground for nationalist attitudes that transcended tribal loyalties. In later years, students used to boast when they left, "I come from a nationalistic school."

It was also at this time in my life that I first met Idi Amin. My elder brother Kisajja and Amin were in love with two sisters, Mary and Malyamu, the daughters of my old headmaster, Mr. Kibedi. Malyamu was later to become Amin's senior wife, and my brother was to have a son by Mary, Mrs. Amin's sister. In Ugandan terms, therefore, I am of the same family as Amin.

I met Amin a number of times while attending Busoga College. The first meeting I remember well. One of my brothers was running a shop next to my old school; there Amin was introduced to me as the prospective son-in-law of the headmaster. It was a very casual visit, but I remember being very struck by his size—6'4"—large even for a soldier. He was only a sergeant in the King's African Rifles at the time, but he had already earned notoriety as Uganda's heavyweight boxing champion, a title he was to hold for nine years. He was a good solider, renowned, as I later learned, for his willingness and smartness—"a tremendous chap to have around," in the words of one British officer. So enthusiastic were his superiors that they turned a blind eye to his inability to speak much English. He was to rise rapidly through the ranks.

I saw little of him after that. The troops were well disciplined and seen very rarely. Uganda was a quiet and peaceful place then—you saw soldiers in the town only in groups of twos and threes or on ceremonial occasions.

In 1957 I went to Makerere University on the outskirts of Kampala to study history. Obote had been there before me and had by now established a wider reputation for his involvement in the major issues of the day—the coming of independence and the status of the Kabaka of Buganda, Mutesa II, better known as King Freddy. The Kabaka had been banished by the British colonial government for advocating greater autonomy for Buganda. By 1957 he was back, and we all knew that independence was not far off.

I was at the university at the time of the elections for the Independence Parliament, in April 1962. I was not much involved in the elections although I was very much aware of what was going on. One of my brothers had joined the Democratic Party and later served briefly as a minister, and I had other friends and relatives who were active in politics. But I was set on joining the civil service; so, despite a sympathy for Obote's Uganda People's Congress, I remained relatively neutral. I was, however, pleased that Obote became Prime Minister.

Immediately after the elections, I joined the civil service as an Administrative Officer. I was asked where I wanted to be posted. I requested Kigezi on the Rwanda border, or Fort Portal in the Toro district, on the Zaire border. I chose these two because the climate and the countryside are beautiful, and because they are relatively remote. In either place, I would have an opportunity to start life in a completely new environment, away from my own relatives.

But Peter Allen, the head of the civil service, had his own ideas about me. He decided to post me to the Prime Minister's office as assistant secretary. It was an unexpected appointment and I was delighted. When I started work in the Prime Minister's office, I found myself in charge of ceremony and protocol, one of a dozen or so bureaucrats deeply involved in the arrangements for independence.

It was at this time that I once again heard of Amin, though not by name. Ugandan troops had been sent to the northern part of Karamoja on one of their regular trips to clamp down on cattle raiding among the Karamojong and Turkana. Many lives had been lost in squabbles as tribesmen sought to enrich themselves at the expense of others. The information received in the Prime Minister's office was that a lieutenant had massacred a number of people in his search for arms. The British were considering prosecuting him. But because independence was near, it would have been politically unwise to take legal action against a black officer. (There were only two; the other was Amin's future commander, Shaban Opolot.) The decision was referred to Obote. He decided not to prosecute. I later learned that the officer involved was Idi Amin.

On October 9, 1962, Uganda became independent, with Obote as Prime Minister, supported temporarily by the powerful Kabaka of Buganda, who became President in the following year. Six months after independence, in May 1963 the Organization for African Unity was founded. I traveled to Addis Ababa as a member of the expert committee set up to establish the organization's headquarters, and also attended the OAU Defense Commission in Accra in Ghana, in October 1963.

After my return from Accra, Obote appointed me his

private secretary. He did so, I think because I was a graduate of Busoga College, and because I was always around trying to make things work as they should at state functions and receptions. Besides, he had never had a good private secretary; he had tried out two of his own tribesmen who were not part of the civil service hierarchy, and both had ended up in prison for embezzlement. It was a demanding job; to perform it properly, I had to take as my residence a house within the compound of the Presidential Lodge.

The most immediate problem facing independent Uganda was the issue of the "lost counties" which had once belonged to Bunyoro and were now part of Buganda. In the 1890s, the British had, with the assistance of the Kabaka of Buganda, fought and beaten Bunyoro, and the British had awarded the Kabaka a chunk of Bunyoro for his efforts. The Banyoro (people of Bunyoro) had always resented this. The British, conveniently for them, left the problem for the new regime to solve. The Independence Constitution called for a referendum to be held within two years so that the inhabitants of the "lost counties" could decide for themselves which area they wished to belong to. The current Kabaka, of course, had little interest in holding the referendum, for the Banyoro in the "lost counties" would undoubtedly vote to be governed by their own people rather than the Baganda. But Obote insisted on the referendum, which was held in 1964. The Kabaka duly lost the counties to Bunyoro, and the tenuous alliance between Obote and the Kabaka collapsed, a split between Prime Minister and President that eventually led to the end of democratic rule in Uganda.

Meanwhile, Amin had not been politically active, but he had begun to make a national impact in other ways. Throughout this period, the Belgian Congo—now Zaire—was in the turmoil of civil war. One aspect of the war, just coming to an end after six years, had peculiar significance for Uganda and Amin. Rebels to whom

Obote was sympathetic were still fighting the new government of Moise Tshombe and Mobutu Sese Seko, Chief of Staff and future President. Mobutu's troops were pressing the rebels hard towards the Ugandan border. Obote wished to aid the rebels to the utmost, and assigned Amin, now Deputy Commander of the Uganda Army, personal responsibility to assist them in and around Amin's own home area of Arua. Obote established a direct link with Amin, bypassing the Army Commander, Brigadier Shaban Opolot. He did this first because he wished Amin's activities to remain as secret as possible, and second because he regarded Opolot as a potential ally of Obote's old rival, the Kabaka.

I was closely involved with this operation. Obote and I had a personal radio link with Amin. Ours was code-named "Sparrow"; Amin's was "Kisu." The rebels often came to Entebbe, stayed in Amin's house, and saw Obote. Their greatest need was for arms and transport. They had no cash, but they did have truckloads of gold and ivory, seized as they retreated from towns they had once controlled. Amin, as the rebel's contact man, sold their gold and ivory and bought arms for them.

This was a considerable operation which revealed for the first time Amin's chief characteristics. To me, he was always charming and easy to work with, but he also displayed a ruthless practicality, individuality and enterprise. For the first time I saw the effects of his particular intelligence which enabled him to snatch any advantage unconsciously offered and turn it to his own benefit.

In Amin's dealings with the Congolese gold and ivory, no records were ever kept. The goods came by truck to his house. He did not have to account for what he sold. He simply began to bank for himself very large sums, regularly and in cash—up to 300,000 shillings at a time—amounting to something like a million dollars in all. He also kept large amounts in his house to avoid undue publicity. (A few days before my wedding in 1965, he pulled about 2,000 shillings from his pocket and gave it to me as a wedding present.)

News of his sudden wealth began to leak out. His account at the Ottoman Bank was photocopied and handed out in Parliament by an MP, Daudi Ocheng, who demanded an inquiry. A debate followed, and the inquiry was authorized. Soon afterward, however, Obote seized control of the government, arrested five ministers, four of whom supported the charges against Amin, suspended the Constitution, fired the Kabaka and assumed his title of President. The inquiry would clearly have embarrassed Obote. He persuaded some of the Congolese rebels, who were in exile in Uganda, to speak on Amin's behalf and exonerate him.

For the second time, Obote had saved the man who was eventually to overthrow him. He did so because, at the time, Amin seemed indispensable. He was needed for the showdown that was clearly at hand between the Kabaka and Obote. Amin was still only deputy commander, but Opolot had by this time married a member of the Buganda royal family, and Obote would never trust him again. Amin was therefore the President's only hope.

On May 22, 1966, Obote arrested some of the chief supporters of the Kabaka. As news of the arrests spread, government cars were stoned and the Kabaka's people threw up barricades on the roads leading into the capital from the Kabaka's palace just outside Kampala. Unless action was taken rapidly, Buganda would declare itself independent, and the government would be faced with the embarrassment of being told to get out of its own capital.

The same day, Obote called a meeting in the President's Lodge in Kampala. The meeting was attended by Obote, the Inspector General of Police, the Chief General Service Officer, the Minister of Internal Affairs, the Minister of Defense, and myself. After some discussion, Obote told us that the disturbance was no longer a civil matter but a military one. He would ask Amin to move in on the palace, which stood just three miles outside Kampala.

Unknown to us, Obote had already tipped off Amin. He now telephoned him and asked him to come to the President's Lodge immediately. Amin arrived soon afterwards in uniform and received verbal instructions to attack the palace the following morning, and to arrest the Kabaka. Meanwhile, the Kabaka's supporters, eager to ensure his protection, had poured into the palace compound, which was built like a fortified village. It had six-foot walls, and contained several office buildings, a school, and various residences (and even later, an airstrip).

Very early the next morning, Amin's troops attacked. The Kabaka must have been warned, for his supporters had arms and put up an unexpected resistance for several hours. At 3:30 P.M., Amin went to the President's Lodge in his open jeep, with its six-foot-long 122-mm gun, to report to Obote and to ask for permission to shell the Kabaka's main residence. He was in a jolly mood and obviously enjoying the fight. Permission was granted. He jumped into his jeep and drove off.

Within a few minutes, there were two large explosions. Shells punched holes in the Kabaka's main official residence. Smoke billowed up. Then, as if this was a signal to the heavens, it began to rain, torrentially. The fighting stopped. After the storm, the troops moved in quickly to find the Kabaka. At about 5:30, Amin, jovial as ever, came back to the Lodge bearing his trophies: the Kabaka's Presidential flag and the ceremonial cap that marked him as Commander in Chief of the Uganda Army. He did not know, he said, whether the Kabaka had been killed or had escaped. The Kabaka had in fact seized his opportunity during the storm and had escaped through a side entrance into one of the nearby houses. From there he eventually made his escape to Burundi and then to Britain, where he died three years later.

The Kabaka later claimed that thousands had died in

the assault; the official toll, based on Amin's own figures, was put at forty-seven; it was in fact much higher—certainly several hundred, perhaps as high as four hundred.

For several days afterward, Amin's troops looted the palace. I visited it while the looting was still in progress, and the dead were still being unearthed from the ruins. The Kabaka's other palaces, at Bamunanika and Masaka, were also ransacked.

Amin was now Obote's undisputed favorite. Obote had little civilian political support left and would have to rely heavily on the army, which was a significant political force in its own right, supplied and trained as it was largely by Israel and Britain. It seemed safe to trust Amin. He was, after all, nearly illiterate and showed no signs of political ambition. Indeed, Obote foresaw a danger, not from Amin, but from some of the younger officers who had been trained by the British and Israelis. Obote believed that Amin would act as a first line of defense against their ambitions.

Amin, now promoted to Army Commander, became Obote's principal means of preventing further unrest. I remember the many route marches ordered by Obote. I would often phone Amin with instructions to take a trip through one or another corner of Buganda. These route marches, commonly described as "map reading exercises," were really missions to cow the populace in areas where Obote feared there might be opposition.

In the space of just a few months, Uganda had gone from a peaceful democracy to something very close to a military dictatorship. With the Kabaka gone, and the Baganda quelled by force, there was no possibility of a lasting, working, parliamentary majority for Obote. Hundreds of prominent citizens were imprisoned without trial (including the former Army Commander, Shaban Opolot). Regular lists of political detainees—often up to eighty names at a time—were published, as demanded by law, in the weekly *Uganda Gazette*. Obote, backed by his security forces, ruled supreme. It is ironic that the system later developed by Amin, an illiterate killer who strikes at random, was inherited half-formed from a man raised in the best democratic traditions.

Amin's preeminence at this time allowed him to forge another link in the chain with which he was later to fetter the country. In his support of the Congolese rebels, Amin had recruited many Nubians and Southern Sudanese, who were themselves in revolt against their government. He recruited them initially because they were people he could trust and because they came from the area where the operations were taking place—along the north-western border of Uganda. They therefore had an interest in fighting there. But Amin and the Southern Sudanese had other mutual interests. Amin was supporting them in their long civil war against the Sudanese government. They, in their turn, provided Amin with an immediate ready-made corps which was steadily absorbed into many Uganda Army units. Amin even placed some of these men in the General Service Unit, the Secret Service institution close to President Obote. There they provided vital information to Amin. Their careers in the army depended on Amin alone. They owed him a personal loyalty, and felt no loyalty whatsoever to Obote.

For three years, Amin remained indispensable. At the same time—as Obote himself saw—he posed a steadily growing threat. Their nascent rivalry erupted into open enmity in December 1969.

On December 19, of that year, Obote attended an evening meeting of the Uganda People's Congress in a Kampala hall. After the meeting, Obote and I led the way out of the hall into the night air. Obote was slightly ahead of me to my right. A crowd followed behind, clapping and cheering in the happy mood that accompanies a suc-cessful meeting. As we came within ten feet or so of a tree on our right, a shot was fired. The would-be assassin had positioned himself behind the tree, presumably leaning over a lower branch to support his pistol. Immediately we all threw ourselves to the ground, knowing it could only have been directed at us. At the same time, a grenade rolled out beside us. I was lying next to Obote. After perhaps five seconds, I realized that he had been hit. The bodyguards lifted him from the ground, seemingly lifeless, carried him to his car and drove off. The grenade had failed to explode. I hardly even registered my good fortune.

I ran to the Vice President's car and shouted to the driver to follow the President to the hospital. It was only when I got there that I realized that I too had been hit. The bullet had just grazed my neck; blood was staining my shirt.

The President had had an extraordinarily lucky escape. He had been turning back and forth to see the people cheering and clapping on either side of him. This—as well as the bad light—must have spoiled the assassin's aim. The bullet missed Obote's brain by a few inches, entering his jaw. It tore through one lip, took out two teeth in his right lower jaw, emerged through his open mouth and finally nicked me in the neck. My wound was slight, but I had been badly shaken and was kept in the hospital overnight. The President was out of the hospital within a week.

The attempt marked a turning point. Amin, who for some reason was not at the meeting, was immediately suspected. Soldiers ran to his residence, which was only a quarter of a mile from the scene of the incident. When they arrived, Amin simply fled without waiting to hear why they had come. In his haste, he did not even stop to put on his shoes. He scrambled over a barbed wire fence, badly tearing his feet in the process. He stopped a passing car and hitched a lift to Bombo, a place twenty miles away, predominantly occupied by a Nubian community, and a strong base for him today. From there, he phoned some junior officers to find out what was going on. It was several hours before he was traced by senior officers. Then, on the telephone, he said that he thought that the soldiers had come to assassinate him. He was persuaded to come back to the capital and an army vehicle was sent to fetch him.

A month later, at a meeting of senior officers, Amin's No. 2, Brigadier Pierino Okoya, an Acholi, quarrelled violently with Amin on the subject of army discipline as it related to Amin's behavior after the attempted assassination. Among other things, Okoya accused Amin of desertion. A few days afterward, on January 25, 1970, the brigadier and his wife were shot dead at close range in the brigadier's home town of Gulu. Amin was again suspected, and inquiries were started.

For several months no evidence was found against him. He was in a position to block investigations that seemed to pose a threat. Every time the police began to question people in the army, where their investigations usually led, Amin knew of their activities and frustrated them. He would say that the men required for questioning were not available, or he would send them on holiday, or tie them up with other duties, or post them to other units.

In June 1970, there was another attempt on Obote's life. We were on our way to Entebbe, via Kampala, from Luzira Prison Officers' Mess at about 8:30 in the evening. We were in a Daimler. Obote was sitting in the back with a cousin. I was sitting in the middle row on one of the folding seats, facing inward, my back to the window, talking to the two of them. We had a police car to lead us. Normally it drove along with its roof light flashing. Not wishing to draw attention to the President's car, I instructed the police, just before we left, to switch off their light. We arrived in Kampala without incident.

But following us into Kampala, about a mile behind, was the Vice President, John Babiiha, in a convoy similar to ours, and also with a police escort. He had allowed his police to keep their light flashing. When he got to a point opposite the Silver Springs Hotel, there was a rattle of machine gun fire and several bullets smashed in through

the rear window on one side, and out the other.
Fortunately, the Vice President was sitting well back in
his seat and was unhurt, if badly shaken. Obviously the
volley was intended for Obote, but if the bullets had hit
our car in the same place, I would have been the only one
killed.

After the two attempts and the murder of Brigadier
Okoya, Obote became increasingly suspicious and
remote from reality. He appeared less and less often in
public and relied increasingly on the Secret Police,
mainly on the General Service Unit, headed by his cousin
Akena Adoko. They knew precisely what he wanted to
hear. File upon file of foiled "Obote assassination
attempts" were compiled and delivered to me for passing
on to him. Every day he would receive the Unit's green
folders—sometimes containing many sheets, sometimes
one typewritten page, sometimes a handwritten note. For
a time, Obote kept them to himself, but after several
weeks this clearly became impossible and he began to
turn them over to me for filing.

One day Obote called for me around lunch time. I
walked into the lounge where he was sitting. Without any
hesitation, he looked at me and asked, "Kyemba, tell me,
were you really shot during the attempt? The General
Service Unit thinks that you were faking." For seconds I
was speechless. When I found my voice, all I could do was
shout "What!?" and storm out of the room. I sat in my
office for several minutes to calm down, then gathered
my briefcase and papers and left. I thought bitterly of
resigning, but eventually decided that nothing would be
gained by doing so. Anyway, if he was serious, he would
throw me into prison whatever I did. As it happened, he
was so embarrassed he never mentioned the incident
again.

When I had the time, I looked through the files of
General Service reports. There was the one on me. It
stated that I was implicated, and that I had scratched my
neck with a stone to fake the bullet wound. This was sheer

stupidity. If I wanted to kill Obote, I would have at least have arranged for my accomplices to make the attempt when I was not in the firing line and not within a yard or two of the grenade that was to finish the deed. (If it had been sent to me, as an accusation against someone else, I would have thrown it away, as I did with many obviously fabricated reports on high-ranking officials.)

In September 1970, Amin fulfilled a long-standing official invitation to visit Cairo. In his absence, Obote finally acted to outflank him. He planned several new Army appointments and tried desperately to conclude the eight-month-old investigation into the Okoya murder so that Amin, against whom there was now hard evidence, could be arrested soon after his return. In fact, Amin was instructed to extend his stay in Cairo, so that Obote would have the time he needed. But Amin's information service was good. His Secret Service contacts sent word of what was in the wind, and he returned unexpectedly and without ceremony. I happened to see him as I was driving to Entebbe. His car passed me going in the opposite direction. We waved at each other. Later, I telephoned Obote to tell him the commander was back from Cairo. He was astounded.

This was the first time I saw the way Amin could exploit his genius for unpredictability, a quality that has served him in good stead ever since.

All Obote could do now was to go ahead with the new appointments. But it was not enough. Amin was now in a position to exploit Obote's unpopularity and turn it to his own advantage. He began attending Moslem prayers with one of the Kabaka's uncles to reestablish some credibility with the Baganda. When he appeared at a graduation ceremony at Makerere University, he was cheered. He also stated publicly that he "feared no one but God"—a deliberate challenge to Obote.

Obote never told me directly that he was going to arrest Amin. But as principal private secretary I was in charge of the President's office, and I saw who came and went

and who was posted where. The signs were clear enough.
No one actually said anything, but the maneuvers
themselves revealed the long-term strategy of the two
contestants.

One incident in particular showed the rivalry between
them and illustrated Amin's growing superiority. Obote
asked Amin to place a unit at Bamunanika, the country
residence of the late Kabaka, to guard against further
troubles among the Baganda. Amin selected a number of
his own Southern Sudanese soldiers, headed by a
Lieutenant Hussein Marella, who after the coup was to
be promoted to Brigadier and Chief of Staff of the army.
Obote, seeing Amin's purpose, bypassed the army
hierarchy and ordered Marella to disband the unit.
Marella refused to take any action without consulting
Amin. Obote was forced to admit that the order should
have gone through the army commander. The unit was
then disbanded with Amin's cooperation. But Amin's
men, who should have been sent back to the Sudan, were
in fact distributed to several other units, thereby ensuring
a vider and less obvious distribution of Amin's influence.

Obote, however, now felt secure enough to go to
Singapore for the Commonwealth Conference of
January 1971. I was certain that he was not as secure as he
felt and acted accordingly. I moved my more valuable
personal property out of my residence, together with my
car, a BMW, and took them to Jinja. This will be news to
Obote; but I would like him to know that my activity was
prompted by an intuitive interpretation of what was
happening, and not by my prior knowledge of Amin's
moves.

As we were preparing to leave Entebbe, I had a long
chat with Amin. Obote was closeted in a small VIP room,
with some selected army officers, the Minister of Internal
Affairs and other General Service personnel. Amin, the
commander of the army, was in another room, almost
alone, with no one eager to talk to him in case they were
suspected of collaborating with him. Feeling that this was

no way to treat the army commander, I spent some time talking to him. During the conversation he asked me to bring him something from Singapore. I promised I would.

Soon after we had gone, Amin called a number of meetings of senior officers at the army headquarters and addressed them to show that he was still in charge. The Minister of Affairs and the Vice President, who had remained in Kampala, received reports that an assassination attempt was to be made on Obote's life when he returned. Another report linked Amin with two other ministers—the Minister of Defense, Felix Onama, and the Minister of Education, Dr. Luyimbazi-Zake. But neither minister exercised any influence after the coup, and the second fled in the following year. I have grave doubts that either report was true.

Obote was told of the two plots, in reports of which I saw copies, and ordered the Minister of Internal Affairs, Basil Bataringaya, to supervise the arrest of Amin and his supposed collaborators. At once, Amin heard of the order from his contacts. He told me later that he had had a detailed report of a meeting in which the Minister of Internal Affairs and the Inspector General, and other senior officers of the army, planned his arrest. Amin acted quickly. In the early afternoon of January 24, he contacted a few of his most trusted officers and ordered them to take immediate command of the armories, a few tanks and the radio station. There was no plan of attack, no meetings, no formal strategy—and nothing, therefore, for Obote's men to fight against. Few people in the army even knew of the coup before it started. Again, Amin had proved a master of unpredictability.

In Singapore, I first got to know that something was wrong at home when Chris Ntende, who was then permanent secretary in the Ministry of Internal Affairs, arrived just after the Commonwealth Conference had ended. He told me that he had come to brief Obote on the discussions with the British Government on the non-Ugandan Asians resident in Uganda. He said he wanted Obote to brief his colleagues from Zambia and Tanzania. The reason for his mission seemed unlikely. The Presidents of Zambia and Tanzania had left Singapore days before.

According to a later report, Obote came to believe that Ntende had told me of the plans to arrest Amin and that I had phoned through a warning to a fellow tribesman, Amin's brother-in-law Wanume Kibedi, in Kampala. This is nonsense. It would have been ridiculous for Ntende to travel to Singapore to deliver such a warning when he could have told any number of Basoga people— Kibedi included—in Kampala. (As it happened, the accusation was not a bad thing for me. It proved to Amin that I had no covert dealings with Obote, and thus assured my safety when I returned.)

That night, Ntende stayed in my room because the hotel was full. He told me that he was to speak to the President at 2:00 in the morning. I asked no questions, but it was certainly an odd time to see a head of state. Later that night I heard voices raised from the President's suite, which was not very far from my own. I had no doubt that they were trying to reach Kampala. As it happend, Obote was trying to contact Bataringaya to see how his plans for the arrest were going. He never did get through. There had been no arrest—Amin had already struck. Obote's men—who, Amin told me later, had been watched as they arrived for their meeting—had fled, abandoning their cars in the street. On my return I saw the cars, bullet-riddled, standing where they had been left.

At 10:00 A.M., just before our departure, one of the Singapore government officials attached to our delegation called me aside and told me that the radio had reported some problem at home. Immediately after, Obote called the senior members of the delegation into a meeting. He announced that there had been fighting in Kampala, but that all was not yet lost. He had tried to find out the true situation, he said, by calling a number of places in Kampala, but had failed to get anyone. Then, while we were waiting to leave, Obote in desperation telephoned the Kampala Central Police Station. He spoke to a senior officer, Suleiman Dusman, now retired, who told him that the police were on standby. Obote asked "Standby for what?" The officer replied that the army was on the move. Obote asked why the police were not on the move if the army was; Dusman's reply reflected the confusion that reigned in Kampala.

We then caught the plane for Bombay and Nairobi. A couple of hours out of Bombay, when I was sitting in the cockpit having a snack and monitoring the radio, the BBC quoted a Uganda Radio report that Obote had been overthrown, that the army had taken over the country, and that his delegation was on its way back from Singapore. The last part, at least, was true—I assumed the rest was. The pilot asked whether he should tell the President. I thought that perhaps I should. I got up and walked back to the first-class compartment. As soon as Obote saw me, he leaned forward and asked if there was anything to report. I said "Yes, Your Excellency—not very good news." He asked me to hurry up and tell him. I said, "The Army has taken over." He said nothing. He just collapsed back into his seat without comment. I moved on to the other ministers repeating the information to them. One, Sam Odaka, the Foreign Minister, said in his jocular way, "Well, we now have no country."

I knew at the time that the reaction to the news would be mixed. Some delegates would welcome it because they had relatives in prison. Others, like myself, had simply become disenchanted with Obote's regime. And then there were those—Obote's own men, mostly his own tribesmen—who feared change.

We arrived at Nairobi airport at about 8:00 in the evening. Clearly the Kenyans had already decided that Obote was to be treated as a deposed leader. We were all shuttled into waiting cars, which sped us off to a hotel. The next day, we were put on board a new East African

Airways DC-9. It was to have made its inaugural flight to Entebbe that day. Instead, we left unceremoniously for Dar-es-Salaam. I left all my luggage—two suitcases and the presents I had bought in Singapore—in Nairobi, at a relative's house.

Our reception in Dar-es-Salaam was in marked contrast to the one we had experienced in Kenya. The then Vice President of Tanzania, Rashid Kawawa, was waiting for us (President Julius Nyerere was on a state visit to India). Cars stood by with the Ugandan Presidential flag waving. We were all given individual cars and taken to State House, Nyerere's official residence.

For the next several hours, we followed the news back home over the various news agency wires. We began to discuss who was going to do what. I was anxious to return to Uganda—if possible—and retire into private life. Obote did not realize that I would like to go home at all, let alone so soon, for my return would give a boost to the new regime. But I had my own plans, and contacted Kampala by telephone. I spoke to my office. Oddly enough, my secretary was still at her post. I told her I wanted to speak to Amin. He was out. I told her to ask him if I could come home or not. I also spoke to my family and several friends and told them that I was all right. I called again later. This time Amin was in. He said that he had already given instructions for me to be welcomed if I wanted to come back. "We're celebrating," he said. "When are you coming home?" This open-handed invitation took me completely by surprise. Scarcely concealing my delight, I booked a flight, called Amin back, and told him my arrival time. I left early the next morning, a Friday, just four days after the coup, without seeing Obote again. I was accompanied by one of Obote's own bodyguards who wanted very much to go with me.

When we arrived at the airport, I was met by one of Amin's men, with the President's BMW waiting on the runway. The driver, Ismail, was a man I had known before and had recommended to Amin as an army driver the previous year. (He is now a major and Deputy Commander of Kifaru Battalion in Arua. He recently became the son-in-law of the Vice President, General Mustafa Adrisi.) Amin had clearly wanted to put me at ease by sending a familiar face to greet me—a thoughtful gesture which seems out of keeping with his brutal character, but is in fact typical of him. On the way Ismail told me that my residence in the Presidential compound had been looted. I was not particularly perturbed. They could have taken only the few small items that remained.

I was taken straight to Amin's residence (which he renamed "Command Post"). He was still in a meeting with a number of religious leaders, briefing them about the takeover. After his meeting, Amin called me upstairs. There were still several government officials in the room.

The first question he asked me was, "What have you brought me from Singapore?" I was thoroughly nonplussed. Considering what we had all been through, it was an incongruous greeting. I said, "I did bring something for you—a small radio and a piece of cloth for your wife—but I do not have it here because my luggage is in Nairobi. I'll let you have it when I get my luggage."

He said "Thank you very much," then turned to the officials and added, "I asked him to get me something and he did."

Then he asked me, "Have you seen your family?" I replied that I hadn't.

"I am sure they are all worried about you," he said. "If you don't have a car, you take the Mercedes."

Then he added, "Go home for the weekend and come back on Monday. Go back to your office and continue as if nothing had happened." I could hardly believe my ears. I knew he had no reason to distrust me, but this seemed extraordinary. His driver took me in the Mercedes to meet Teresa, who had brought our own car from Jinja. We drove back home together, laughing and talking as we each heard the details of the other's life over the previous three weeks.

2

The Tyrant Emerges

IMMEDIATELY AFTER THE coup, in January 1971, the country greeted Amin as a hero. For several weeks, celebrations took up almost all of his time. He was not the type of man to sit at a desk and it was pure joy for him to be constantly on the move by car and helicopter. Wherever he went, his Cabinet and senior officials went: he wanted to show us off. For days at a time, there were hardly any leaders left in Kampala to run the country.

His visits developed a certain pattern. People would hear on the radio that Amin planned to be in their particular area. The local inhabitants would build a platform overnight, and the following morning would gather and await Amin's address. He would arrive by helicopter, make a speech, watch some dancing, receive presents (once, he was given nine hundred head of cattle), go to a reception, jump back into his helicopter and be off again—along with his government entourage. Our job was to sit on the platform while he spoke, socialize with him, and then follow him to the next stop.

Amin was greeted with delight; he had overthrown an unpopular regime. He had also, significantly, released Obote's detainees. Among them were the former Prime Minister and leader of the Democratic Party, Benedicto Kiwanuka, who was later appointed Chief Justice (and, later still, murdered); Brigadier Shaban Opolot, once Amin's commander and rival (Amin magnanimously granted him all the back pay that had accumulated during his five-year prison stay); and Grace Ibingira, who was a minister and prominent lawyer, and was recently Amin's United Nations Ambassador in New York. He also released many of the late Kabaka's relatives, who had been imprisoned since 1966, arranged for the return of the Kabaka's body from London for reburial, and, in fact, even claimed he had saved the Kabaka's life by allowing him to escape.

The country seemed set for a return to peace. True, there was one early incident that shocked me. On my first day back in office, there was a car chase outside the President's Lodge. Major Emmanuel Ogwal, a pro-Obote officer, was chased through the center of Kampala by Amin's soldiers. He took refuge in a doctor's house and was killed during a shoot-out that we all heard from our offices. (The unsuspecting owner of the house, Dr. George Ebine, was—I learned later—traced to his hospital, taken to Malire barracks and crushed by a tank.) Amin's boys triumphantly brought Ogwal's driving license to Amin in my presence, as proof of their success. The incident was disturbing, but it seemed natural that there should be some dangerous opposition to be dealt with. It did not strike me as ominous.

At first the administration was delighted with Amin. He insisted on appointing only a few of his own people, like Lieutenant Colonel Obitre-Gama (Internal Affairs) and Charles Oboth-Ofumbi (Ministry of Defense). For the most part, he took considerable care to select the most capable people for the Cabinet, frequently seeking advice about the qualifications of possible appointees. Because he asked the advice of professionals like myself, the Cabinet was filled with experienced and efficient men, like Nyonyi Zikusoka, a brilliant engineer who became Minister of Works; Nkambo Mugerwa, Solicitor General, who became Minister of Justice; and Professor William Banage, Department Head of Zoology at Makerere University, who became Minister of Animal

Resources. The tribes were all fairly represented, and there was a good balance of Christians and Moslems.

I was Amin's principal private secretary, the secretary to the Cabinet, and permanent secretary to the office of the President. As secretary to the Cabinet, I was responsible for taking the minutes at Cabinet meetings, and for following up Cabinet decisions. As permanent secretary to the office of the President, I was head of the civil service, and responsible for informing the President of the activities of all departments. These three different jobs—which were later divided among three people— put me in a unique position. But it was also an impossible position: I could not do all the tasks efficiently on my own. I soon suggested that I be replaced as principal private secretary as quickly as possible.

At the first Cabinet meeting, Amin turned his mainly civilian Cabinet into a pseudo-military one. He swore all the ministers in as officer-cadets and gave them all uniforms. None of them was ever to rise above the rank of officer-cadet; all of them would now be subject to military discipline. At the time, however, this ominous implication did not register fully.

For that first meeting, I prepared a brief document on Cabinet procedures detailing how the President's office and Secretariat should be kept informed of all actions to be taken on Cabinet decisions. Copies were distributed. The President, in military uniform, spent some time talking about his trust in the new Cabinet, saying that he wanted them to run the country as well as possible. He said he wasn't a politician, and that it was the job of his expert advisers to get the country running smoothly. He announced that each minister should be assigned a black Mercedes Benz, and each car marked "Military Government." In the discussions that followed, Amin sat quietly and listened to the ministers' suggestions. When someone finished speaking, he would ask if anyone had anything to add. In fact, he was a model of decorum and generosity. We all left happy, convinced of both his good nature and his good sense.

Over the next few days, there were some hints that all was not as it seemed. It puzzled us that Amin never spoke of military matters to his Cabinet except in the vaguest terms. We were angered when he announced on the radio on February 22 that the military government was to be in power for five years. (Following our protests, he declared that his was a caretaker administration only. He did not, however, mention a timetable.) But he had promised political freedom. He was clearly going to be a reasonable fellow. We were prepared to forgive him any small lapses.

Disillusion followed swiftly. To start with, the Cabinet and I prepared most of Amin's speeches. But his English is poor. The speeches were a great labor for him to read and a great bore for people to listen to. It was obvious that he was reading words he hadn't written, and the foreign press criticized him. He felt much more relaxed when he was talking off the cuff, and after a short while, he found he could make a greater impact that way.

Thereafter, everywhere he went on his jubilant tours, he promised paradise. If he found that a place needed a hospital, he would promise one. "The Minister of Health is here," he would say, and turn to the poor man. "You build one." Or, "Here is the Minister of Works and Communications—he will build you a road from here to there." It was an exhilarating time for him. Incapable of detailed administrative duties, he preferred grass-roots contact. He liked to joke with ordinary people. He liked to make a show of praising and blaming his ministers in public. He could really play "Big Daddy"—or "Dada" (grandfather)—as he liked to call himself. Yet, because we were constantly on the move, there was no time to follow up on these "immediate action" directives.

The ministers were, of course, taken completely by surprise by his random announcements, made both in speeches and on the radio. (He would brief the radio's news editors personally, without telling the Minister of Information.) The ministers took to carrying notebooks, and as soon as he started to talk, began scribbling down what they were meant to do. I was supposed to coordinate the instructions to various ministries. This was fine to start with, because it followed, more or less, the procedures laid down by the colonial civil service, but soon it became impossible to keep track of all the orders. We had to read the newspapers and listen to Uganda Radio to learn the decisions he had made. Government officials began to use the radio as their guide. Colleagues often explained their actions to me by saying, "The President told me to do it—didn't you hear it on the radio?"

At first there was nothing sinister associated with these announcements. They were even amusing—as long as they concerned someone else. They became less amusing when you were the victim, as I soon was in a minor way. In March 1971, Amin decided to replace me as principal private secretary, as I had requested. He chose to announce this, and the name of my successor, on the radio. I wasn't particularly upset at his high-handedness, since I would in any case remain in my old office with control of the whole establishment. (Indeed, in one small way, I still am in control. As far as I know, I am the only person who possesses the combinations to the State House safes. They contain only some old files which may one day be of interest to academicians.)

From January 1971 to July (when I went on leave), I was extremely close to Amin. He knew my family well and we had worked together for many years. He used to call me to his bedroom, even when he was in bed, to sit down and have a chat. He would talk a lot about his girlfriends. (He had—and still has—an extraordinary sex life). I often traveled with him, and I was in constant touch with him. If he had something to say to a minister, he would normally contact him personally, but he often channelled information through my office.

Despite my intimacy with Amin, I was unaware of the terrible events that were then going on in the barracks, events that presaged a yet more terrible future. Although the coup itself had not been particularly bloody, the murders started immeditely. His "enemies" at this stage were principally the Acholi and Langi. Obote was a Langi—sufficient reason for Amin to suspect the entire tribe— and the Acholis also formed a large proportion of the armed forces; Amin lumped them both together. He used to tell his Cabinet that there were "mopping-up" operations going on, but we had no idea what this meant until later. These early murders have been documented in some detail, by the journalist David Martin, in his book *General Amin*.

Of those officers who held the rank of lieutenant colonel or above at the time of the coup, most have been murdered. I was later told that on the night of the coup, Amin's troops bludgeoned several officers to death with rifle butts and bottles in the Malire officers' mess. Also killed was Brigadier Suleiman Hussein, the Army Chief of Staff. He had been ordered, along with Bataringaya, to arrest Amin. After the coup he went into hiding, but was soon arrested, taken to Luzira prison, and beaten to death with rifle butts. It was rumored that his head was later taken to Amin, who kept it in a refrigerator overnight.

A picture of what was happening in Uganda's prisons in those first months was later given to David Martin by Joshua Wakholi, who had been Minister of Public Service and Cabinet Affairs in Obote's government for almost five years. He retired into private life, but was arrested in early March and taken to Makindye prison. He was placed next door to the notorious cell called "Singapore," reserved for those condemned to death. Wakholi reported that thirty-six army officers and one corporal were shot and slashed to death by three or four soldiers. The next morning, he was among those told to go into Singapore cell and scrub up the remains. The floor was a quarter of an inch deep in blood. It took six hours to clean. Along with the blood, there were pieces of skull and teeth, brain tissue and empty shell cases. A number of other accounts confirm that Singapore cell was often used for such brutal killings.

Many other atrocities were taking place throughout the country. In May, Amin told his troops that they could shoot on sight anyone suspected of having committed or being about to commit a crime. He also issued a decree providing for detention without trial. The deaths mounted into the hundreds. At Malire, thirty-two senior Langi and Acholi officers were herded into a room and blown up with explosives. Of several hundred Langi soldiers who had obeyed Amin's call to report back to their barracks at Lira, scores were bayoneted and thrown into the Nile. On another occasion, several hundred people—soldiers and civilians—fled into Sudan, intending to join Obote. They were stopped by Sudanese guerrillas, and later executed on Amin's orders. In early July, scores of Acholi and Langi soldiers were killed in two massacres, at the Mbarara and Jinja barracks.

Also in early July, two Americans, Nicholas Stroh and Robert Siedle, began to investigate reports of the massacres. Stroh was the son of a wealthy Detroit brewer. He had left his job on the *Philadelphia Evening Bulletin* to work as a freelance journalist in Africa. On July 9, 1971, he and Siedle, a sociology lecturer at Makerere, went to ask questions about the massacre at Mbarara barracks. They saw the second-in-command, Major Juma Aiga (a taxi driver at the time of the coup and now District Commissioner in Toro). The Commander, Lieutenant Colonel Ali Fadhul Warriss, was in Kampala at the time, and was in close contact with Amin. Stroh and Juma got into a heated argument. The two Americans were killed, and were buried in a shallow grave nearby. Major Juma was later seen driving Stroh's blue Volkswagen in Mbarara. When the American Embassy in Kampala began inquiries a week later, the bodies were dug up from their grave, put into sacks and burned in the barracks. Their remains were then dumped in a river. The car was burned and thrown into a mountain valley.

In April 1972, in unwilling response to American efforts to find out what had happened to the two men, Amin appointed a judicial inquiry headed by a British judge, Mr. Justice David Jefferys Jones. After reading a report of the killing—written by one of the men involved, who had fled—the judge managed to trace the car. Amin was furious and ordered that the inquiry be wound up. In May, Mr. Justice Jones—a friend of mine to whom I remarked, "This will be your last job in Uganda"—completed his report, as well as he could under the circumstances, and left the country. He had concluded that Ali and Juma were responsible for the two deaths. Amin dismissed the judge's findings, calling them the result of a "prejudiced mind." He later successively promoted Ali to Brigadier, Army Chief of Staff, provincial governor, and, more recently, minister.

Amin never gave explicit instructions to kill in my presence. But he had certain euphemisms that were recognized as orders for execution. One phrase was "Give him the VIP treatment," which meant death after torture, a phrase I heard him use when he was ordering the death of the Minister of Information, Alex Ojera, in September 1972. Other code phrases were "Take him to Malire" and "*Kalasi,*" which means "death" in Nubian, a language few Ugandans speak. I was also aware that many units and army personnel were moving from place to place to carry out executions. There were never any written instructions. First, he cannot write (no one I know has ever received a handwritten letter from him); and second, he always preferred to give his orders verbally, so that later, if necessary, he could deny any personal involvement.

To further escape responsibility, Amin preferred to be abroad when his massacres took place. He used this tactic in July 1971. The killing started in Jinja barracks half a mile from my own home, on July 11, the day Amin left for a trip to Israel and Britain, seeking arms and cash. He was to use this tactic time and again; any journey abroad immediately threatened an increase in the level of violence at home.

On this occasion, a group of Acholi and Langi soldiers—the number has never been established—were rounded up and crammed into a guardroom near the entrance to the barracks. Fearing for their lives, they broke out into an adjoining room and seized a machine gun. Throughout the night they fought their guards. A few soldiers managed to escape, but most were killed. News of the battle spread throughout the Jinja area; bullets flew from the army barracks over the main road, and a number of passersby had very narrow escapes. During the battle, a military vehicle knocked a hole in the barrack wall in an attempt to flush out the prisoners.

Afterward, bulldozers arrived to clear out the bodies and demolish the buildings. Trucks were commandeered from the Jinja municipal council to cart the bodies away. I can vouch for this because Amin, on his return from abroad, wanted to see the barracks, and I went there on July 19 to make the arrangements. The building where the prisoners had been penned was a pile of rubble. The brickwork was splattered with blood. I was told that some of the army officers had tried to take over the barracks. I did not believe the story, and later learned the true details from an army contact.

Amin cannot avoid responsibility for these killings. The acting commander at Jinja was Colonel Suleiman, a relative of Amin's. It is inconceivable that he would have acted on his own initiative.

Another case of which I had direct knowledge—a case that brought home to me Amin's dangerously inconsistent and deceptive nature—concerned the Police Bandmaster, Ahmed Oduka. He was one of the men who had reported that Amin planned to assassinate Obote on the latter's return from Singapore. He had fled immediately after the coup, to Mombasa. One of Amin's men visited him there in March and told Oduka that it would be safe to return. When he arrived, he was taken to see Amin, who asked him to record a statement at Makindye prison. The meeting was friendly, but as soon as Oduka left, Amin ordered him to be "taken to Malire." There his skull was smashed in with a club. News of the murder reached Amin while I was with him. He was telephoned by the chief medical officer of the army, Brigadier Bogere, who reported the facts of Oduka's death. Amin turned to me and said coldly, "Oduka is dead," as if reporting the completion of some trivial task. I already knew better than to react in any way.

Immediately after the coup, about eight hundred officers from the police, army, and Obote's secret police, the General Service unit, had been arrested and detained in Luzira prison. Among them was a friend of mine, who told me what happened. On December 29, 1971—after almost a year's detention, and many futile attempts to have them released—they were all blindfolded and transferred by buses under army escort to Mutukula prison. There, forty-five officers and between two hundred and two hundred and fifty noncommissioned officers were slaughtered. They were buried by those who still survived. On January 25, the first anniversary of the coup, Amin announced a general amnesty for all detainees, including the survivors in Mutukula.

It seems unbelievable, but ordinary people knew little of what was going on. The killings in the first few months after the coup were almost exclusively confined to the army and the details were kept secret. Reports of massacres appeared only abroad, where they were not taken all that seriously. In Uganda itself, we were mostly inclined to give Amin the benefit of the doubt. We accepted his talk of anti-Obote operations and of happenings over which he did not yet have control.

The secret killings did, however, have some obvious effects. To make up for the gaps in the officer corps, Amin began to appoint new officers. His choices were ludicrously inadequate. He put sergeants and sergeant majors in charge of battalions. He appointed tank and car drivers—the people he most enjoyed chatting with—as majors or intelligence officers. Sergeant Musa Eyega, a tank driver, was put in charge of the Malire Mechanized Regiment. (He is now a lieutenant colonel and Ambassador to Saudi Arabia). Private Ismail—the driver who had met me at the airport upon my return—was made the temporary head of the Intelligence Service, and a captain. His promotion came about in April when I had to introduce Ismail to a British officer. I did not feel I could introduce a private as the Secret Service chief. When I mentioned this to Amin before the meeting, he said, "You say he is a captain." From then on, he was a captain (until his further promotion).

Such promotions were never confirmed in writing. Men would simply confront the paymaster and say, "I am a captain," or "I'm a major," and ask to be paid accordingly from that date. Confusion followed. When Amin realized the administrative trouble caused by his orders, he decided that new promotions should be backdated to January 25, the day of the coup. His decision was naturally abused. People simply promoted themselves, knowing that the paymaster would never dare check back with Amin.

By mid-1971, an inexperienced junior officer corps virtually ran the country. One of the most feared of these men was—and is—Lieutenant Malyamungu who was in charge of quelling dissent in the army. Before he joined the army, he had been a gatekeeper at Nyanza Textile Industries, where my brother Kisajja was personnel manager. At the time of the coup, he commandeered a tank with which he shot up the entrance to the Entebbe airport terminal, killing two priests. After the coup he headed Amin's execution gangs, with unlimited power to execute anybody in the army, even officers senior to him. His modes of execution are as atrocious as anything imaginable. He is fond of disemboweling. Along with

several other officers, he is known to have executed his
victims by having them run over by tanks. But perhaps
the grisliest episode concerned Francis Walugembe, who
had previously been Mayor of Masaka. In September
1972, Walugembe was arrested, had his genitals cut off
and was paraded through the streets before being killed
and dismembered. So violent and brutal is Malyamungu
that even Amin once commented to me that he feared he
might be going mad.

To rebuild a real officer corps from Amin's illiterate
sadists, who could hardly speak a word of English, was an
insurmountable problem. The British, however, gave it a
try. Soon after the coup, Amin requested and was
granted a British officer to train the Intelligence Service.
The cadets given to him were Amin's best, yet they were
still totally inadequate. I often met this officer on his way
to and from the President's office and he would tell me of
the difficulties he was having. He doubted that the men
could ever benefit from his presence. "Obviously an
intelligence officer needs some basic intelligence," he
would say. "These chaps have none." Since they were
semi-literate, all he could do was describe the basic tasks
of an intelligence officer. Not that they could ever
perform these tasks, let alone teach others, which was the
long-term aim of the project. He often told me how
ridiculous he felt. He stuck it out for three or four
months, then said he would try to arrange training for
them outside the country, and left.

Amin's other deficiencies became increasingly
apparent as the months passed. One was his total
financial naïveté, exemplified in the way he handled the
construction of the OAU Conference Center and the
nearby Nile Hotel. This major project was started in the
Obote days in preparation for the OAU summit,
scheduled for June 1971. After the coup, no one seriously
believed that the OAU heads of state would come to
Uganda so soon—if ever, given the nature of Amin's
inadequacy as a politician. But Amin pushed ahead

anyway. The Yugoslav company, Energo-Project, which was doing the construction, worked twenty-four hours a day in three shifts to complete the conference center and hotel in time. In May, the OAU decided to hold the June summit in Addis Ababa. By June, the Nile Hotel complex was finished, three hundred percent over budget, with nothing to justify this cost. Not until 1975 did the OAU agree to meet there.

Uncounted millions were spent on other projects as well. The Israelis were heavily committed to a number of large-scale building projects—barracks, roads, airport runways, and apartment buildings. Besides these, Amin ordered the constuction of what he later named Field Marshal Idi Amin Air Force Base, at Nakasongola, about seventy miles from Kampala. Appalled by the loss of the Egyptian Air Force to the Israelis in 1967, he was taken with the idea of an air base with underground bunkers to protect his so-called air force from a similar fate. Uganda didn't have many planes at the time—no more than two dozen—but he continued with his plan to give the impression that he really did have something to protect. As a matter of fact, he could not bear to have his planes that far away from him—they were always at Entebbe. He did not trust the people in charge of them, and wanted to have them close enough so he could visit them regularly. Hence the destruction of most of the Uganda Air Force during the Israeli raid in 1976.

All these projects were unbudgeted. There was no thought that the country might have to foot the bill some day. Amin was told of the financial limitation, but such warnings meant nothing to him. Obote had allowed for a deficit of 700 million shillings (80 million dollars) in his last budget but Amin could not grasp this fiscal reality. By his definition countries could not go broke, because they printed money and could always print more. In 1977, Uganda's deficit ran to three billion shillings. The ministers are still under orders to blame Obote.

His financial irresponsibility and total ignorance of

economic realities also has a personal dimension. He does not differentiate between personal and government expenditure. The government was required to maintain him and his several family establishments in food, clothing, furniture, cars, any luxury goods he fancied, and just plain cash. This last item is of particular interest. There was, in fact, an official provision that allowed for small amounts to be spent on information gathering at the discretion of the President and the permanent secretary to the President's office (at the time, me). This was normally accounted for by the permanent secretary to the Auditor General.

When Amin realized that such money was available, he began to demand cash for "intelligence missions." At first the sums were modest—a few hundred dollars—but eventually they ran into tens of thousands. In fact, he began to use the Bank of Uganda as a petty cash box. He would just come into the office or call me on the telephone and say, "Get some money ready for such-and-such an intelligence purpose." I would call up the Accounts Office and arrange it. He also used the Ministry of Defense to provide such sums. He carried cash in his briefcase and cash in his pockets—English pounds and American dollars (which are illegal to hold) as well as Uganda shillings. He would happily take a thousand dollars from his pocket at public functions and give it away. It meant nothing to him.

It was a very difficult sitution for me; I could no longer account reasonably for money of this kind, nor did I have the time to do so, so he appointed a man in my office who was in effect his personal cashier.

Fortunately, I did not suffer the indignities imposed on me for long. In July 1971, having heard some gossip that he was perpetuating the Obote regime by being so close to me, Amin told me to go on leave for two months. (A decision I was supposed to hear first on the radio; in fact, a friend tipped me off beforehand.) I was happy to take a holiday—my job had become impossibly demanding. I bought my own dairy farm just outside Jinja, and began to develop an orange orchard on a piece of land twenty miles to the east. I dictated my own hours, and worked hard; I enjoyed myself tremendously.

It was during my leave that the massacres in the army really became a public horror. Amin's troops were no longer killing people by the score but by the hundreds. It was impossible to dispose of the bodies in graves. Instead, truckloads of corpses were taken and dumped in the Nile. Three sites were used—one just above Owen Falls Dam at Jinja, another at Bujagali Falls near the army shooting range, and a third at Karuma Falls near Murchison Falls.

The intention was for the bodies to be eaten by crocodiles. This was an inefficient method of disposal. Bodies were frequently swept to the bank, where they were seen by passersby and fishermen. At Owen Falls many bodies must have been carried through the dam over which the Kampala-Jinja road ran, but many also floated into the still waters to one side, near the power station. Once, while driving across the dam at Jinja, I saw six bodies, revoltingly puffed up and decomposed, floating in the waters. Despite the presence of a boat that was (and is) in permanent use for dragging the bodies to the bank for disposal, workers from Jinja, who travelled daily over the dam between their houses and the many industrial plants on the Kampala side—like Nyanza Textiles, Nile Breweries and Mulbox, as well as the Njeru municipal offices—told me that they saw dozens of bodies almost every day.

Toward the end of my leave, one incident—the murder of Michael Kagwa, President of the Industrial Court—revealed to the country as a whole that the massacres were not to be limited to the army, or to the Acholi and Langi. Kagwa, who was extremely rich (he had a Mercedes sports car with its own television), had a girlfriend, Helen Ogwang, in whom Amin was interested. In September 1971, Kagwa was seized by Amin's bodyguards at the Kampala International Hotel swimming pool. They shot him and burnt his body, together with his Mercedes, on the outskirts of the capital near Namirembe Cathedral. No attempt was made to discover who the murderers were. The senior police officers had already been arrested for investigating the Okoya murder. No one would risk death by asking questions that could lead only to Amin. The government "offered" a 50,000-shilling reward for information. So far it has gone unclaimed. Helen Ogwang was later posted to the Uganda Embassy in Paris, where she defected.

At the end of September 1971, when I was due to return to work, I asked where I should report for duty. No one knew. My successor as permanent secretary suggested that I take over an empty office somewhere in the Parliament building and bring myself up to date by reading files. I said there was no point in my reading files I might not have to deal with, and added that I would stay at my house in Jinja until I was required. Within two days, Amin summoned me. I found that I was to take over as permanent secretary in the Ministry of Culture and Community Development. This was a relatively unimportant ministry, and it suited me perfectly. In the President's office it had been hard enough to follow what was going on before I went on leave; to resume the work after a two-month absence would have been extremely difficult.

In my new role, I had some time to continue the development of my farm, but my official responsibilities were wide-ranging and interesting. At various times, I dealt with the National Theater, museums, the preservation of historical monuments, cultural activities, youth activities, the Probation and Welfare Department, the rehabilitation of the physically handicapped, refugees from Rwanda, Sudan and Zaire, and sports. I also administered the Heartbeat of Africa, Uganda's national dance group, which then included the future Mrs. Amin, Medina, wife number four. I now had much less contact with Amin, although he did ask me to employ as a secretary one of his girlfriends (whose husband, a doctor, he had murdered).

I was not, therefore, directly involved in the extraordinary developments of early 1972, when Amin broke with Israel and began his love affair with Libya. But I was to see their effects, and a brief summary is essential for an understanding of Uganda's recent history. The events were dictated by Amin's need for ready cash. Britain was still willing to help, but most of her funds were tied up with specific projects, and British officials always wanted feasibility studies before funds were allocated. Similarly, the Israelis, apart from the fact that they had limited funds and were deeply involved in a number of projects, gave serious consideration to new ideas strictly on merit. That was not the kind of money Amin wanted. He saw his chance while on a state visit to West Germany in February 1972. Shortly before his return, he decided to visit Libya's head of state, Gaddafi. Since he was flying an Israeli jet, many ministers were shocked at the prospect of his dropping in on an extremist Arab dictator, but he went, met with Gaddafi, and received promises of massive financial and military aid. It was an attractive prospect for Gaddafi as well, for he was suddenly presented with an opportunity to have Israel thrown out of an African country.

The first indication of Amin's switch in allegiance came in a joint communiqué attacking Israel, published and broadcasted in Uganda after Amin's return. The Israelis—indeed all in Uganda—were taken aback. Things then moved very swiftly. The Israeli ambassador complained about the remarks. Amin retaliated by broadcasting more violent statements against the Israelis. He refused to see the ambassador, and began to attack Zionism, blaming Israel for not returning Arab lands seized in 1967, and demanding that the Arabs be granted their rights. Finally, Amin accused the Israelis of milking Uganda of three million shillings a day in the projects they were undertaking, stated that Israel must be wiped off the face of the earth, and ordered them out of the country.

Cleverly, the Israelis managed to drive much of their heavy construction equipment into neighboring Kenya. I passed some of these machines—cranes, trucks, bulldozers, scrapers—while driving between Kampala and Jinja. The Israelis were picnicking by the side of the road. By the time Amin realized that very valuable equipment was there for the taking and gave the order to stop the Israelis, most of the equipment had rumbled over the border. By the end of March 1972, the Israelis had gone.

The oil money from Libya was good for Amin personally, but it did little to sustain the loyalty of the army. To ensure this, he needed to offer cash or goods. He soon found a way to provide both.

On August 4, Amin appeared at the barracks at Tororo, near the Kenyan border, and announced to the troops that he had had a dream the previous night in which God instructed him to order the 50,000 Asians out of Uganda within ninety days. This he proceeded to do.

The Asian community was an ideal target. Asians almost totally controlled Uganda's trade, factories, plantations and industries. They were the managers, the bureaucrats, the accountants, the technicians, the doctors, the engineers, the lawyers. They formed an affluent middle class, a distinctive element in the population, with their own language, behavior patterns, names and occupations. On the whole they were not popular with the Africans. They have been described as the Jews of East Africa. They were, in other words, ideal targets.

By the 1970's, 30,000 of Uganda's Asians had British passports, but the other 20,000 were legally Ugandans. At the time of Amin's original announcement, nobody thought that he intended to expel both Ugandan Asians and British Asians. But it soon became clear that he did not intend to make a distinction between passports. He wanted the Asians' property to hand over to his troops. It was a brutal and thoroughly racist decision, and one that was to deal the Ugandan economy a terrible blow.

The Asians were sent out of the country with nothing except a hundred-dollar personal allowance. A stop was put on their bank accounts. Amin did not care where the Asians went as long as they went, and he stuck to his deadline—November 8, 1972—with a countdown that proceeded remorselessly day by day on the radio. He announced that any Asians remaining after the deadline would be sent to detention camps. Informed that some Asians were attempting to avoid deportation by blacking their faces with shoe polish, he issued a dire warning to anyone found guilty of such practices. Understandably, all the Asians made every effort to move out of the country.

On the pretext of helping the Asians pack, Amin's soldiers snatched household goods for themselves. As the deadline approached, the army moved from house to abandoned house taking anything they could carry.

The Asians left all their Ugandan property behind (although some had wealth in Britain and in other East African countries). Amin told them they were allowed to airfreight out a few personal belongings. Boxes of goods began to pile up outside the airport under army guard "to prevent looting." Day by day, the number of boxes mounted into the hundreds and then into the thousands. The Asians left, but the boxes stayed. Passersby could see that the boxes had been split open and the goods removed. Gradually, the boxes themselves vanished. Eventually, all the crates were carried off by the soldiers who were supposed to be guarding them. Nothing was ever sent to its owners.

Meanwhile, there occurred the event that finally revealed to all Ugandans, civilian as well as military, Amin's true nature. In September 1972, a small army of Obote guerrillas invaded Uganda from Tanzania. The invasion was a farce. There were only a thousand men; they were badly equipped and ill prepared. They were delayed crossing the frontier and attacked Amin's troops late in the morning, when there was no possibility of surprise. If Amin had ignored it, the whole thing might easily have collapsed of its own accord.

Obote's attack was a pure gift to Amin. His troops were anyway incensed at the invasion, which they saw as an attempt to stop them from seizing Asian property. Since the guerrillas were no conceivable threat, Amin could safely exaggerate the danger and thus show himself to be his country's savior. He could also, more ominously, use the invasion as a pretext to move against those members of the population whom he saw as a threat.

Early in the morning of Sunday, September 17, having spent the previous night at home in Jinja, I was preparing to drive out to my orchard when I heard the first reports of the invasion on the radio, which announced that people should go to church and pray. I found this announcement intriguing. Clearly the situation was not serious. Otherwise the government would have asked people to be on the lookout and ordered troops to report to the barracks.

I drove the twenty miles to my orange orchard. On my way I passed the ordnance depot at Magamaga. Soldiers in camouflage and army fatigues were rushing into the depot from the surrounding areas. I began to wonder if things were more serious than had been implied, so I returned to Jinja around lunch time and then left for Kampala.

There were a number of Army roadblocks between Jinja and Kampala. The troops said they were looking for Obote guerrillas, but it was clear that they were more interested in harassing the Asians who were passing through.

In Kampala the next day I began to find out what was really happening. The Obote guerrillas had attacked Mutukula, near the Tanzanian border, and the barracks at Mbarara. Announcements on the radio, however, gave the impression that countless other towns had been captured by Obote's troops. Friends of mine, when they heard the reports, drove out to see what was happening. There were road blocks all right, but once clear of them the drive was uneventful. It was clear that Amin's reports on the radio were pure lies. To further dramatize his "victory," he even wildly asserted that the Tanzanian Army, the British and the Israelis were all involved in the invasion.

During the first few days after the invasion, Amin was reported to have appeared at the battlefront, where there was supposed to be heavy fighting, with one of his favorite sons, five-year-old Moses. More evidence that the danger was slight. He would hardly have risked his own life and that of a favorite son unnecessarily.

The truth was that he now had nothing to fear from Obote or from anyone else. Terror reigned across most of the country. The killings had already extended from the army deep into the population at large.

It is almost impossible to estimate the numbers of the dead. As early as 1973, the former Foreign Minister Wanume Kibedi, who fled in that year, estimated that 90,000 to 100,000 had been killed. My calculations—done on the basis of the sights witnessed by hundreds at the Owen Falls Dam—give a comparable figure. A boatman at Owen Falls works full-time removing corpses from the water. If he retrieved twenty bodies a day between July 1971 and my departure in April 1977—a reasonable assumption—then, in round figures, this would amount to over 40,000 dead. But this figure doesn't include those that must have been eaten by crocodiles or swept through the dam—at least another 10,000. Moreover, Owen Falls was only one of three dumping areas. Multiplying the Owen Falls numbers by three gives a total of 150,000 dead by mid-1977. There were in addition many, many other dead, abandoned in forests, and hidden in pits near barracks.

The dead are literally innumerable: all their names will never be known, their numbers never counted. My own list is but a small indication of the true horror. And day by day the total grows.

3
Coming Chaos

I FIRST BECAME a minister in November 1972. The terror of indiscriminate killing continued unabated in the country as a whole, but in government circles it was quiet enough, for the Cabinet was cowed and submissive. Nor was there any trouble from the army, which was totally taken up with the absorption of Asian property. I thus had an extended opportunity to see Amin the administrator. I watched his brute ignorance and wily deceptiveness in action, and began to see how impossible it would be to change things from within.

The way I became a minister typifies Amin's method of making decisions. On November 4, 1972, at about 1:15 P.M., I was on my way from Kampala to Entebbe to attend a graduation ceremony at an institute attached to the Ministry of Culture, of which I had been the permanent secretary for just over a year. My minister, Yekosfati Engur, was to officiate at the ceremony, due to start at 2:15 P.M.. Halfway to Entebbe, I heard an announcement on the car radio stating that four ministers had been fired for inefficiency and slowness. One of them was Engur.

I did not feel there was anything particularly sinister in these firings. Engur was the only Langi in the cabinet, which—in the wake of the September invasion—was reason enough for him to be fired. But he was also slow, as Amin said, and hardly of ministerial quality. (He was arrested and imprisoned in 1974, kept in prison for about two years and then killed along with other prominent Langi in early 1977.) The only dismissal into which I could read a deeper motive was that of Professor Banage, Minister of Animal Resources, who had been a zoology professor at Makerere University. Amin was now painfully aware of his own reputation for stupidity, and to fire a professor would have given him considerable satisfaction.

I continued to the ceremony. It was to take place on a hill overlooking the airport and State House. As soon as I arrived, I telephoned the personal secretary in the Command Post to find out who the new minister was so he could come immediately to officiate. The secretary told me the President was in a meeting, but said she would pass on my message. I left the number and asked for Amin to call me back. I telephoned a few friends, including the Minister of Foreign Affairs, Wanume Kibedi, to see if any of them knew. No luck.

There was no chance of cancelling the ceremony, for hundreds of guests had been invited from all parts of Uganda and the proceedings were to be covered by the press and television. I decided that I would have to officiate. Fortunately I had prepared the minister's speech, and had a copy with me. I put on my academic gown, took my place at the head of the procession and led the way into the main hall. The ceremony continued without incident for about half an hour, with students coming up to the platform to receive their graduation scrolls from me. Then a policeman made his way to the rostrum, and asked me to go to the telephone. The assembled guests must have been wondering what was going on. First, Engur had not appeared; now I was being called away. As I rose, there was a murmur of uneasiness.

It was Amin on the phone. He asked me where I was. I told him, and added that I was having to officiate, because my minister hadn't arrived.

He said, "That's very good. The minister has been fired. You take over. After the ceremony come and see me at Command Post." I replied, "Right, Your Excellency," and went back to the main hall. My return was greeted by loud clapping as the audience saw that everything was all right. In Uganda, people who leave rooms escorted by policemen seldom come back.

After the ceremony I returned to Kampala where the President officially told me to take over the ministry. I did so at once, disguising the reluctance I felt at joining a disgruntled and disillusioned Cabinet. In the ministry, little changed. I did not even change offices. I had been preparing papers for the forthcoming Commonwealth Youth Ministers' meeting, due to be held in Zambia in January 1973. I simply went ahead with the work and got ready to go to the meeting myself.

Knowing what I did about the nature of Amin's rule, why did I serve? Mainly because I was not yet ready for the only alternative: flight. It was an alternative that several senior ministers chose at this time. Early in 1973 the Minister of Education, Edward Rugumayo, went to a meeting in Mombasa and decided not to return. He was able to arrange for his fiancée to join him in Nairobi, on the pretext of shopping for their wedding. He sent a telegram from Nairobi, stating that he could no longer be a party to mass killing, for which he blamed Amin. After Amin received the telegram, he appeared at a Cabinet meeting in a towering rage and demanded that any similarly dissenting minister leave at once. No one moved. The chairman of the East African Railways, Dan Nabudere, also fled, saying that he could no longer see officials killed without protest. My replacement as Amin's permanent secretary, Z. Bigirwenkya ("Big" to his friends), who had been on leave for several months, thought Amin was about to move against him, and vanished.

In March 1973, Uganda's Ambassador to Germany, John Barigye, refused to return home after the murder of his brother. His letter of resignation was a classic: he spoke of Amin's reign of terror, of the death of innocent people, of Amin's own complicity in "these barbarous acts" and concluded: "I have no alternative but to hereby tender my resignation, for this I believe is the only way I can listen to the dictates of my conscience and to universally held principles of civilized conduct."

All Amin could do in retaliation was to tell us that he had, "with immediate effect," stopped Barigye's salary. The following month the Foreign Minister, Wanume Kibedi, fled to Kenya. From there he went to London where, a year later, on June 21, 1974, in the form of an open letter of Amin, he issued a scathing denunciation of the regime. This was subsequently presented to the UN Secretary General as evidence of the gross violation of human rights in Uganda since Amin came to power.

Throughout 1973, the administration was preoccupied with the chaos resulting from the distribution of the Asians' property, an operation that began in late December 1972, when I was fortunately already in Zambia for the Commonwealth Youth Ministers' meeting. Amin appointed committees, run by ministers and officers from the army and police, to allocate the abandoned Asian property (although many properties he presented as gifts directly to family and friends). It was a chaotic business. There were no lists of applicants. The committees just moved from building to abandoned building, with applicants lining up outside in crowds, to be interviewed publicly. The properties were allocated on the spot. Each committee dealt rigidly with a particular area. One committee might allocate a shop on the main street, while around the corner another committee would dispose of its warehouse, and a third would hand out the cars from its garages. One furniture store had its showroom allocated separately from its workshop.

When the committees arrived to allocate the businesses, there was supposed to be someone to assess the goods in the shop, but this was an impossible task. In practice, the new owners just took down some of the goods or broke open the safes, and paid off the officials.

Officials in various ministries daily took home piles of shirts, shoes, jewelry, instruments, kitchenware furniture, food—anything they could lay their hands on. With this loot, the officials would then start their own businesses.

Haste and confusion notwithstanding, the ministers insisted on looking into the applicants' qualifications too closely for Amin's liking. A few weeks after the work started, he told the ministers to go back to their ministries and hand the whole job over to the army officers. This meant that the army—in effect Amin's Nubian friends— got everything from then on.

Thus people with no education, and no knowledge of business, were given big firms like the furnishing store Fazal Abdullah on Kampala Road, or General Motors on Bombo Road, the main importers of Peugeots. Some army officers became fabulously wealthy. One is reputed to have taken over about twenty houses in various parts of Uganda. Another reputedly acquired two dozen trailers, cars and trucks. Many officers neglected their duties to manage their new businesses, and could be seen in full uniform behind their counters, selling off their goods.

The new owners were completely at a loss. They did not know the prices of the items in their shops, and would ask customers, "How much did you pay for this before?" The purchaser simply named his own price. Goods were sold off for a fraction of their true value. The owner of one clothes shop took the collar size of his shirts as their price; a size 15 shirt sold for 15 shillings. Pharmacies were given to totally unqualified people, who sold off their drugs— poisons included—to anyone who asked. The army officer who received Kampala's top dental surgery, near Portal Avenue, ripped out the equipment and sold it. Many of the owners simply plundered the stocks and left, locking the buildings and sending the keys to the Ministry of Commerce. There was no way of tracing the vanished owners—there were no lists of who got what, and

THE RISE TO POWER

Amin, aged thirty-five, chats with General Sir Richard Hull, together with the then Lt. Col. Mulinge, now commander of Kenya's armed forces. Amin was then a lieutenant colonel.
KEYSTONE PRESS AGENCY LTD.

Watched by President Milton Obote (with walking stick), Amin directs army exercises in 1966. I am on the left, my back to the camera.
CAMERA PRESS LTD.

ABOVE: Obote is lifted by his jubilant cabinet after his success in the elections of 1962. Just behind him, wearing glasses, is Alex Ojera, then Minister of Information, murdered by Amin in 1972.

Two days after Amin's seizure of power on January 25, 1971, Amin's troops beat up an Obote supporter in their armored car.
ASSOCIATED PRESS LTD.

The early days: jubilant crowds throng the Kololo airstrip, as Amin drives a jeep–one of his favorite pastimes.
CAMERA PRESS LTD.

Amin stands to attention before the coffin bearing the body of the Kabaka of Buganda (1971). He had arranged for the Kabaka's body to be returned from London, to win over the Baganda, his former enemies.

THE NEW OVERLORD

The new head of state, playing the role of jovial "Big Daddy," bangs out one of the only two tunes he knows on the melodeon.

Celebrating the first anniversary of the coup; some of Amin's tanks tear up the pavement of City Square, Kampala.

CAMERA PRESS LTD.

LEFT: At a reception in Tel Aviv in 1971, Colonel Bar-Lev, then head of the Israeli Military Mission in Uganda, shows Amin an Israeli sub-machine gun, complete with silencer, which can be fitted into a briefcase. After the demonstration, guests-including the then Israeli Defense Minister, Moshe Dayan-toasted Uganda-Israeli friendship.

JOHN HILLELSON AGENCY LTD.

The head of the military police, the Southern Sudanese Hussein Marella (in cap, see also inset) – one of the most vicious men I have ever met – supervises the display of 200,000 shillings, found hidden in water pipes by an Asian exile.

Customs officials and State Research personnel delve into Asian property left at Entebbe Airport. The goods never left. This, and much more, was looted by the army.
ASSOCIATED PRESS LTD.

Amin strolls past Asian shops – like the one shown barred and shuttered (LEFT) accompanied by the then Minister of Commerce, Wilson Lutara, prior to allocating choice property to his own friends.

MASSACRE

ASSOCIATED PRESS LTD.

CAMERA PRESS LTD.

The corpses of Obote's guerrillas, bullet-riddled after mass execution, litter the compound of Mbarara Barracks, 50 miles from the Tanzanian border.
ASSOCIATED PRESS LTD.

OPPOSITE, ABOVE: Amin entertains two guerrillas, captured after the abortive invasion of September 1972, organized by Obote from Tanzania. After giving them drinks, Amin had the two men-one of whom, Pincho Ali (ABOVE, *left*) had worked with me in the President's Office-taken to prison (BELOW), where they were battered to death together with other guerrillas.

Bodies of slaughtered guerrillas slung into the back of a truck prior to mass burial.

OVERLEAF: In a double execution, Captain Tom Masaba, an alleged guerrilla, and Sebastiano Namirundu, a 16-year-old schoolboy, were killed before crowds forced to watch the execution. Namirundu's only crime was to flee from Amin's marauding troops.

CAMERA PRESS LTD.

Slain "guerrillas" are put on public view in Gulu, capital of
the Acholi tribe, who Amin considered supporters of Obote.
No armed opposition existed in Uganda.
There was nowhere to hide and no one would have risked the
lives of the local populace by working among them.

FRANK SPOONER PICTURES.

OVERLEAF: An alleged guerrilla is tied to a tree prior to execution, beneath a poster that adds a touch of macabre irony. Note that priests stand by. The scene of the execution is an open space beside the main Entebbe road.

for a longer
and better life!

One of Amin's first prominent civilian victims was Benedicto Kiwanuka, Prime Minister immediately before independence, and Chief Justice at the time of his murder, in September 1972; seen here on his arrival back from London.

FAMILY MAN

Sarah, shortly to become wife No. 5 (LEFT), stands with Aliga
(son of Kay, wife No. 2) and Mwanga (son of Medina, wife No. 4),
while "Big Daddy" looks benignly on, his pockets bulging as
usual with cash. Behind stands Amin's Maserati, one of his
many cars.
POPPERFOTO

Medina, formerly Amin's wife No. 4, now wife No. 1, stands in a formal reception for a visiting head of state. Her agile dancer's figure is disguised by her padded African dress.

STERN ARCHIVE

Kay Amin, wife No. 2, was a personal friend of mine for 9 years.
She later died in peculiar and mysterious circumstances.

Amin poses with Sarah in 1975. He had murdered her lover and
the father of her child. He married her twice: one ceremony for
the OAU heads of state, the other ceremony for a TV film.

Mwanga, Medina's son. Like Amin's other favorite sons on official occassions, he is dressed up as a miniature version of his father.

WHITE MAN'S SCOURGE

Amin, always eager to humiliate whites, especially his former British masters, stands with his then Chief of Staff, Mustafa Adrisi, while British residents in Kampala kneel to take oath as army reserves. Normally it is taken standing. To force the whites to kneel was – as he told me – a deliberate insult.

In another scene staged to humiliate local Britons, Amin sets himself up as a literal white man's burden. The occasion was a reception during the OAU summit conference in 1975.

OPPOSITE, ABOVE: James Callaghan, then British Foreign Secretary, concludes a 1975 visit that ensured the release of author Dennis Hills (RIGHT), who had been threatened with death by Amin for calling him a "village tyrant" in his book *The White Pumpkin*.

BELOW: Bob Astles, the Englishman who has for years been Amin's professional lapdog, was originally his pilot. He has no official post but is used for various errands and public relations jobs. His wife, Mary, a Ugandan, was recently made a minister.

The black dictator takes a salute at a review of soldiers wearing regulation issue jungle hats, at Masaka in 1976.

certainly no serious valuations of the properties involved.

The new owners had no interest in the future of their businesses and nobody was prepared to reinvest even if they knew how. They took all they could and built houses in their home villages. Soon all that tremendous wealth—millions upon millions of invested pounds which had been sustaining the country for decades—was to be scattered and lost for good. For a few months, however, Amin's henchmen, the army and countless government employees, were happy.

Among the richest prizes were the huge estates of the multimillionaire Madhvani family at Kakira and those of the Mehta family at Lugazi. Both were looted. The main Madhvani estate—apart from the vast Madhvani empire of companies and factories—employed several thousand people. The three main houses were palatial, with fountains in the living rooms and chairs with fitted stereophonic speakers. The property—furniture, carpets, draperies, pictures, works of art by the score—was taken to the vacant car showroom in Jinja, where an "auction" was held and the goods simply handed out to the troops. The houses, which could have been used for state visitors, were left empty. Amin himself took over one of the Madhvani houses in Jinja, a beautiful place with luxurious bathrooms and a massage parlor. He also took the Madhvani cars—the Mercedes and Cadillacs—and kept them at State House. It became commonplace to see him driving them around Kampala, to the considerable embarrassment of his ministers and officials. It showed the head of state to be what he was: a robber chief.

By mid-1973, the huge amounts of Asian wealth and property, which could have continued to support the country, had almost vanished. Dairy farms had been allocated to butchers, who slaughtered the milk animals and sold off the meat; since then the country has had little milk. Salt and sugar; bread, cheese; cars and their accessories; household goods—all the essentials of civilian life became increasingly rare.

The fate of Nakasero Soap Works—one of the biggest soap factories in the country—was typical of the effects of the reallocation. In 1973, the new owner was given nearly 25 million shillings' worth of foreign currency to import raw materials. Yet that year the factory produced just 15 million shillings' worth of goods. It would have saved ten million shillings for Uganda to have imported soap instead. But that would have been impossible: the import companies had collapsed also. They were abandoned by the new owners, who feared they would be imprisoned or killed if they did not do a good job. Few foreign suppliers would agree to do business except on cash terms. Today soap, if you can get it, costs 40 shillings (five dollars) a cake. In some villages, they crush pawpaw leaves to make a soap substitute.

Amin was amazed at what was happening. He never realized that businesses needed educated people to keep them running. He thought you just had to press a button and sit back. To save face, he instructed his ministers to blame the economic chaos on the old machinery left behind by the departed Asians. His attempted remedies only made matters worse. Some new owners were dispossessed and their assets seized. The businesses were either taken over by the government or allocated to other friends of Amin. Consequently all the new owners felt thoroughly unsafe, and made sure that if they were ever dispossessed, there would be very little that they could be dispossessed of. Nobody put any money in the banks; people preferred to keep it in their own houses in mattresses or in boxes.

Throughout 1973, and thereafter, the country's economic plight was accentuated by a massive brain drain. We had already lost the doctors, lawyers, accountants and other professionals of Asian origin. Now thousands of Ugandan professional men and women, on whose training the government had spent millions of shillings, fled. By 1977, fifteen ministers, six ambassadors and high commissioners, and eight permanent secretaries—in effect deputy ministers—had fled into exile. Two Vice Chancellors of Makerere University fled. Professors, heads of departments and lecturers fled by the score. Makerere lost professors of medicine, physics, agriculture and history. The dean of the medical school fled. Consultants and doctors fled. Nurses, midwives, teachers, and professionals of all kinds vanished in uncounted thousands. Today more of Uganda's professional talent live out of the country than in it.

The new generation of professionals that should be in training hardly exists. Schools cannot reorder books or needed equipment. Makerere University itself cannot supply books or pencils or pens. Paper is hard to get. Light bulbs are a rarity, and are stolen if not kept under lock and key. Under such conditions study becomes almost impossible.

From 1974 onward, signs of economic chaos multiplied. We used to export sugar, and have an export quota under the Lome Convention, which links a number of African, Caribbean and Pacific countries with the EEC. Now we can preserve our export quota only by importing an equivalent amount. The official price is seven shillings a kilo; the black market price is fifty.

We used to export cotton, but now we are producing about as much cotton nationally as we produced in one district, Busoga, in 1948.

No one in Uganda ever thought he would be short of salt; now it is a luxury. Many wash the crude salt from lakeside pans in order to live.

It is often impossible to get bread, for the wheat imports are erratic. Many foreign airlines have abandoned restocking facilities at Entebbe Airport, because bread, butter, sugar and eggs are very seldom available.

Tea, a traditional staple of the economy, is almost unobtainable. (The manager of the Brooke Bond Tea Factory, Mr. Masembe, was executed for his failure to provide sufficient quantities.) Amin exports whatever he can to London to pay for his imported luxury.

Before I left, I had not seen butter in the shops for many months. I hadn't seen bacon or cheese for years, both once local products.

This is the way things are in Uganda in 1977. In 1973, the process of collapse had already begun. Early that year, Amin moved against his own Cabinet. On February 22, he sent most of the ministers away for a month's holiday. He just announced on the radio that all the surviving ministers of his first Cabinet—which excluded me and a couple of other recent appointees—were to go on leave, and that all permanent secretaries were to take charge as ministers, "with immediate effect." Suddenly, the government had two sets of ministers in most Cabinet posts. In part, his decision reflected his bitterness at the defections by senior officials. But largely it came about because the Cabinet, long since reduced to impotence, was still reputedly a force to be reckoned with. He had heard once too often that he was lucky to have such a capable Cabinet, when he himself was such a hopeless fellow.

At the first meeting of the new Cabinet in early March Amin told his ministers that they were doing much better than their predecessors. The following week he announced that the displaced ministers were to take a second month's leave, since their replacements were doing so well. Finally, all the old ministers were retired (except four—Charles Oboth-Ofumbi, Emanuel Wakweya, Justus Byagagaire, and Erinayo Oryema— who were told to take on the demeaning task of assessing Asian property.)

In some ways the new Cabinet resembled Amin's first, in that it was made up largely of permanent secretaries with civilian backgrounds and considerable experience in government. But at the same time, Amin started to appoint military personnel as ministers without specific responsibilities. They were clearly being held in the wings to take over office later. This did not bother many of the civilians in the Cabinet, because we hoped privately that army officers would be able to exercise more influence on Amin than civilians could. But it soon became apparent that this hope was a false one: Amin would never allow any minister—military or civilian—to establish a power base that would threaten him or limit his arbitrary rule. He began to use Cabinet appointments as a way of cutting officers off from their military contacts. He even ordered those officers in nonmilitary posts to wear civilian clothes and to stay away from their army units, an order that was so unpopular he had to rescind it rapidly.

Cabinet meetings, which were rarely attended by Amin, were generally quiet affairs, despite the slaughter in the country at large. We all heard regularly enough of the arrests and killings. Sometimes these atrocities touched our daily lives, when our friends or our staff were affected. But we could do nothing. Any comment to Amin would risk our lives, and the lives of our families. We therefore kept our heads down and got on with the routine business of government.

And routine it was. Ministers were reduced to little more than ciphers. We were forbidden to discuss anything of significance, because such subjects were classed as security matters. Since nearly half the country's budget was devoted to the armed forces, we could not discuss the budget seriously. (The published figures, then and now, bear no relation to the realities.) We were not allowed to discuss Amin's decision to buy American planes (although we would have preferred to spend the money on buses) because he declared the purchases a security matter. We could not even talk about inflation—currently running at over four hundred per cent—because military men were running the businesses. The beating and murdering of civilians was declared a security matter. Even the murder of our own colleagues in the Cabinet was classified "security."

Amin seemed to enjoy humiliating his officials. This was typified by his treatment of his new Foreign Minister, Michael Ondoga. Ondoga, a plump little man, who made no great impression on first acquaintance, had been appointed Ambassador to the Soviet Union in 1971. In mid-1973, he was recalled by Amin to take charge of the Ministry of Foreign Affairs following the defection of Wanume Kibedi. Ondoga came to Kampala to receive his appointment, then returned briefly to the Soviet Union to collect his luggage and make his official farewells. He had been there just two days, when Amin announced on the radio that his new Foreign Minister would be dismissed even before he took office unless he returned immediately to start his work within forty-eight hours. He did return within the allotted time, bringing with him an accordion as a conciliatory gift to Amin. (Amin can in fact play two songs, both love songs, and both with calypso-like tunes. To one of them he puts his own words: "I love this slim girl from Kyaggwe"—Kyaggwe is the part of the country his fourth wife, Medina, comes from. He often entertains visitors by singing these songs. He can't play much else.)

Ondoga got off to a bad start in office with his near dismissal in Moscow, but I never did discover why Amin conceived such a violent dislike of him. Clearly, though, he had made up his mind to get rid of Ondoga. At the end of 1973, Ondoga took over an abandoned Asian house near Amin's Command Post. It had become established practice for senior officials and ministers to move at will into any such property they fancied. But when Amin found out what Ondoga had done, he was furious; without even telephoning to ask him to move elsewhere, he ordered the Military Police to go to the house and throw him out. If the Minister of Foreign Affairs cannot live in a house of his choice, I thought, he won't last long. Ondoga must have had the same thought. For security's sake, he began going out only in the company of friends.

Amin made his move at the end of February 1974, one

week after I was made Minister of Health. He marched into a Cabinet meeting, and remarked that some ministers thought they were too important, and that one of them, Ondoga, thought he could make himself immune by "appointing extra bodyguards." It immediately struck me that Amin must have tried to have Ondoga arrested, but had been foiled by Ondoga's own security precautions. No doubt he was smarting under the irritation of being unable to have him killed discreetly.

Fresh from this sudden castigation of one of our number, we all moved on to a graduation ceremony at Makerere University. As we walked together to the ceremony, I joined up briefly with a senior member of the Ugandan Foreign Service, Princess Elizabeth Bagaya of Toro, who had trained as a lawyer and was at that time acting as a roving ambassador. She was a good-looking, capable woman. It was widely known that Amin admired her, and that she had rejected his advances. I suggested that she sit with us. She hesitated; "Well," she said, "no, thank you." To open the ceremony in front of several hundred diplomats, academics, and guests, Amin rose to speak. He called Elizabeth Bagaya up to the rostrum. Out of the blue, he announced that he had fired Ondoga as Foreign Minister, and proceeded to introduce his new Foreign Minister, Elizabeth Bagaya. I looked across at Ondoga who was sitting not far away. He was clearly shocked and horribly humiliated, yet he had no alternative but to clap like everyone else. Amin never told him what he was supposed to have done wrong.

After this, Ondoga's days were numbered. Unlike Wanume Kibedi, he had waited too long to flee. He was followed everywhere. Eventually, they waylaid him while he was taking his daughter, Peace, to her school, which happens to be close to the headquarters of the State Research Bureau. As he drew up in his car, a State Research vehicle pulled alongside. Several men leapt out, surrounded Ondoga's car, and ordered him to get out.

Then in front of his daughter, several teachers, and many parents they beat him up. He tried to resist, but he was a small man, and nobody came to his aid. It was clear to all those watching that this was another bird for the kill. One of the attackers was a Nubian Presidential bodyguard, a notorious killer known as Hassan. He and his henchmen forced Ondoga into the State Research car which then sped away, while one of the thugs helped himself to Ondoga's car. (Hassan is now a senior official with Transocean Uganda Ltd., a government transport company.)

On the following Sunday, I came home from a reception to find a message awaiting me from the President. He asked me to check the identity of a body, reportedly that of the former Foreign Minister, which had been taken to the Jinja Hospital mortuary. Since I had not been available, the chief medical officer there had arranged for identification and for a post mortem. The doctor, an Englishman named Crawden, told me that Ondoga had been shot and stabbed. His head had been battered in and some ribs broken by a heavy, blunt instrument. The body had been immersed in water. (One of my contacts told me later that, two days after Ondoga's arrest, he had seen a helicopter hovering over the source of the Nile. Something—he thought it was probably a body—had been thrown out. It could well have been Ondoga.)

I told the President about the state of the body. He clearly knew already and made no comment. He simply sent Colonel Malyamungu to check the identification. A guard was placed at the hospital mortuary to prevent the relatives from taking the body away. I assumed that this was a temporary measure, but to my surprise, I learned that the army had been told to place the body in a coffin and fly it to the West Nile for burial. I doubt if the relatives had a chance to see it.

Ondoga's successor, Princess Elizabeth, never seemed particularly popular with Amin. The job was an impossible one. Amin always acts as his own Foreign Minister. He may have appointed her in the hope of winning her affections, but if so he was disappointed. Her intelligence, beauty and independence probably only served to anger him further. His treatment of her was oddly contradictory. In November 1974, he sent her to New York to defend him before the UN. Perhaps fearing she might defect, he praised her inordinately even before she delivered her speech. He announced that she was far more intelligent than Secretary of State Henry Kissinger. She did, indeed, make a most impressive defense of Amin, and received an ovation in the Assembly. To make doubly certain of her return, Amin awarded her the Order of the Source of the Nile, Second Class (the Order of the Source of the Nile, First Class, is reserved for heads of state), announcing that she was to receive it on her return. She never did receive it. Instead, she was placed under house arrest. A few days later, she was allowed to come to a Cabinet meeting. During this meeting she was summoned from it to the President's office. She came back after only a few minutes, picked up her bag and left without a word. It was obvious something was wrong.

Later that day, the President announced that he had dismissed his Minister of Foreign Affairs, for the most extraordinary reason: he said that she had had sexual intercourse in the bathroom of Charles de Gaulle Airport, Paris, on her return from New York. He never said who with. This was both a deliberate insult and a deliberate lie, but it was also comically nonsensical. One may, I suppose, have sex anywhere—but a public toilet? In private we laughed ourselves to tears at Amin's action. We also knew, however, that it had a sinister dimension. Fortunately for Elizabeth Bagaya, she was able to flee to Kenya.

My tenure as Minister of Culture, 1972-74, was not particularly demanding. Within my own ministry there were few problems. I had to ensure that football matches between army teams and civilians were properly controlled, otherwise the bitterness towards the army tended to erupt into open violence. One particular club, the Express (since banned by Amin), was nicknamed the "Club of the Dead" because so many of its officials and supporters had been murdered. In any Army-Express match the army team had to win. If it lost, the crowd would be in for a beating for being "anti-army."

I also had to organize the Heartbeat of Africa, Uganda's national dance troupe. After the coup, Amin took considerable interest in this troupe—his wife Medina was a Heartbeat dancer. The troupe had to be immensely expanded—from forty to about four hundred—to ensure the inclusion of dancers from all parts of Uganda. The Heartbeat troupe almost became synonymous, in Amin's mind, with the Ministry of Culture. Amin insisted on having them with him when he went on tours, both nationally and internationally.

By early 1973, Amin had already established the routine that has been a feature of his government ever since. Being semi-literate, Amin finds it difficult to do office work—reading, writing and dictating. He signs his official papers wherever he happens to be, for he has no files and seldom takes notes. He may talk to a minister for hours and jot down no more than one or two words. His secretary's job is mainly to make abstracts of his conversations for broadcast on the radio.

He administers the country by talking to people on the telephone, which allows him to dramatize his own importance. "I am meeting here with the Defense Council . . ." he will begin, when in fact he is alone or with a girlfriend. I have been the "Defense Council" on several occasions. In my experience, the phrase—when it is not an outright lie—means that he is with one or two people from whom he has had a report about the person he has just telephoned. Everyone knows that if he says he is with the Vice President or the Chief of Staff he may well not be.

The atmosphere that he creates, therefore, is thick with

lies and distortion. Sometimes though, when it suits him, he tells the truth. This interweaving of truth and falsehood engenders a universal suspicion in which people will volunteer information, true or false, in an effort to remain in his good graces. Such information never buys his favor for long, for he distrusts everyone and betrays all confidences. Several times he has said to me, "You think so-and-so is your friend? Wait till you hear what he is saying about you." He accepts reports with equal interest and equal distrust whether they come from drivers or ministers, privates or senior officers.

Amin mostly operates from his residences and hotels. He moves around constantly for security purposes. When he calls you on the telephone, you can never tell where he is. If you ask where he is, he will immediately suspect you. He has telephones everywhere—in every room, at the swimming pools, at the places where he takes warm baths and massages. They have direct lines, with their own numbers. But if anyone phones him at those numbers, he will suspect them of spying. The only safe way to contact him is to call State House and allow the operator to make the connection.

Knowing his methods, the Cabinet kept quiet and tried not to attract his attention. Indeed, 1973 was the quietest year I ever had in government. But underneath, as the Asian wealth was dissipated and the shortages rose, forces were at work that were to transform the country. It was a deceptive and ominous peace.

4
Reign of Terror

To understand Amin's reign of terror it is necessary to realize that he is not an ordinary political tyrant. He does more than murder those whom he considers his enemies: he also subjects them to barbarisms even after they are dead. These barbarisms are well attested. It is common knowledge in the Ugandan medical profession that many of the bodies dumped in hospital mortuaries are terribly mutilated, with livers, noses, lips, genitals or eyes missing. Amin's killers do this on his specific instructions; the mutilations follow a well-defined pattern. After a foreign service officer, Godfrey Kiggala, was shot in June 1974, his eyes were gouged out and his body was partially skinned before it was dumped in a wood outside Kampala. Medical reports on the deaths of the Minister of Works, Shabani Nkutu, in January 1973, and the Minister of Foreign Affairs, Lt. Col. Ondoga, in March 1974, stated that the bodies had been cut open and that a number of internal organs had been tampered with.

On several occasions when I was Minister of Health, Amin insisted on being left alone with his victims' bodies. Such was the case when the acting Chief of Staff, Brigadier Charles Arube, was murdered in March 1974. Amin came to see the body while it was in the mortuary of Mulago Hospital; he ordered the deputy medical superintendent, Dr. Kyewalabaye, to "wait outside"; Amin then went in by himself for two or three minutes.

There is of course no evidence for what he does in private, but it is universally believed in Uganda that he engages in blood rituals. Hardly any Ugandan doubts that Amin has, quite literally, a taste for blood.

Amin's bizarre behavior has much to do with the peculiarities of his own aberrant personality. It also derives partly from his tribal background. Like many other warrior societies, the Kakwa, Amin's tribe, are known to have practiced blood rituals on slain enemies. These involve cutting a piece of flesh from the body to subdue the dead man's spirit or tasting the victim's blood to render the spirit harmless—a spirit, it is believed, will not revenge itself on a body that has become in effect its own. Such rituals still exist among the Kakwa. If they kill a man, it is their practice to insert a knife in the body and touch the bloody blade to their lips.

The ritual has been observed even in the upper ranks of the government. The driver of a Kakwa official, a senior member of the administration, told me that he was driving his boss through the Murchison Falls National Park in 1976, when they came upon some big-game poachers. The official, armed with a rifle and a knife (as is common for Amin's men), shot two of the poachers. He then went up to the corpses, stabbed each one with his knife and licked the blade.

I have reason to believe that Amin's practices do not stop at tasting blood: on several occasions he has boasted to me and others that he has eaten human flesh. One day, in August 1975, he was talking to some senior officials about a trip to Zaire, and said that he had been served monkey meat there. Seeing that his audience was rather shocked by this (eating monkey meat is unacceptable to Ugandans), and clearly deciding to dramatize the occasion further, he added, "I have also eaten human meat." I heard the others catch their breath in horror. We all looked at each other, bewildered, uncertain how to react. A silence fell. Realizing he had gone too far, he went on to say that eating human flesh is not uncommon in his home area. He justified the practice in coolly practical terms: "In warfare, if you do not have food, and your fellow soldier is wounded, you may as well kill him and eat him to survive."

On another occasion in September 1976, when I was with him at the President's Lodge at Nakasero, we were talking with a Ugandan doctor who was due to go overseas shortly. We started to talk about eating habits. Amin mentioned various unusual types of meat he had eaten—for instance, leopard and monkey—and then went on to say: "I have eaten human meat. It is very salty, even more salty than leopard meat."

Amin is certainly superstitious enough to engage in blood rituals. He regularly visits witch doctors, both in Jinja, where friends of mine have seen him entering the witch doctor's house, and in Kampala. Witch doctors are consulted in Uganda, particularly by Moslems, as astrologers and psychiatrists are consulted in the West. Amin usually goes to them because he needs advice on some problem or other—he may wish to have an "enemy" named, for instance, or he may want to know what action to take to avoid assassination. No doubt his sessions follow the same pattern as other, similar consultations: the client comes bearing a chicken, goat or some other offering. The witch doctor tells the client to sit in a darkened room, then asks a number of questions, to elicit the information that will later form the basis of his advice. He then mumbles a few incantations, before telling the client what he should do. He may also provide the client with some beads to be worn as amulets or he may give him a magic chant to be used on particular occasions. The consultation is then at an end.

Amin also frequently consults the head of the Moslem religion in the army, Colonel Khamis Saafi, who is himself a firm believer in witchcraft. The colonel once came to me with a request to transfer a Mulago nurse because, as he put it, she was bewitching a former lover to make him impotent. He said that if she was sent to a

remote area the spell would be broken. I did not oblige
him.

Amin's extraordinary sadism and cruelty have often
been said to be a direct result of syphilis, which in its final
stages affects the brain, driving the victim insane. Amin's
records show that he has indeed suffered from syphilis.
One of his girlfriends, a nurse, complained to me that she
had been infected by him and rendered infertile.

It is rumored that the disease is progressive in Amin
and that he will eventually succumb to it. I have seen no
medical evidence of this. But even if it is true, in my
judgment it cannot explain his behavior. His extreme
brutality is not the result of brain damage but a long-term
phenomenon. His orders are premeditated and consistent. I have seem him dangerously angry. I have
heard him lash out in apparently uncontrollable rage,
ordering indiscriminate arrest and death. But he knows
well enough how to stage-manage his rages. The most
telling example of this occurred in mid-1973 when, for the
benefit of a French television crew, he exploded in rage,
threatening to shoot all recalcitrant ministers. He
behaved like a wild animal. The tribal scars on his
temple—the three vertical marks which have earned the
Kakwas the nickname "One-Elevens"—stood out
sharply, as they always do when he is angry. Yet
immediately after the television crew had left, he joked
about his performance. "How did it come out?" he asked
me, laughing.

Such is the extraordinary personality that is
responsible for Uganda's current state of terror. His rule
depends for its effectiveness on the Southern Sudanese he
has imported, on members of his own Kakwa tribe, and
on recruits from the Nubian community scattered
throughout Uganda.

Amin's thugs, who must now number more than
15,000, are placed at every level in the army and
administration. But first they are trained in one of three

units, whose total roll is around 3,000 at any one time. In
ascending order of power, these are the Military Police; a
police intelligence group known as the Public Safety
Unit; and Amin's dreaded corps of "bodyguards," the
State Research Bureau. Theoretically, the three units
have different responsibilities. But they are all staffed by
Southern Sudanese, Kakwas and Nubians; they all
respond to Amin's direct orders; and their activities
overlap to comprise a powerful, merciless machine of
terror that reaches into every corner of Uganda and seizes
victims from even the highest level of Ugandan society, at
will and with impunity.

The Southern Sudanese are recruited from the
northwest in an odd but effective way. At night
truckloads of Sudanese trained by the State Research
Bureau and other terror units are driven through the bush
across the undemarcated border. The men are dropped
off in their home territories, where they offer their friends
work, promising them high rewards in wages and luxury
goods. The next day the trucks return to ferry the new
recruits back into Uganda.

These Sudanese mercenaries have no compunction
about their actions. They are, after all, foreigners. But the
Kakwa and Nubians are not much better. They actually
have more in common with the Sudanese than with their
fellow Ugandans. Often they do not speak the language
of the people among whom they come to work; they own
no local property; they do not bring their families with
them; most of the houses they occupy belong to expelled
Asians or Ugandan exiles. (In fact, people are often
forced to flee so that their houses may be seized and
looted.)

Immediately after the coup, Amin had to have an
organization he could rely on. He found it in the Military
Police, established in Obote's day for disciplining army
personnel. It had been quite small and not particularly
feared. Its headquarters at Makindye are not outwardly
forbidding: the compound of single-story buildings

stands right on the main road leading from Kampala to Entebbe. It was only in late 1971, when a Nubian, Major Hussein Marella, took the force over that it became a notorious terror unit. It executes Amin's will both among the civilian population and within the armed forces.

The second organization that acts as Amin's instrument of terror is the Public Safety Unit, which also acquired its notoriety in late 1971, when the murderous Ali Towelli, another Nubian, took over. Originally it was set up as part of the civil police to deal with armed robbery, which grew to epidemic proportions in the capital after the coup. The unit was equipped with submachine guns and allowed to shoot robbers on sight. At that time, anyone who found a thief could kill him with impunity. Once, the guard at my house killed a thief prowling around outside. The following morning, I telephoned Amin and told him; he gave my guard 500 shillings for doing a good job.

The Public Safety Unit is based at Naguru, next to the police college, about three miles from the center of the capital on the Kampala-Jinja road. Much of the activity that goes on in the compound takes place in full public view; this is intentional and meant to serve as a warning to any potential "enemies" of Amin. Opposite the headquarters stands a high-rise management training center that towers over the compound, giving everyone there a commanding view over Naguru. The cries of prisoners can often be heard from the roads that run alongside. (One is a particularly busy road leading to a housing development; my own bodyguard, Vincent Masiga, lives there). Sometimes a crowd will gather to watch an execution.

A peculiarly sadistic form of death has been developed at Naguru by Ali Towelli. To save ammunition, one prisoner is forced to batter out the brains of another with a heavy hammer on the promise of a reprieve. The "executioner" is then killed in the same way by another prisoner brought from the cells with the same promise. (In fact, such atrocities at Naguru will be even more public in the future: by a grotesque irony, part of the area has been designated holy ground in preparation for the construction of a mosque, to be supervised by Ali Towelli himself.)

Under Ali Towelli, the Public Safety Unit has become an instrument of terrifying public menace. Like the Military Police, its activities reach deeper and deeper into the civilian population, increasingly overlapping those of the most feared and most powerful of the three terror units—the State Research Bureau.

The State Research Bureau—the secret police—was set up as a military intelligence agency to replace Obote's bodyguards, and its successor fulfills the same function for Amin. These people—about 2,000 at any one time, under the effective command of another Nubian, Major Farouk Minawa—are Amin's keys to power. The Bureau headquarters, is next to the President's Lodge at Nakasero. During the construction of the three-story building by a Yugoslav firm, a tunnel was built between it and the Lodge, as an escape route in case the President is surrounded. It is also next door to the French Embassy, which must cause the French considerable embarrassment. In the last six years, some 12,000 men have passed through the Bureau. After their tours of duty, the men are sent on to posts in the army, the government, or embassies abroad.

In the army, Bureau "graduates" within each battalion have formed small terror gangs which are responsible for operations within their own barracks and for public executions in the surrounding areas. Crowds of 10,000 and more were ordered to attend several public executions in 1973.

Within the administration, some Bureau men have even become provincial governors. These people—who have never made a sensible speech, are semi-literate, and speak hardly a word of English—are in charge of the provincial planning committees and security committees, and control all the other local administrative business. Of course, they are not there to administer. They retain their firearms; they are in constant touch with the State Research Bureau headquarters; and they act as reserves to carry out Amin's orders.

The State Research staff are on the official payroll, but their salaries are negligible compared to the loot they get from their jobs. They steal money from their victims; they are paid lavish funds by Amin as a reward for gathering information; and they are given fantastic sums to spend when they go overseas. Many of these young men keep two or three cars in overseas missions, plus several more in Kampala. They lead a life that no other Ugandan can now afford. They do not wear uniforms. Typically, they dress flamboyantly in flowered shirts, bellbottomed trousers and dark glasses. For any young Kakwa or Southern Sudanese it is an exceptionally attractive proposition.

The thugs in these three units operate anywhere, at any time, and in full public view. They arrest people in offices, at public functions, and in restaurants. They drive the Datsuns, Toyotas, Peugeots and Range Rovers that form the Presidential escort. Victims are picked up in these cars—which usually carry the registration letters UVS (I mention the registrations whenever possible as a further embarrassment to Amin)—and bundled into the boots (trunks) of the cars. "To put someone in the boot" has become a phrase equated with a humiliating public arrest. Amin has claimed that the disappearances are organized by Obote guerrillas, but no one has ever believed him.

It is possible, from the numbers of men who have passed through the three units and on into the army and the administration, to gain some idea of the extraordinary machine Amin has built up. Elsewhere in this book, I have estimated the number of deaths over the past six years as 150,000 plus. This is well within the range of killings that Amin's thugs could have achieved.

Among them, the three units employ some 3,000 people at any one time. Since a tour of duty averages a year, the number of men trained to kill increases at a rate of 3,000 per year, making a current total of 18,000. Assuming that each trained killer is responsible for three murders a year, the numbers mount annually from a theoretical 9,000 in the first year (1971, when in fact the death toll was much higher) to 54,000 in 1977. This makes a total of 189,000.

But cold figures can never convey adequately the savagery of the system that has ravaged my country. I have listed in the dedication to this book one hundred of the dead, mostly prominent people whom I knew personally. What follows is an attempt to show what the system means in practice. The cases I cite come from my personal experience and cover the range of terror—from murder to theft with violence—which is now a part of everyday life in Uganda.

In September 1972, Amin gave terrifying notice to us all that no one, however prominent, would be safe. On the twenty-first of that month, Benedicto Kiwanuka, Chief Justice and former Prime Minister, was murdered. Kiwanuka was an experienced, highly respected politician and lawyer who had been imprisoned by Obote and released by Amin. Later he had angered Amin by releasing, for lack of evidence, a Briton arrested by Amin's men. Amin had subsequently criticized in public "a prominent Ugandan from Masaka"—Kiwanuka's home.

At about 3:00 P.M. on September 21, State Research personnel drove up to the High Court in a Peugeot 504 (registration UUU 171), seized Kiwanuka, removed his shoes to humiliate him, forced him downstairs in full view of other judges, pushed him into the car and drove off. He was never seen again, and his body has never been found. Amin later accused Kiwanuka of working with Obote; then, with startling inconsistency, blamed Obote's guerrillas for Kiwanuka's disappearance. I heard of the arrest within minutes, as did all of Kampala. It was a totally sickening event.

But for me there was greater horror to come. That same afternoon, my own brother, Kisajja, was seized. He knew Amin well. It was he who had been in love with Mary, Amin's first wife's sister. He was also well known by Amin's men. As personnel manager of Nyanza Textile Industries he had recruited a number of Kakwas and Nubians as unskilled labor—people like Charles Arube (later a brigadier), and Isaac Malyamungu (later a colonel in the army).

Kisajja was picked up from his office at 3:00 P.M. in full view of his colleagues. I do not know why. The only reason I can think of is that he was a great friend of Amin's brother-in-law, the Minister of Foreign Affairs, Wanume Kibedi, who had too strong a political base in Jinja for Amin's liking. (Some of Kibedi's other supporters, such as the Jinja town engineer and the treasurer of the municipal council, were killed around this time.) Kisajja was bundled into a Peugeot 404, a Public Safety Unit car and driven to Kampala. I was notified of his arrest within half an hour. I immediately telephoned the Minister of Internal Affairs, Charles Oboth-Ofumbi; the head of the Military Police, Colonel Hussein Marella; and several other officials to try to bring pressure on Amin. Amin was informed at once. Later an acquaintance of mine at the Public Safety Unit headquarters at Naguru called to say that Kisajja had been brought in and that I should notify higher authorities as quickly as possible to prevent his murder. I again called the same people and told them that my brother had just arrived at Naguru. I was told not to worry—things would be all right. I waited, but heard nothing.

On the third day, September 24, increasingly desperate, I again called Naguru. I was told that Kisajja had been removed from there and taken to Makindye, the Military Police headquarters. I contacted Colonel

Marella who promised to telephone as soon as he had
checked. He never called back. The next day I called him
again. He told me Kisajja had not been transferred from
Naguru to Makindye. I knew then that my brother must
already have been killed at Naguru.

I never did learn anything officially. Later, a former
inmate who had been at Naguru at the time, told me—
after he had successfully bought his way out—that he saw
my brother in prison, and that the Public Safety Unit
thugs were killing people at random. He did not see how
my brother could have survived.

After the death of my brother, it did not seem possible
to continue in government service. I was in a position of
some authority. Was I not by my very presence
sanctioning the terror? How could I ignore the sense of
moral outrage that all decent people were beginning to
feel? My dilemma was shared by many of the ministers.
One obvious solution was to resign. But it was not
possible to resign and remain in Uganda: that would have
been an invitation to execution. If I resigned I would have
had to go into exile, as many ministers had done already.
But it seemed to me that such action could only be
justified if my family and I were in danger or if defection
would make a significant impact on Amin's regime. I was
in no personal danger and, as a permanent secretary in a
relatively minor ministry, my departure in 1972 would
not have had much effect.

Shortly after Kisajja's death, I left the country
officially for about two weeks, and postponed my
decision. When I returned I was made a minister. Now
there seemed to be valid reasons for staying. Like many
newly appointed ministers, I believed that, for me, things
would be different. I thought it might really be possible to
exercise some influence on the course of government.
Given my personal relationship with Amin I believed I
could be of more use inside Uganda than outside it.

I did not think Amin would ride over me as he did over

so many others. I did not believe I would ever be in any personal danger. I had known Amin for years. He usually listened to anything I had to say. The best way of serving my country, I thought, was to do what little I could to try and limit the terror. It took another change of job and another five years for me to learn how impotent—and how dispensable—I really was.

In October of 1972, I learned that the Vice Chancellor of Makerere University, Frank Kalimuzo, had fallen victim to Amin's terror. Kalimuzo had been permanent secretary in the President's office before me, and I used to work closely with him. He had been appointed Vice Chancellor by Obote, who called him "the donkey" for his capacity for hard work. (The nickname was adopted by the students for different reasons). During 1972, he came under attack from Amin for "collaborating" with Obote, and passing government information to forces outside the country. The invasion of September 1972 provided Amin with the excuse he needed to move against Kalimuzo. The arrangements were bungled: before the police had time to pick the Vice Chancellor up, the radio announced that he had disappeared. Immediately, Kalimuzo telephoned Amin to say that the radio announcement was incorrect. Friends told him to leave before it became correct, but he had done nothing wrong, and determined, donkey-like, to stay put. He was arrested soon afterwards. His body has never been found.

The disappearances are so numerous now that a woman will fear for her husband's safety if he is late coming home from work. So many have vanished never to be seen again, dead or alive, that an extraordinary new profession has sprung up—"body-finding"—of which Amin's men are the chief beneficiaries. Uganda is a religious country and it is vital for religious reasons—let alone personal ones—that the bodies should be properly buried. Body-finders work in teams. If anyone disappears, relatives immediately contact the team and arrange a fee for the tracing of the body. The teams are in daily contact with the murder squads. Sometimes news will come directly from the murderers, via the bodyfinders, who offer assistance to the relatives in finding the body. The fee varies depending on the status of the victim. To trace a junior official, the family might be asked for 5,000 shillings (600 dollars); it could take anything from 25,000 shillings (3,000 dollars) upwards to find the body of a senior member of the administration. There are also many bogus-finders who offer their services, take the money and vanish. When my own brother disappeared, my family spent some 30,000 shillings (4,000 dollars) in a futile attempt to trace his body. My contact at that time is still one of Amin's bodyguards.

In January 1973, Shabani Nkutu was murdered. He had been Minister of Works in the Obote government and was now a shopkeeper. Nkutu was arrested one evening at his home, not far from my own house in Jinja. We had known each other for many years. He was a scrupulously law-abiding, gentle individual.

Just before Nkutu's arrest, a State Research car was seen driving up and down outside his grocery shop. Forewarned, relatives and friends put up a fight on his behalf. The thugs fired a few shots into the air to scare off the opposition and seized Nkutu. The following morning, Radio Uganda announced that he had fled to Tanzania. Shortly afterward his body was recovered near the source of the Nile and taken to Jinja Hospital mortuary, where it was placed under guard. Nkutu's relatives, who had learned the body was in the mortuary, made attempts to recover it, but it could not be officially released since Nkutu was supposed to have fled. In fact, Amin had ordered the body to be buried secretly in a common grave at Masese. Amin then attempted to seize Nkutu's property on the now customary pretext that Nkutu had run away. The family insisted, "You tell us where Nkutu is—since you claim to know—then we can go and bring him back." Amin eventually gave up.

The next incident of which I have personal knowledge concerned the National Insurance Corporation, which has an almost total monopoly in Uganda of insurance of all types. As is usual for such corporations, it is headed by a chairman, who is the chief executive, and under him, a board of directors and a corporation secretary. One afternoon in early 1973, members of the Public Safety Unit burst into the corporation's ten-story building in the center of Kampala, arrested the chairman, Mr. Wekiro, and the secretary, Mr. Tidhamulala. They hit them repeatedly in front of their staff, forced them downstairs past a crowd of onlookers, and shoved them into waiting cars. They drove them to the headquarters of the Public Safety Unit at Naguru. By the time the cars arrived, the secretary was almost dead. He died soon afterward.

The same evening, Radio Uganda announced that the police had arrested two people from the insurance corporation; "the secretary," the radio reported, "was unwell." Knowing that he must have been killed, his relatives, who are well known to me, made desperate attempts to recover the body; it was never released. Having murdered the secretary, the army went on to dispossess his wife of their private house, and handed it over to the then Commander of the Air Force, Brigadier Smuts Guweddeko. (Guweddeko, formerly a telephone operator at Mulago Hospital, had already been given an abandoned Asian house, complete with swimming pool and tennis court, as his official residence.) The victim's wife and children were evicted. They subsequently returned to their home village.

The chairman, Mr. Wekiro, was detained in Naguru prison for several weeks. He was assigned the task of looking after Ali Towelli's goats and sheep, which Towelli had received as bribes. Eventually, he managed to buy his way out. Nothing was mentioned again about his arrest or his release.

Another incident I know about concerned one of Uganda's only two qualified pharmacologists, Dr. Mawerere. On August 5, 1976, Dr. Mawerere was in the doctors' club near Mulago Hospital, when one of Amin's Nubian thugs from the Military Police came in. He demanded that the club sell him huge quantities of beer and cigarettes.

Dr. Mawerere ordered the intruder to leave. The thug, in retaliation, struck him down and kicked him, breaking his jaw and knocking him unconscious. He then fled. Dr. Mawerere was taken at once to the hospital and given medical treatment. His colleagues reported the beating to the police, but the police took no action. The thug had meanwhile gone back to the Military Police, and complained that he had been insulted by the doctor. The following day, the Military Police sent in a unit to arrest the doctor, who was still only semiconscious—he had clips in his jaw and was incapable of speech. I was infuriated beyond measure when I heard what was happening. I drove straight to the hospital, walked up to the ward (6C) and found half-a-dozen military men with automatic rifles guarding Dr. Mawerere's bed. The doctors and other staff gathered around and asked me how they could be expected to work when one of their profession was being humiliated in this fashion. With some difficulty, I persuaded them not to walk out but to allow me to see what could be done.

Seething with anger, I walked downstairs to the office, telephoned Amin and told him, "I cannot have the army coming to arrest people who are unconscious, let alone a doctor in the hospital, and still expect other doctors to work. It is inhuman." In normal circumstances I would not have allowed my anger to run away with me in this way. Fortunately, Amin did not take offense. He had clearly been informed of the situation in advance because he refused to see its urgency. He pointed out that doctors should not be above the law. I agreed but added, "If Dr. Mawerere has broken the law, then the arrest should be properly conducted."

After a few days, the troops were withdrawn and the patient left to recover in peace. Dr. Mawerere later fled the country, as did the other pharmacologist, Dr. Anakabong. Now, Uganda has none.

At the end of January 1977 (just three months before my escape), some Makerere students organized a party to which many hospital nurses were invited. After the dance, around midnight or soon after, the nurses were on their way home in an official Uganda Transport bus, hired for the occasion. They were accompanied by some students and by a university security officer.

The bus was stopped by a State Research vehicle, a Volkswagen. Inside were two men. They came out holding guns and demanded from the driver proof of his authority to travel at night. Since driving at night was part of his job, he had no special authorization papers. The university security officer tried to explain why they were out so late, but one of the State Research thugs just punched him and took over the wheel. Escorted by the Volkswagen, he drove the bus back to the State Research Bureau.

As they pulled in, at about 2:00 A.M., the new driver damaged the bus on the compound gate. He ordered all the nurses and the students to file out, remove their shoes, and file into the State Research headquarters. Several other State Research men now appeared. They ordered the male students into a room on one side of the building, and the women into another some distance away. The women were told to undress, to stand up holding their clothes and to march around to be viewed. They were then raped. There was not enough room for them all to be raped in the room, so several were raped in the cars, in the bus, and in small, temporary office cabins. The men kept calling their friends to come and help themselves to the nurses. Many of the State Research patrols were returning after the night's operations, so anyone who wanted, joined in. Afterward, some of the women managed to run out. Some were put in a State Research vehicle and driven back to the hospital. Others simply walked down to the bus stop and hid until daylight, when they took buses back to the hospitals. The boys, after being roughed up, were released. The bus remained at Nakasero.

I heard of the incident only two or three days later, from a friend of mine who was responsible for the buses. One of his vehicles was missing; he wanted to find out what had happened to it, and to the nurses it was carrying. I contacted the hospital authorities to find out. It was then that I heard of the trouble. None of the nurses wanted to talk about it. Many of them feared admitting that they had been in the bus, and it was not until I questioned them thoroughly that I learned exactly what had gone on.

When I heard the full story, I contacted Vice President Mustafa Adrisi, told him what had happened and asked him to have the State Research Bureau men arrested. I followed this request up with a very long memorandum detailing the events and pointing out that the evidence was clear cut: the commandeered bus was still at their headquarters. Adrisi said something would be done, but nothing ever was. Not one of the thugs concerned was ever disciplined.

The theft of private property is in no way so hideous as the assault on human life, but the impunity with which the State Research Bureau can steal demonstrates another aspect of their unassailable power. One of their most common practices is car theft. One case is particularly well known to me.

On December 31, a group of Amin's bodyguards, traveling in one of his own escort cars, a blue left-hand drive Peugeot 504 (registration UVV 015), decided that they wanted another car. Early in the morning—about 7:00 A.M.—they parked almost opposite Kira Police

Station, intending to waylay any suitable car that passed.

That day, one of Mulago Hospital's two neuro-surgeons, Dr. Kahwa, happened to be driving in early to see a patient. As his Mercedes approached the Peugeot, it pulled out in front of him. The doctor, suspecting trouble, swung his car around the Peugeot and sped away. The bodyguards immediately gave chase. They tried to overtake him, but he refused to allow them to pull abreast. The two cars approached a traffic circle at which Dr. Kahwa should have turned right toward the hospital. He realized that it would be difficult to get into the hospital compound in safety, since he would have to stop at the gate. So, instead of turning right, he veered left into a wider road. There the bodyguards were able to overtake him. As they forced him onto the side, the cars came abreast of a minor road to the left, which Dr. Kahwa, with considerable presence of mind, immediately took, doubling back to the hospital in time to enter the compound safely. When Amin's bodyguards arrived at the hospital gates they argued with the gatekeepers and forced their way in. Meanwhile, Dr. Kahwa was at the casualty department, where he had had time to summon a crowd of hospital staff to back him up.

As soon as the bodyguards had parked their car, one of them ran into the casualty department and tried to arrest Dr. Kahwa. The doctor refused to go with him and boldly inquired the reason for his arrest. Not having a reason to give, the bodyguard threatened him with a pistol, then, at a loss, ran back to the car to collect a submachine gun. Dr. Kahwa went and hid in an operating room. By the time Amin's man had discovered from the frightened staff where he was, the hospital authorities had telephoned the police. A patrol car arrived shortly afterward. The police entered to find the bodyguard struggling with Kahwa. The police officer then demanded to know what the doctor had done. The bodyguard had nothing to say for himself. Obviously the policeman knew it had been an attempted car snatching. The policeman simply told the bodyguard to leave and then drove off himself. I reported the matter to the State Research Bureau chief, but nothing was done. Dr. Kahwa confessed to me later that he would never feel safe again. We discussed the possibility of an official trip to London, but on second thought, I realized this might draw attention to him and lead to his arrest. He wisely fled to Kenya shortly afterward.

As a final note I should mention an incident that, although quite horrible enough, has been overplayed by the international press. This is the so-called Makerere Massacre of August 1976.

The true story begins in March of that year, when a student, Paul Serwanga, was shot on the outskirts of the campus by Public Safety Unit personnel who were attempting to rape his girlfriend. The incident was so well publicized that Amin was forced to appoint a "commission of inquiry." The commission never completed its task; one chairman after another was fired.

In June, a principal witness, Mrs. Bukenya Nanziri, who was six months pregnant, was dragged from her office and shot in the neck. Her body was dumped in the river. When the body was found and brought to Mulago Hospital mortuary, we were appalled for—in addition to the barbarity of the murder itself—the fetus had to be removed from the body for separate burial, in conformity with Ugandan custom.

As if this were not enough to enrage the increasingly restless students, in July Amin imposed one of his sons, Taban, on the university campus. Taban had been thrown out of Moscow, where he had been sent for training, after Amin accused the Soviet ambassador in Uganda of being drunk. Amin wanted his son to take an engineering course at Makerere. Taban was just a stupid, happy-go-lucky eighteen-year-old with a style of life far beyond that of other students. He had a car, a lecturer's apartment, food and other luxuries from State House, and bodyguards. He always carried a pistol with him. He was openly reviled by his fellow students.

On August 3, 1976, the students demonstrated in protest at the various outrages they had suffered. The Minister of Education, Brigadier Barnabas Kili, tried to calm them down, but without success. Police and army personnel were ordered to break up the demonstration. Many students were beaten; many women raped, both by soldiers and by police; there were several incidents of torture—in one case, women were made to crawl barekneed on concrete. But although many of the students had to have medical treatment, both at government and at mission hospitals, and seven were subsequently detained at Mulago Hospital, mostly with fractures and sprains received when escaping from the troops, nothing more serious occurred. There were no fatalities.

The reports of this incident in the international press spoke of up to 700 dead, and of soldiers slicing off women's breasts. This is absolutely untrue. No one involved in the incident has ever produced evidence of any killings on this occasion. If any had occurred, I should have known. One girl, who was listed as dead, was in fact at her parents' house, where I found her fit and well. Another, who reportedly had a breast cut off, I also found, uninjured. The reports began, I imagine, because so many students fled and were then too frightened to come back for the rest of the term.

Gross misrepresentation of this kind does nothing to aid the cause of justice in Uganda. The truth is horrific enough.

5

My Country's Agony

ON FEBRUARY 24, 1974, I was appointed Minister of Health. I found the ministry in a state of growing disorganization. It had not had a minister for over a year; Amin himself had been in charge since the retirement of the former minister, Dr. Justin Gesa. In all the months that Amin was his own Health Minister, he never once visited the ministry. When he appointed me, he told me that there were many problems in the ministry. "But I know you," he added, "and I have no doubt that you will do a good job."

The Health Ministry was the only one Amin treated with any respect. He was aware that doctors required a long training, that they did vital work and that they could not be easily coerced. Besides, it flattered his ego to think that he could call at will on medical experts. Finally, he knew that doctors and Health Ministry officials had good reason to know what was going on in the country: they dealt with the dead and injured. The Health Minister had it in his power to be a severe embarrassment to him. He had to have someone he trusted, and he trusted me.

As Health Minister, I found that our relationship became, once again, exceptionally close. I could talk to him at any time of the day or night. Over the three years, until my defection, his attitude remained the same. He was generous to the ministry. He handed over Asian houses to a number of doctors, and often allocated cars to the ministry for use as ambulances.

My first task as minister was to analyze the problems facing the department. The ministry was still running on sound civil service lines, and I had a considerable body of information to call upon. But I wanted to see at first hand the conditions in which the doctors and other medical staff were working, so I immediately began a tour of the country's hospitals.

The country had inherited a fine medical system. There was a good foundation of forty-eight government hospitals, twenty-eight mission hospitals, one hundred and fifty health centers (small units with about thirty beds each) and three hundred dispensaries. The government hospitals were administered in British fashion. Treatment was free. Doctors could, however, set aside part of their time and some of their beds for private practice. The mission hospitals levied a small charge; the government defrayed their running costs. At the time of the coup, these institutions were staffed by experienced teams of doctors, nurses and paramedical staff. Salaries were low by Western standards—23,000 shillings (2,900 dollars) per year for an intern, and for a medical assistant, only 9,200 shillings (900 dollars) per year. But until 1971—when Uganda first began to feel the effects of galloping inflation—these salaries had been adequate enough.

By 1974, Uganda's excellent medical infrastructure was in a steep decline. The problems reflected the ills of the country as a whole; they were common to every hospital in the country and were the same as those affecting other public institutions. With the steady flight of professional people, essential services—for instance the water supply system—were threatened. The maintenance of Kampala's main water station at Gaba was neglected. While the demand for water increased, supplies dwindled. By 1974, water shortages had become a perpetual feature of everyday life, both in the hospitals and in the homes (and in Amin's residences, for that matter). There was not enough water for cleaning floors, for washing, for sterilizing, for bathing, or for flushing toilets. We had to hire tankers (we later bought our own) to bring water to Mulago Hospital from standpipes near Lake Victoria. On more than one occasion, we seriously thought of closing the hospital for fear of infection.

Maintaining supplies of water to private houses was another headache. People took to collecting a few cans of water in basins or baths overnight, and then using it for the rest of the day to flush toilets, to cook and to wash. Most of my doctors had water in their houses only for one or two hours a day. I arranged for a water tanker to distribute a can or two to each household.

Nothing has been done to improve this situation. Nor is it the only way in which medical staff and patients suffer. Amin's thugs think nothing of bursting in on hospitals and medical institutions, at any time of the day or night, to get immediate attention. They force patients aside and insist on being treated first. If the relative of a Nubian dies in a hospital—from whatever cause—the doctor concerned has no choice but to flee the country.

Patients' diets have become poorer and poorer. At Mulago we could not provide eggs, bread, sugar or butter. Nor were such items available in the doctors' mess. With so many shortages, medical staff—even consultants—are forced to waste time lining up for essential household goods.

Most of my time at the ministry was spent coping with these day-to-day problems—shortages of drugs, anesthetics, bandages, needles, uniforms; the collapse of electric or water systems; and staff shortages.

Eventually, difficulties with staff led me to make a major policy decision: the abolition of private practice. Under the old system, government doctors were allowed to engage in private practice on their own time. This worked well enough until the Asian exodus. When the Asian doctors left the country, many clinics became available and were given to Ugandan doctors. As the cost of living rose, the Ugandan doctors began to spend more and more time in the private clinics to supplement their meager incomes. Naturally, many of them began to neglect their hospital duties. They could not afford not to. There was only one solution: to force doctors back into full-time government service by abolishing the clinics. The ministry discussed this step with Amin. We knew it would do little to offset the effects of the chaos created by his rule, but there was no other way open to us.

For some time Amin took no action. Then, in October, he discovered that a woman he had impregnated had procured an abortion at a private clinic. This infuriated him. He announced that all private clinics must be closed down. Suddenly, "with immediate effect," no doctor was allowed to engage in private practice. Patients in such clinics had to be quickly discharged and reabsorbed into the government and mission hospitals. Anyone wishing to run a private clinic had to get permission from me. (I had licensed about fifty by the time I left.)

It was a harsh measure, and one that only temporarily eased the situation, for all the most talented doctors—those who could have given their skills at least part-time to the government—now faced certain poverty. Consequently they fled the country in even greater numbers. The only thing I managed to do was to persuade Amin to agree to an increase in salary for the lowest paid doctors: the interns were given a seventeen percent raise, and the medical assistants, who were by then living on the poverty line, had their salaries more than doubled.

In 1976 I began to investigate the possibility of reintroducing private practice for doctors. But there was—and is—no answer to the problem while Amin remains in power.

My deepest involvement in the day-to-day lives of Uganda's medical staff came through the special relationship I developed with Kampala's main hospital, Mulago. It had 1,800 beds and it was the country's best and largest hospital. It was also the teaching hospital of Makerere University. To keep in close contact I developed the habit of making my own hospital rounds at Mulago to talk to staff and patients alike. People used to tell me that I knew the hospital and its problems better than some of the senior medics.

Amin considers Mulago his own personal clinic. If any of his staff or family need treatment, he sends them to Mulago. If he needs a doctor at the President's Lodge or State House, he calls Mulago.

Before my appointment, Amin had quarrelled with one superintendent of Mulago after another. Eventually he ended up with someone he could control, whose job was simply to dole out drugs to him, find him beds and send him doctors on demand. One of my first actions was to fire the superintendent. Thereafter, the hospital was run by a man of my own choice who answered directly to me. In his dealings with the hospital, Amin seldom bypassed this hierarchy. (Something he did with impunity in the army and other ministries.) I became in effect Amin's own medical superintendent. If he needed medical help, he would telephone me.

My experience as Minister of Health gave me an even deeper insight into the way Amin worked. I found myself, after some years of service, in a unique position. I had seen the system from the inside in the civil service, the President's office, and as a senior Cabinet minister. Now, finally, I saw what it was like to be face to face with Amin in the highest ranks of government. It was an unedifying spectacle. Here is one rather typical day, selected at random from the early months of my ministry.

I am sitting in my ministry office, opposite State House. I know that Amin is there today. I can see his officials going in and out. At 11:00 he calls me up and says, "Will you come over? I have someone you should see. We'll get doctors later—you just come first." I go across to State House.

I find Amin sitting on the verandah overlooking my ministry. He offers me tea and roast chicken. We sit on deckchairs around the table and start talking. He says, "Some of the children are sick. Can we get a doctor to come and look at them some time?" I say, "Certainly." I pick up a nearby telephone, dial one of my doctors in Entebbe and tell him to come along with a nurse. In the meantime, the President tells an *ayah* (nanny) to prepare the sick children for the doctor's visit. (Each wife's children has a separate nanny.)

We chat briefly, then he says, "Mr. Zigler (a commercial contact in Zurich) is here. I'll let him come in. You stay here." So I stay. Zigler comes in and the two men discuss the purchase of a Boeing airplane. In the Cabinet we have already discussed this and advised that we need more buses, bicycles and tires for cars before we purchase any more planes. But he is obviously not prepared to listen to us. "I want it, and quickly," he tells Zigler. "Can I have it in two months?" Zigler says, "It will be ready by then. I have already had my people start work on it. I'll telephone them now and tell them to go ahead." Amin picks up the telephone and informs the Minister of Finance, "I have ordered another Boeing from Zigler. Can you prepare the necessary payments?" The transaction concluded, Zigler leaves.

A secretary comes in and tells Amin that an aide is due to leave for London the next day to do some shopping for the children. He says, "Call him in and fetch my briefcase from inside." The briefcase is fetched. The aide comes in. Amin opens the case, takes out several thousand dollars, gives it to the aide and tells him what to buy in London. The briefcase is then closed and the secretary takes it back inside.

The phone rings. The doctor and nurse have arrived. Amin orders them to be admitted to examine the sick children.

Amin suggests a walk around the garden. He takes

me to see his new Land Rover, which contains transmitting equipment. He shows me how it works. He says proudly, "If Kampala Radio station is surrounded and I can't transmit from there, I can broadcast from this car, and people will not know that I have lost the radio station."

We stroll around to the swimming pool. It is half full. "We are having it refilled," he explains.

A phone by the pool rings. He tells me the doctor and nurse have finished their examination.

"You should do a bit of swimming," he says, "and you could do with some massage. Massage is very good for you." He tells me to visit the massage parlor he has had installed at the Kampala International Hotel. He regales me with the benefits of massage. I look at my watch. It is 4:00 P.M. and I have lost the best part of the day.

In March 1974, there was a mutiny in the army. It proved that the spirit of rebellion was not completely dead. When it broke out, I was touring hospitals in the West Nile district, and had spent the night in Amin's home town, Arua. In the morning, I set out for Moyo which is about one hundred miles from Arua, near the Sudan border. On my way I was stopped by army road-blocks and my identity checked before I was allowed to continue. Puzzled, I arrived in Moyo, toured the hospital, and began to address the staff. During my address, I was told that my wife Teresa had called from Kampala. I called her back. She spoke guardedly because she was afraid the line was tapped, but her message was clear enought: "The cocks are fighting here—you'd better come back." I understood immediately that the army was in conflict; hence the roadblocks.

Although I was worried about my family, I did not think an army rebellion would spread immediately to the civilian population. I decided not to rush home. It would be impossible to tell which unit was fighting which, and I could find myself running the gauntlet of both sides. So I took my time. I returned to Arua for the night, then drove down to the Murchison Falls National Park for another night. While I was there, I switched on my radio to hear the news. There was nothing about the revolt—but out of the blue, to a nation waiting for news of a potential civil war, came the extraordinary announcement that Amin had divorced three of his wives! I just burst out laughing at the incongruity of it.

In Kampala the next day, I heard the full story. The Lubiri Mechanized Battalion, headed by its former commander, Lt. Col. Elly, with the backing of the Chief of Staff, Brigadier Charles Arube, had attacked the military police headquarters at Makindye, which was commanded by the Southern Sudanese Brigadier Hussein Marella. Other units were despatched to seek out the Public Safety Unit's Ali Towelli. One reason for the revolt was that Arube and a number of senior officers resented the rule of the Southern Sudanese and the way in which they were bringing the army into disrepute. The revolt was an attempt to drive them out. It may also have been the start of an attempted coup. During the fighting, the Makindye headquarters was badly damaged by tanks, and a number of soldiers were killed or injured. Many of the injured were admitted to Mulago Hospital.

The attempt was nipped in the bud—Arube himself was captured. The following morning, he was taken by armed soldiers to Mulago Hospital with three or four bullet wounds in his stomach. He was wearing civilian clothes. He died on the operating table, and his body was wheeled down to the mortuary. Amin was contacted and went to the mortuary, where he insisted on being left alone with the corpse.

It has been said that Amin practiced some rite on Arube's corpse. Perhaps. I was told by one deputy medical superintendent that (through a half-opened door) he saw Amin saluting the body. To non-Africans this may seem a respectful gesture, but knowing Amin, I am convinced it was intended ironically, to humiliate Arube, even in death. Had he genuinely respected Arube, he would have given him a burial with full military honors.

The outcome of this strife in the army was very much to Amin's satisfaction. As soon as the fighting had stopped, he drove his jeep—easily identifiable by its long aerials—around town to show that he was in full control. He did, subsequently, relieve Brigadier Marella of his post, shocked perhaps by the extent of the opposition to the Southern Sudanese. But it was a meaningless gesture. Marella was retired with full benefits, and resounding praise. He packed up his belongings, went to the Bank of Uganda, collected as many bags of American dollars as he and his aides could carry (he couldn't write, so he couldn't take travelers' checks) and left for Juba, in the Southern Sudan, with his white Mercedes Benz and several lorries.

Elly, who was a Kakwa, and a fine professional soldier, fled to his home area, where he lived in hiding for some time. Later Amin rehabilitated him. He is now Ambassador to the USSR.

With the death of Brigadier Charles Arube, Amin appointed Brigadier Mustafa Adrisi as Chief of Staff, in effect Commander of the Army. Adrisi, who is from the West Nile district, is a Moslem and a Lugbara. He also has Kakwa relatives. For many years he was a sergeant in the army, and known as a strict disciplinarian. He speaks Lugbara, Kakwa and Swahili, but no English (though he understands a little). Virtually his only words of English—the country's official language—are "my colleague." He is now Vice President.

If my theory about Arube is correct, he was in revolt against what was then emerging as the one consistent, long-term aim of Amin's administration: to turn Uganda from a Christian country into a Moslem one. Amin's thugs are Moslem, his officers are Moslem, and, slowly, his Cabinet is being taken over by Moslems.

Yet Moslems constitute only ten per cent of the population. By 1974, Uganda was virtually ruled by a foreign elite of Southern Sudanese, who at best are sympathetic only to the Moslem elements of the population. The majority—the Christians and Bantu—meant nothing to them. Since then, as the country's economic problems have intensified, Amin has reinforced his pro-Arab stance to insure a continued flow of oil money. To do this, he has attempted to demonstrate to the Arabs and to the world at large that Uganda is, through and through, a Moslem country.

In 1971, Amin's Cabinet had only two Moslems: Amin himself and the Minister of Education. The remainder of the Cabinet were Christian. Between 1972 and 1977, progressively more Moslems were appointed. As of now, August 1977, fourteen out of twenty-one ministers are Moslem.

But the introduction of Moslems was a gradual business, not at first much remarked upon. In fact Amin tried to play it down, a fact that was brought home to me early in 1977, when Amin, addressing an international conference, complained about the foreign media's attacks on him for his Moslemization policy. He told the assembled guests that he had no more than five Moslem ministers. Yet at the table where he sat were four Moslem ministers, and there were another nine in the audience.

Moslemization in the army has been a deliberate policy from the start. The Moslem Nubians and Southern Sudanese are, after all, the only people he can really rely on. Now Moslems, mostly Nubians, command all except two of the seventeen armed forces units—the thirteen battalions; the Military Police; the State Research Bureau; the Air Force; and the Ordnance Depot at Magamaga. A Moslem also heads the Civil Police. The State Research Bureau actually has a nominal head who is from Busoga, but the real power is held by Major Farouk Minawa, a Nubian and a Moslem. Amin's government is, in every sense, a minority regime. Only a handful of men, drawn from one small section of Ugandan society, wield any real power: the rest are foreigners.

But to have Moslem officers and administrators is not enough for Amin. At the 1975 annual conference of Moslem countries in Lahore, Pakistan, Amin's right to attend was questioned, on the grounds that Uganda had only a small number of Moslems. Amin replied that virtually the whole country was Moslem, a reflection of his strenuous efforts to make it so. Numbers of Amin's junior staff in the State House have announced their conversions. Indeed, many hundreds with career aspirations have decided that they cannot afford *not* to become Moslem.

Paradoxically, the effect of Amin's campaign has been disastrous for Islam, while the Christian faith has been strengthened by the onslaught (which included the murder of Clement Kiggundu, editor of the Catholic newspaper *Munno*, on January 16, 1973). Moslems had previously been looked down upon as representing an uneducated minority, but this intolerance was social, not religious. Everyone knew that Islam was a great religion and respected it. Now ordinary people—and I have talked to drivers, nurses, patients, and office workers almost daily on the subject—see Islam as the religion of Amin's domination. They believe that the slaughter initiated by Amin is licensed by Mecca, as are the humiliations piled on the Christian Church. For the first time, ordinary people became distrustful of one another, simply because of their religion.

There are other aspects of Amin's Moslemization policy. The radio now makes announcements in Arabic, a language understood only by the Nubian community and Arab diplomats. Amin has announced that Moslems should have Fridays off for prayer. This is in line with the practice in other Arab countries—but Arab countries work on Sundays; since Uganda is largely Christian,

Uganda may well end up with a three-day weekend. Amin has also authorized Moslem public holidays, such as the birth of Mohammed. He has even directed that the Arab slave trade—suppressed by the British in the late nineteenth century—be excised from the schools curriculum, because it gives Moslems and Arabs a bad name. (He ordered this after watching a television program on nineteenth-century history, which described the Arab slave trade in East Africa. The Minister of Education, a Christian, nearly lost his job over it.)

Meanwhile, the country's suffering has intensified; the economy has virtually been split in two. On one side, there is the mass of the people living at subsistence level; on the other are Amin's thugs—a rich elite. The thugs have the money; the people have the food—the maize, potatoes, fruit and fresh vegetables that grow so well in Uganda. Ordinary people have abandoned export crops like coffee and cotton to grow basic foodstuffs which they can sell in Kampala at the exorbitant prices they need to cope with Uganda's inflation. In retaliation, the thugs terrorize the traders in an attempt to dissuade them from charging such high prices. This leads to the temporary disappearance of goods from the market. When the goods reappear, the prices are as high as before.

In so many of the details of day-to-day life, Uganda's tragedy is apparent. In addition to the terrible shortages, everything that can be stolen is stolen. A mass of manhole covers disappeared from Mulago Hospital compound overnight; a piece of welding equipment—it must have weighed a ton or more—vanished one weekend. Telephones are prime targets—all the accessories can be used in other electronic equipment. It is almost impossible to find a public telephone in Uganda that works. In Mulago Hospital, even the microscope light bulbs and the hearing aid equipment vanish. So do linen, spoons, cups and plates.

Tires and other accessories are stolen off cars. I tried

very hard to get my ambulance service working properly by importing new vehicles and spare parts, and keeping them all in the ministry garage under guard. One morning, I discovered sixty new tires missing; there was no sign of the guard. I then ordered an armed policeman to guard the place. Three months later, on January 26, 1977, a mass of spares—and the guard—vanished again. I drove to the garage myself and found there the policeman's rifle and ammunition. I handed the weapon back to the Commissioner of Police in disgust. Thereafter, the doors were firmly locked and the guards left outside without keys.

Inflation is rampant. Officially the Ugandan shilling is on a par with the Kenya shilling and the Tanzanian shilling, and officially the Ugandan pound is stronger than the English pound. But "officially" in Uganda means "according to Amin." Amin orders the banks to keep the exchange rates static. This enables his men to buy foreign currency and sell it on the black market at up to eight times the official rate. In this way, a dollar, which exchanges officially for eight shillings, can be sold for fifty.

There is no remedy for all this. I have witnessed the death throes of a whole society. It is the same as when a person dies. No one section or department can ever recover on its own. The Ministry of Health cannot work properly if the machinery for importing spare parts no longer exists. Even if arrangements can be made to import the vehicles, and spares, the goods will be seized as soon as they appear on the street. The hospitals cannot work properly if the junior hospital staff can make more money by stealing drugs and equipment and selling them on the black market, than they do by working for the government. The whole system has to be rebuilt from scratch.

Economic collapse, combined with Amin's rule of terror, has not been accepted passively. There is, in suffering Uganda, still a spark of resistance—there are many in the army and the police who would gladly kill Amin themselves. The risks are great, not so much for individuals, as for the community: any hint of a plot against Amin leads to widespread reprisals.

But there have been a few attempts on his life. Little is known about most of them, for Amin likes to deny their existence (to preserve the myth of his popularity) or to dismiss them as doomed in advance by his "invulnerability." As a result of these attacks, he changes his plans frequently and travels with a wide variety of weapons. He has always carried a knife and a pistol. He now puts grenades in his briefcase and submachine guns in his car. One day he proudly showed me a new knife, which doubled as a wirecutter. "If they have you surrounded," he said, "you can cut wires and escape through the fence." Perhaps he was thinking of the time, after the attack on Obote in December 1969, when he scrambled over a fence to escape from Obote's soldiers.

I had direct experience of one major attempt on Amin's life. It occurred on June 10, 1976, at a police review at Nsambya Police Recreation Ground. Amin was obviously more than usually nervous about the function, because he changed the site four times before he finally settled on Nsambya. The function started at about 4:00 in the afternoon with a police review watched by a crowd of thousands. I sat with Amin and other ministers in a covered stand. The parade involved every section of the police, and included a demonstration by a *tae-kondo*, an armed self-defense group, trained by South Koreans. During this demonstration, Amin took out a rifle with fixed bayonet. He chose a constable as an opponent, pretended to stab him and ordered him to defend himself.

After the show, the VIP's—Amin, ministers, police officers and army officers—went to a recreation hall next to the sports ground, for a reception. I had not planned to stay long: that morning I had just opened a meeting of the Medical Research Council in Kampala, and I was to host a party for the delegates at the Imperial Hotel in Kampala.

The reception started at 6:15. At about 6:45, Amin decided to leave for Entebbe. It was surprisingly early. I have no doubt this is what saved him: the would-be assassins were not ready for him. With the other VIP's, I accompanied Amin to the compound, which was packed with cars and people. It was twilight, but Amin was plainly visible. He planned to travel in an open jeep with no windshield. He often did this when there were crowds around and he wanted to dramatize his departure by taking the wheel.

He told his driver to move over to the passenger seat on the left-hand side. Followed closely by an escort car, he swung the jeep toward the gate of the compound, where further crowds were waiting to see him. We stood by the entrance to the hall and watched him go.

The moment Amin's jeep turned right onto the main road, just out of our sight behind the crowd, there was an explosion, followed, seconds later, by another. We saw dust and debris fly up. The escort car, which was still in view, came to a sudden halt. Then I heard two shots.

One of the ministers turned to me and said, "They have got him." Then the crowd in the road began to scatter, screaming. I realized the explosions were caused by grenades. Some of the slightly injured started running toward us. Others were picked up and brought into the compound. Amazingly, no one in the crowd was killed, although thirty-five were subsequently treated at the hospital.

Those of us standing outside the recreation hall made no move. We just looked at each other, waiting for somebody to do something. I thought at the time that we might be in the midst of a coup. I half expected some new army chief to take control and order us to put up our hands.

Then, suddenly, we were all trying to get away. One of the senior air force officers suggested that we had better go through the same entrance, "otherwise someone will accuse us of knowing what was going to happen in advance." We began making our way through the milling crowd to our cars. The drivers, also bewildered, edged their way to the exit. I told my driver to take me to the party at the Imperial Hotel. Fearing more violence, I lay down on the back seat as we went through the gate. We swung left, and I looked up. The police were beginning to pick out "suspects."

I stopped briefly at the hotel to instruct a senior doctor to stand in for me at the party and to ask for some senior surgeons to go to the hospital for emergency duty. Then I went to the hospital myself.

When I arrived at Mulago I found out from doctors and aides what had happened. My picture of events was completed in a talk with Amin later that evening. The first grenade had exploded on the left-hand side of the jeep, at the front, where Amin was supposed to have been sitting. The jeep shielded both occupants from the main force of the blast, but a splinter struck the driver between the eyes. He slumped down, unconscious. The blast also lacerated the offside front tire. The second grenade landed to the rear of the jeep, and immobilized the escort car.

Amin realized that the only thing to do was to get away. He put his foot on the accelerator, and his jeep roared off. He told me he heard the two shots, "but they were wide of the mark." The unconscious driver, shaken by the movement of the jeep, almost fell out. Amin hauled him in and drove on. As he went, he opened his briefcase with one hand and pulled out a grenade, which he raised to his mouth, ready to pull out the pin with his teeth and toss it over his shoulder at anyone who tried to pursue him. A hundred yards down the road, he stopped, waved down a passing car—the driver, a governmental official, later told me about this incident—and asked for assistance for his own driver. But before the official had time to respond, Amin, sweating and gasping from his narrow escape, drove off again in the direction of Mulago.

Amin got his driver to the hospital, where he was whisked into the operating theater. His wound was an odd one. The x-ray showed that the minute splinter had entered his skull like an inch-long needle, leaving hardly a mark, and penetrated to the back of his brain. There was no way to save him. He died two days later.

After Amin had dropped off his driver, he jumped into an official car that had followed him to the hospital, and drove straight to Entebbe, where he mobilized his army. He had no more idea who was responsible for the attempt on his life than his commanding officers did. But the officers, anxious to show their loyalty, sent their troops out to arrest and beat up civilians at random. Tanks and armored personnel carriers took to the streets. A number of people were killed. The troops were ordered back to their barracks shortly after midnight; by that time Amin realized that there had been no organized attempt to topple him.

However, Amin pretended he knew who was responsible. He went on television and announced the release of a dozen or so suspects. He said that they had wanted to kill him, but he had forgiven them. Everyone knew that none of them had anything to do with the assassination attempt. They were arrested simply because they were near the scene at the time.

No one ever did discover who was responsible.

6

Amin and His Women

THE STORY OF Amin and his women is one that is by
turns bizarre, comic and brutal. To have five wives—and
all beautiful—is peculiar enough in itself. To have thirty
or so mistresses—and about thirty-four children (the
figure varies, even officially)—is even more extraordinary. That one wife should die in mysterious and horrifying circumstances seems to overstep the bounds of
credibility. Certainly in Amin's behavior toward women
his maniacal personality is most clearly distilled.

The first of his wives was Malyamu, the daughter of my
old headmaster, Mr. Kibedi, and the sister of the former
Foreign Minister, Wanume Kibedi. I knew her when I
was a teenager, at the time when Amin, then a
twenty-eight-year-old sergeant in the King's African
Rifles, was first in love with her. She was a statuesque six-
footer in her early twenties, physically a fine match for
the powerful young boxing champion. She was also
self-possessed, with an intelligence and maturity that
stood her in good stead later in life. To marry a Kakwa
soldier, face the disapproval of her family and move to an
unfamiliar area took considerable courage.

Although he had several children by her, he was not
formally married to her until 1966, the year he stormed
the Kabaka's palace and became a national figure. The
rearing of illegitimate children is not unusual in Uganda,

145

where children can always find a home, and marriage
bonds are looser than in the West. In fact, there never was
a wedding in the ordinary sense. Amin simply paid the
bride price and the marriage was formally recognized.
Obote visited the couple at Amin's house at Mbuya, on
the outskirts of the capital, and was officially introduced
to Malyamu, then in her early thirties, and their children.

By this time Amin had been "married" to her, in all but
name, for thirteen years. He was quite ready, therefore, to
look for a junior wife, as was the custom. He wanted one
from his own tribal area. In fact, even before the
formalization of his relationship with Malyamu, he had
chosen Kay Adroa. Kay was a natural choice for she was
the daughter of a clergyman, an intelligent girl (a student
at Makerere University) and a beauty with striking
looks—her skin was not the usual African brown, but a
rich ebony. She was also a dignified, quiet and
self-possessed girl.

Amin knew her family well, and in February 1966,
when Parliament demanded the suspension of Amin over
the gold scandal, he went into hiding with Kay. Three
months later, as he was formalizing his marriage to
Malyamu, he was already planning his marriage to Kay.
Kay was, like Malyamu, a Christian, and the marriage
was conducted in a registry office, followed by a
reception, which I attended. Kay was wearing a white
Western-style bridal dress, I remember, and Amin was
in full army uniform. The ceremony was held at Arua,
Amin's home town; the best man was Erinayo Oryema,
who later became Minister of Land and Water
Resources, and later still, was murdered.

To marry two wives almost simultaneously is, of
course, extraordinary by Western standards, and even in
Uganda it would have caused comment, except that
everyone knew Malyamu had in effect been Amin's
senior wife for many years (hence her title "Mama," an
affectionate recognition of her seniority).

Within a year, Amin had acquired wife No. 3, Nora, a

Langi from Obote's home area. Amin's marriage to Nora was one of political convenience. After Amin's rise to national prominence and popularity, Obote became suspicious of Amin's intentions. To marry a Langi would reassure Obote that their tribal differences were insignificant, and thus allay his suspicions. In 1967, Nora joined the household, and later bore him several children. By the late 1960s he had ten or fifteen offspring.

Wife No. 4 was Medina, a dancer from Buganda with the Heartbeat of Africa Troupe. Even before I joined the Ministry of Culture and took responsibility for the troupe's affairs, Medina was very much in evidence. I noticed her first within a few days of the coup. She was one of the dancers that Amin used for entertaining dignitaries at state functions. Indeed, it would have been impossible not to notice her. Medina was, quite simply, stunning. Although she has now put on a few pounds, she had a figure then that was dramatically sexy by any standards. Many Ugandan women have rather large backsides (a feature traditionally regarded as beautiful), but not Medina; she was slim-hipped, with well-formed breasts, and was a ferociously agile dancer. She was in a class by herself. Being the troupe's star, she appeared in all the official tourist films. (Amin had the relevant sections of the films deleted after they were married.) Amin could hardly take his eyes off her.

The troupe was popular with Amin from the start, and group of dancers travelled with him at his request all over the country. I got to know Medina quite well. She was extremely pleasant, but lacking the intelligence of Kay and the authority of Malyamu.

Soon after the coup, it became obvious that Amin had serious designs on her. It was at this time that I spent long periods with Amin, often in his bedroom, and often late into the night. One night, when we were on tour in Moyo, I had stayed with Amin until about 12:45, discussing the arrangements for the following day. Amin got undressed—he was completely uninhibited about stripping in front of me—and climbed into bed. I said goodnight and left. As I went out, one of Amin's bodyguards ushered Medina in. I just said "hello" to her and walked on. I wasn't surprised. Amin never worried about me seeing his women joining him at night. At that moment I realized that any man who touched Medina would have problems.

Amin enjoyed telling his ministers that if anyone wanted her, they could take her—she was readily "available." She attracted the admiring glances of every man in Amin's entourage. One of them—I will not embarrass him by naming him—actually wanted to try. "Kyemba, do you think it's safe?" he asked me. I told him to forget it. He tried anyway, without success. I suspect very strongly that that was one of the reasons for his subsequent transfer to another ministry and his final dismissal.

Medina's status was soon clearly established. I had to fly back with some other officials to do some Cabinet work before the end of that particular tour. Medina was on my flight, accompanied by one of Amin's bodyguards. When we landed at Kampala, an official car was there to pick her up. If any confirmation of Medina's status with Amin was needed, that was it.

Amin announced his marriage to Medina in September 1972, the same month as the invasion by Obote's ill-fated force from Tanzania. It was a strangely inept time to make such an announcement. People were tensely listening to the radio to hear news of the operations at the "front" when they suddenly heard that Amin had taken a fourth wife. He said that she had been given to him by the Baganda in appreciation of all that he had done for them since the takeover. This was a terrible insult to the Baganda, for everybody knew that Amin had been responsible for the deaths of many of them.

During 1973, Amin's household of four wives and children—which then numbered about twenty, including those by his numerous mistresses—was little in the news.

On March 26, 1974, with no warning to the public, the government or the women concerned, Amin divorced Malyamu, Kay and Nora. It was done Moslem style, by simply stating, "I divorce thee. I divorce thee. I divorce thee." The first news of the divorces came over the radio. (Coinciding with the fighting that followed the mutiny of Brigadier Charles Arube, the announcement was once again incongruously out of keeping with the tense political situation.) Amin also announced that he intended to remain monogamously with Medina.

The reasons given by Amin for the divorce action were absurd. He accused Malyamu and Nora of being involved in businesses. (This was true—Amin himself had given them both textile shops in 1973, the time of the redistribution of Asian property.) Of Kay, he said that she was a cousin, and that he was complying with complaints he had received saying that their kinship was too close to sustain marriage. In the case of Malyamu, he had another hidden reason; her brother, Wanume Kibedi, Minister of Foreign Affairs, had recently fled into exile, and it was clearly an embarrassment for Amin to be married to his sister.

I later learned that there was yet another reason for his action. Amin's womanizing had not left him any time to spend with his first three wives. For two years they had lived in virtual isolation in his two Presidential Lodges, bored, and increasingly frustrated. Eventually, they all took lovers. Kay's was a doctor, Peter Mbalu-Mukasa, a senior member of the Mulago Hospital staff, married with several children. Kay became pregnant by him.

On March 25, the three women—united in their hatred of their husband—threw a party for their lovers. Amin's bodyguards, fearful that he would find out about the party, telephoned him. Furious, he got on the phone to his recalcitrant wives, threatening to come over directly and throw them out. The women, who had all been drinking, told him he could keep Medina and go to hell. They then dismissed the bodyguards and locked the doors.

The next day Amin dictated letters of dismissal to all three and had them delivered to the house at the same time as the radio announced their divorces.

But this was not the end of the matter. Amin was clearly angered beyond endurance by his wives' rejection of him, and was ready to humiliate—even kill— the two divorced women to whom he was closest—Malyamu and Kay.

On April 11, less than a month after her dismissal, Malyamu was arrested near Tororo on the Kenyan border, allegedly for smuggling a bolt of fabric into Kenya. The arrest could only have been made on Amin's orders. He ordered that she be kept in prison until her hearing, and not granted bail. On April 30, she was taken to court, fined and released. She retired into private life.

The following year, on March 13, Malyamu was involved in a car accident outside Kampala. I later learned that her car was rammed by Amin's bodyguards, clearly in revenge for her unfaithfulness. When Amin was told of the accident he asked: "Is she dead?" In fact, she sustained a fractured leg and arm, and was taken to Mulago Hospital. I was immediately notified by the authorities, reported it to the President, and had her admitted to the private ward at her own expense. She arrived in very great pain. Her limbs were placed in plaster casts and raised on pulleys.

The following morning, Amin told me he was going to see Malyamu. I was then in Entebbe, and by the time I arrived at the hospital, Amin had already been in to see her with his Presidential press unit. There, in the presence of his journalists and the hospital medical staff, he started quarrelling with her and insulting her. "You're a very unlucky woman," he shouted at her: "You cannot run your own life properly." It was a most callous performance by Amin, and a degrading experience for Malyamu. Amin went on to advise Malyamu to visit a witch doctor whose magic might save her from further misfortune.

Later that day, Amin telephoned me and ordered me to have Malyamu transferred from the private ward into a public one. This was an extraordinarily cruel order, considering her condition. I explained to Amin that she was paying her own way, and was fully entitled to stay where she was. Amin would not listen, and told me to have her removed immediately.

I contacted the hospital authorities and passed along the order. They explained the difficulty of moving Malyamu in her present condition. I decided to disobey Amin's orders for that night, but told the staff to do as directed the next morning. I also instructed them to choose a corner bed and place some screens around her so that she could have some privacy. The next morning, after this had been done, I telephoned Amin and advised him. He expressed his satisfaction.

Malyamu remained in the hospital for several weeks. During that period I visited her a number of times. We talked a good deal about her experience. She was very philosophical. "I understand Amin," she would say, "Don't worry about it." For some time she had been worried that Amin's men would take her and kill her, but lately she had felt more secure. She had an extraordinary capacity to accept Amin's character without bitterness. She would tell me that she knew he had many problems— that she had lived with him for many years, and looked after him during his painful attacks of gout. "When he gets gout," she told me, "he cries like a baby, and I have to comfort him."

In June, when Malyamu had recovered sufficiently, she was discharged from the hospital and left the country for further treatment. She never returned. In November 1975, she flew to London, leaving her six children to be looked after by Amin's other wives.

After Malyamu left, her shop was looted, obviously on Amin's orders. But then, typically inconsistent, he told Malyamu's father, Mr. Kibedi, then aged about seventy, to take over the shop. It was ramshackle and empty of goods, and Mr. Kibedi could not hope to build up the business again, but he was too afraid to give it back to Amin or to abandon it. He still gets up every morning, and minds the place as best he can.

After Kay's dismissal, her father, Reverend Adroa, wishing to save the good name of his family, interceded for her with Amin, begging him to reinstate her. Eventually, Amin, who had no idea that Kay was pregnant, agreed to build a house for her in her home town, Arua. She was, not surprisingly, unwilling to go. Amin visited her several times but her attitudes toward him only hardened. He took to driving past her apartment, hoping perhaps to catch her with a lover.

Then in early August 1974, she was arrested, allegedly for being in possession of a pistol and ammunition. Clearly, this was on Amin's orders, for the charge was trumped up—the weapon was one Amin had given her. She was taken to the police station, where, as I learned from a number of people who were there at the time, Amin visited her. They started quarrelling through the bars of the cell, in the presence of the police and other security men. She shouted at him, "You can't get me arrested for keeping a pistol and ammunition which you yourself left in my house." Amin shouted back, calling her a whore and saying she deserved her punishment.

After these exchanges, Amin left, leaving Kay behind bars until the following morning, when she was formally questioned by a magistrate. When asked whether she had a gun and ammunition, she said, "Yes, they are my husband's." She was simply cautioned and released.

Not long after this, on Sunday, August 13, she died. The circumstances of her death are both obscure and horrific.

On the morning of Monday, August 14, at about 9:00, Mulago Hospital telephoned me in my ministry office in Entebbe. I was told that one of my doctors, Dr.

Mbalu-Mukasa, was in a critical condition in the hospital, and that his wife and five of his children were also there, seriously ill. He had overdosed himself, his wife and the children with sleeping pills. (The youngest—a baby—was found later in a cupboard with a blanket over her head). I was shocked and anxious, for I knew the doctor well. He was my age (thirty-seven), and we had been at university together. Soon afterward, the hospital telephoned me again to tell me that Mbalu-Mukasa had died, but that his wife and children would probably survive. I informed the President—Mbalu-Mukasa was a senior member of the profession—and drove to Mulago.

When I arrived at the hospital, I was surprised to find Kay's father outside the emergency ward where Mbalu-Mukasa had just died. He told me he had been staying with his daughter for the past few days, but since the previous day, Sunday, Kay had disappeared. He said she had left her apartment with Dr. Mbalu-Mukasa. There was nothing strange in that—Dr. Mbalu-Mukasa had recently become Kay's doctor. But Kay never returned. Worried and puzzled, he had traced the doctor to his hospital and come there to find out what was happening. He had just been told the doctor was dead, and was bewildered and panicky. I left him with some reassuring words, but I too was puzzled. The suicide of the doctor and Kay's disappearance were certainly odd events—although they had occurred so close together, I could see no logical connection between them, and thought them merely coincidental. It was only three years later that I learned that they were lovers.

About 6:00 the same evening, my wife Teresa, who was then matron in charge of Mulago Hospital, returned home and told me that just before she left work the dismembered body of a woman had been brought into the mortuary. It was, she had been told, the body of Kay Amin. I was astounded. I telephoned Amin at Nakasero Lodge and told him that I had some urgent information that I wished to discuss. I went immediately to the

Lodge. I was shaking. I got to him and said, "Your Excellency, your former wife is dead, and in terrible circumstances, I understand." There was no reaction. He just said, "What has happened?" I said, "The body is in pieces. It's dismembered in my mortuary." He said, "Have you been there?" I said, "No." He said, "You go there and tell me exactly what it is like."

I drove back to the hospital, had the mortuary unlocked, and went in with two attendants. They opened one of the refrigeration units in which the bodies were kept. The shelf slid open and a body emerged. The sight that confronted me was the most horrible I have ever seen; it is one that still haunts me. The body was indeed that of Kay Amin, but it had been dismembered. The legs and arms had been cut off. Lying on the shelf was the torso, face up, with the head intact. The torso was lying in a burlap sack, which had been slit open and folded back to expose its contents and to ease the task of identification. More sacking lay beside the torso. Underneath were the legs and arms. The dissection had been neatly done; no bones were broken; the ligaments in the joints were carefully cut; there had been no tearing. The job had been done by an expert with the correct surgical instruments. Too appalled even to speak, I took a step back in shock and simply nodded to the attendants to slide the shelf shut.

After taking a few minutes to recover, I drove back to Nakasero Lodge and told Amin what I had seen. He expressed no surprise at all, but simply nodded, saying "Oh, is that what has been done? You go home now." I said that I would, if he had no specific instructions for me. He agreed and I left. Knowing Amin as I did, and having seen the deadpan way he received my news, I immediately came to the conclusion that he was somehow involved in Kay's death, although I was in no state to ask myself how.

Later the same night, Amin telephoned me with an extraordinary order; he asked me to arrange for the limbs to be sewn back on to the body. He wanted the job done the next morning, he said, because he wanted to bring Kay's children to view the body. I assumed he wished the family to be allowed a formal leave-taking. The next day I ordered a postmortem, after which the gruesome task was done.

Kay's body was then laid out on a bed and covered with a sheet up to her chin. At about 11:00 A.M., on Amin's orders, Kay's father and her three children, aged between four and eight, were brought to the hospital. Amin appeared. Then, in front of television cameras and with reporters standing by, they went in to see the body. His behavior was quite appalling; instead of making the customary oration to comfort the family, he reviled his former wife, and used her body to humiliate them. "Your mother was a bad woman," he shouted at the children. "See what has happened to her!" Two days after this scene in the hospital, Kay's body was taken back to her birthplace near Arua by helicopter and buried. Amin did not attend the funeral, and did not even send a representative. He never again mentioned her to me. That was the end of the matter. There were no further investigations by the police, and Kay was never referred to again.

There has never been an explanation of what really happened, but in the week following Kay's death, I discovered a number of details that led me toward a theory. I spoke to the police, who were investigating the doctor's suicide, and I went to his house myself. I spoke to the Mulago doctors. I spoke to Mrs. Mbalu-Mukasa. I learned the following facts.

- Kay's torso had been found in the trunk of the doctor's car, in a sack which was itself in a box. The police had been led to it by blood spots on the garage floor. The limbs were in a sack on the back seat of the car, which was parked in the garage. The house was immaculately clean.
- One of the medical assistants at Mulago Hospital, a Rwandese, who had been questioned by the Military

Police once before, had been arrested, probably on Monday, August 14, but perhaps on Tuesday. The Rwandese used to work part-time at the doctor's clinic, and had been taken to army headquarters, where he had been interrogated by the chief medical officer. He then vanished. I was told he had been released and had gone back to Rwanda. He could just as easily have been murdered.

- The postmortem established the cause of Kay's death. She had died of loss of blood during an attempted surgical abortion. She had been four to five months' pregnant. The fact that Kay had been seeking an abortion was a surprise. That she should have asked Dr. Mbalu-Mukasa's help was not. Although he was not a trained gynecologist, Mbalu-Mukasa had performed a number of illegal abortions.

- Mbalu-Mukasa's maid had arrived early that Monday morning but was sent away by the doctor, who was clearly distraught. She went to see a friend of the doctor's family, who telephoned, heard the groggy voice of the doctor and walked over to find the doctor already deeply unconscious.

- Amin told me that when the police went to Kay's apartment after her death, they found a Tanzanian living in her house. According to Amin the Tanzanian had firearms and ammunition in his possession, and the police had arrested him on suspicion of plotting against the President. This story struck me as very odd. Kay's father, who was also staying in the apartment, had never at any time mentioned that there was a Tanzanian staying there. What is more, apart from the fact that Amin told me about the Tanzanian, not another thing was ever heard about him.

None of this evidence is conclusive, but the pieces could be fitted together to show a pattern, as follows.

In March 1974, Kay is thrown out of the Amin household. She finds herself pregnant. In July she turns to her lover, an abortionist, for help. She is by now more than four months pregnant, well past the three months normally considered safe. Perhaps after some hesitation, the doctor agrees. She is, after all, in deep distress. He arranges for the operation to be done at his clinic with the assistance of his part-time junior, a Rwandese. During the operation, something goes wrong; Kay begins to bleed uncontrollably under the anesthetic, and dies.

The doctor and the assistant dismember the body. The assistant returns home, as does the doctor. The doctor then administers sleeping pills to his family to ensure their ignorance, (the baby he places in a cupboard with blankets over its head), and goes back to the clinic to collect the body. He returns home, planning to dispose of all evidence during the night and then to flee.

Realizing the futility of the scheme, however, he despairs and takes no action. Early in the morning, the maid appears at the door. The doctor sends her away, but she becomes suspicious of his behavior, and the absence of noise from the children. The doctor takes a huge overdose of sleeping pills. The maid meanwhile has walked to a friend of the Mbalu-Mukasas. The friend, worried by the maid's story, calls up the doctor, who answers in a slurred and groggy voice, and hangs up without saying anything more. The friend, now certain that something is amiss, goes over to the doctor's house. There, he finds the doctor lying unconscious on the floor, and the family apparently dying. The friend calls an ambulance, and all the family (excluding the baby) is rushed to the hospital. The police are called in. They arrest the assistant. He tells the whole story. The police hand the assistant over to the army, tip off Amin and later find the doctor's baby still alive. They also find Kay's body. The corpse is taken to the mortuary. The assistant is either sent back to Rwanda or murdered by the army.

This scenario could explain what happened in general terms. It does however, still leave a number of questions unanswered. Who was the mysterious Tanzanian Amin mentioned to me? If the doctor drugged his family that evening, what was he doing the rest of the night? Did he intend to just keep them quiet, or, as the Mulago authorities assumed, to kill them? Did he do the dismembering during the night? Was the dismemberment done at the doctor's clinic or at his home? Having dismembered the body, why did he not dispose of it?

I do not now believe, as I first did, that Amin had a direct hand in Kay's death. If he had ordered her murder, he would never have chosen such a complicated way to have it done. There would have been no need to court publicity when she could have simply disappeared without a trace. The case will probably remain unsolved, a weird backwater in the mainstream of Ugandan affairs.

Kay's children are still with Amin. The oldest is now about ten. They are at school with the children of friends of mine. They tell their school fellows that their daddy killed their mummy. I think they were wrong, but considering their daddy's reputation, I doubt if they would ever believe me. Who would?

Of the three divorced wives, Nora was the luckiest, despite being a Langi—or perhaps because of it. Like Malyamu, she was dismissed for running a business, which Amin had given to her himself after the expulsion of the Asians. She has simply continued with it ever since. She is now in her mid-forties. She has not been disgraced, and has been to see Amin about assistance for her family several times. In fact, she and her family have been flown out to Libya for medical treatment on a number of occasions. It looks as if the relationship between the two of them was more political than passionate. It has suited Amin to treat her decently: if he is accused of being anti-Langi, he can reply, "My former wife is a Langi— and look how well she has been treated."

With three of his four wives dismissed, Amin was left with the delectable Medina. Their relationship has always been passionate. They have fought frequently and violently.

One fight occurred after an assassination attempt in early 1975, when one of Amin's cars was forced off the road on the outskirts of Kampala. Amin was traveling in another car and was unhurt. In fact nobody was killed but Amin was convinced that somebody on his staff had tipped off the would-be assassins. He suspected Medina, and beat her up thoroughly. She was left with a black eye and severe bruises. Somehow during the fight Amin managed to fracture the base of his wrist. If this was done while punching Medina on the head, she is extremely lucky to be alive. Amin contacted me and asked me to send a doctor. I did so. Medina was then taken to Mulago Hospital, but talk started almost at once about Amin's wife looking as if she had been assaulted. She was removed soon afterward, and treated as well as was possible at home. Fortunately, she had no internal injuries.

Amin, too, was given immediate treatment. An x-ray showed that he had a fracture in his wrist. He explained that he had been in a car crash. Doctors put his wrist in a plaster cast to hold it in shape, and told him to keep it there for two or three weeks. But the very next day, Amin—who never likes to display evidence that he can suffer injury like ordinary mortals—went to another doctor and had it removed. As a result, the bone was never joined. It must be very painful—he complained to me several times about it. No doubt it affects what little writing he does although he pretends to have full movement in this wrist. In 1977, I arranged for him to consult another group of doctors—North Koreans—who x-rayed his wrist again. I saw the x-rays; the bone had still not mended. In fact, a splinter had separated from the main bone—but he would not accept any attempt to immobilize his arm.

In January 1977, Amin and Medina had another battle. The cause is unclear, but one weekend Amin beat up Medina, who was then two or three months pregnant, giving her such a clout by her left temple that she was badly cut and suffered from severe headaches for some time afterward. He also kicked her, nearly causing her to miscarry.

I had gone home for the weekend, so Amin contacted the staff of Mulago Hospital, and asked for a doctor. The doctor he reached, Dr. Otiti, had her taken to Mulago. Later Amin telephoned me, and told me that the following day, a Monday, he wanted Dr. Otiti to go with Medina to Tripoli.

Medina was in Libya for several weeks, and returned to Uganda on the morning of January 23, 1977, two days before the sixth anniversary of the coup. Amin asked me to go to the airport and welcome her, which I did. I could not see her injuries, for she arrived wearing huge dark glasses; but she told me that she was all right. On the twenty-fifth she appeared in public, still wearing dark glasses, at a review of the massed army bands in front of the Nile Hotel.

I have only described two assaults, but in fact, violence was a feature of their daily lives. Although Amin loves Medina, his attitude to her is affected by the failure of her colleague, Sarah—wife No. 5, but currently ranking No. 2—to produce a child for him. Medina conceives easily and Amin, uncomprehending, takes out his disappointment with Sarah on Medina—especially when she is pregnant.

Wife No. 5, Sarah Kyolaba, was previously a go-go dancer in the jazz band of the "Suicide" Mechanized Unit (so named solely for dramatic effect) stationed at Masaka, eighty miles from Kampala. It was inevitable that he would be attracted to her for she is strikingly good looking. When Amin became interested in her, in 1974, she was only eighteen, and was living with a young man.

On Christmas Day 1974, Amin telephoned me just after I arrived back from church. He told me that a girl named Sarah had given birth to a baby at the Church of

Uganda Hospital at Namirembe. He asked me to arrange for her to be transferred from her present public ward to a VIP ward at Mulago. I made the arrangements myself because the circumstances were strange: Sarah had had a normal delivery, and there was no reason to risk complications by transferring her at this stage. My wife, Teresa, went to get her and took her to Mulago, where the baby was just marked "BBA" (Born Before Arrival). When I saw her later that day, I realized that she was the dancer from the "Suicide" Mechanized Unit.

I informed Amin that Sarah had been transferred and was comfortable, and he ordered me to issue a statement for the radio announcing that the President had had a baby born to him on Christmas Day, and that both the mother and child were doing well. Sarah's name was not mentioned. The next day, Amin arranged for Medina—at that time his only wife—to visit Sarah and the newborn baby. The visit was covered by television cameras, but again there was no mention of who Sarah was. (This was not the first time Amin had done such a thing; he had once had two of his children, twins, given names Moslemfashion in a mosque, a ceremony which was announced on the radio, without mentioning the mother's name.)

After a few days, Sarah was discharged from the hospital and Amin had her picked up and taken to her home. Later, I learned that Sarah's boyfriend was the father of the child; Amin had publicly claimed paternity for a child he knew was not his.

Thereafter, Amin used to have Sarah brought to him periodically. Finally, probably in March or April, Sarah's boyfriend objected. He refused to allow her to go, saying that Sarah was the mother of their child, and his wife in all but name. Amin was informed. The boy vanished. His body was never found. Sarah was brought to Kampala. She, of course, knew perfectly well Amin had killed her lover, but there was nothing she could do about it.

On August 2, at the OAU Summit, for which occasion he had promoted himself Field Marshall, Amin married Sarah. The ceremony was not held in a mosque; Amin simply summoned the head of the Moslem faith, the Chief Kadhi, to Command Post and had the wedding there, attended by a few OAU heads of state and other dignitaries.

In the meantime, the remaining OAU delegates, myself included, had been asked to proceed to a place called Cape Town View, so named to commemorate Amin's self-proclaimed role as a leader in the fight against white domination in southern Africa. Cape Town View is about six miles out of Kampala on the shores of Lake Victoria. There, the guests were to watch a demonstration—"Operation Cape Town"—in which army and air force units were supposed to act out the destruction of the South African city by bombing an island in the lake. Before the start of the demonstration, Amin and Sarah arrived. He took her into a nearby house, changed from the uniform he was wearing at the wedding, and then dressed in his battle fatigues, joined the crowd on the shores of Lake Victoria. The exercise did not go well; the bombers missed their target island, and all the bombs fell into the lake. Amin was not very happy about this. Soon after, the Commander of the Air Force, Smuts Guweddeko, was dismissed. He was later murdered.

After the demonstration, Amin officially announced that he had just been married again. He then returned to a nearby house, got dressed once again in his ceremonial uniform, and came out with his new bride, still in her white dress, with her bridesmaids. Although it had been a Moslem wedding, Amin had organized all the trimmings of a Western-style reception; Amin and Sarah cut their tiered cake, and everyone gathered around to congratulate them and toast their health.

The next day, Radio Uganda announced that, in response to public demand, the President had decided to have another ceremony so that it could be witnessed live on television. This was held in the International Conference Center attached to the Nile Hotel. Diplomats, ministers and other officials arrived. Again Amin wore a Field Marshal's uniform. Again Sarah was all dressed up in the Western fashion. Again there was a Moslem ceremony. Again there was a reception. The whole spectacle was carefully filmed by Amin's press corps. Thereafter, the film—for which "public demand" is apparently insatiable—has been shown on Uganda television every few days.

Since then, Sarah has been mysteriously barren. She has been examined by countless doctors, both Ugandan and foreign. They have found no physical abnormality. Amin cannot understand why his other wives have conceived easily but not the youthful Sarah.

To me, the answer is straightforward enough. The girl has never forgotten her former boyfriend, nor the circumstances of his death at the hands of Amin's bodyguards. Many doctors have told me of this problem, and asked me how they should confront Amin with it. I told them that it was simply not possible to do so, but if Amin has this passage read to him, as I'm sure he will, he should know that the murder of Sarah's boyfriend and Amin's known brutality have had serious psychological effects. She has told her doctors that she dreams of his murder, and is so thoroughly frightened of Amin that she can never enjoy sexual relations with him.

Besides his five wives, Amin has had countless other women, many of whom have borne him children. His sex life is truly extraordinary. He regards his sexual energy as a sign of his power and authority. He never tries to hide his lust. His eyes lock onto any beautiful woman. His reputation for sexual performance is so startling that women often deliberately make themselves available, and his love affairs have included women of all colors and many nations, from schoolgirls to mature women, from street girls to university lecturers.

Besides his official wives, there are at least ten unofficial ones, who have not been graced with any particular title. Two of them work in his private office as secretaries. One of them, Sauda Amin, uses his name, although he has never mentioned to anyone that he is married to her. It was Sauda who bore him the twins which were publicly named in a mosque. In fact, she has now fallen out of favor, because she objected so strenuously to Amin's wide-ranging sexual interests.

One particularly frightening aspect of his sex life is his readiness to kill to achieve his sexual ends. Sarah is not the only girl whose husband or lover has been murdered. I have come across at least three other cases in which a woman had been taken as a mistress after her man has been killed:

- My personal secretary in the Ministry of Culture and Community Development. Her husband, Professor Emiru, was murdered in 1971.
- The wife of a man named Nshekanabo, manager of Tororo Hotel. In this case, Amin even ordered the insurance company to rush through the payment due the wife on the death of her husband.
- A senior woman police officer whose husband was arrested, and then—when Amin became interested in the wife—murdered.

Amin's behavior is mirrored by his bodyguards. The husband of a senior nurse in a Mulago Hospital was murdered, and the nurse was later seen in the company of one of Amin's senior aides named Abdud. I eventually dismissed her, because the case was becoming so much of an embarrassment.

Amin's casual affairs are too numerous to count. His sex life has extended into all corners of the administration. No ministry or department has been left untouched. In my own ministry, I had to cope with his frequent approaches to nurses. Once he became interested in a student nurse in Jinja Hospital. He asked

me to organize some overseas training for her as an
enticement. The girl saw the danger, left the training
school, abandoned all her possessions and fled to Kenya.
A similar case occurred when Amin expressed interest in
a nurse from Mulago Hospital. One day he sent his
bodyguards to the girl's parents, with a car filled with
sugar, salt and 700 shillings in cash. In Uganda, it is the
custom that if the parents of a young girl accept such gifts
from a suitor, it is a sign that their daughter may go to the
man. When the parents saw the gifts, they began crying in
horror at the implications. Amin's treatment of his wives
and girlfriends is widely known, and nobody would want
a daughter involved with him. The next thing I heard was
that the nurse had vanished from the hospital; I later
understood that she, too, had fled to Kenya.

At any one time, Amin must have a harem of perhaps
thirty women on which he can draw. They are scattered
all around Uganda, in hotels, offices and hospitals. Some
have been sent to foreign missions, awaiting his
summons. While they are away from him they lead very
abnormal lives. They dare not go out with other men.
Even those in foreign embassies are followed by his spies,
and regular reports go back to Amin on their behavior.

Amin's sex life and his working life are two sides of the
same coin. An energy that is expressed in sex as well as
politics infuses both his days and nights. He stays alert
until four or five in the morning in case the army moves
against him in the early hours. His treatment of women
has its counterpart in his treatment of the country. His
urge to dominate by force, his vindictiveness, his peacock
flamboyance—all suggest that he has seized and ravaged
the country as he has possessed his scores of women.

7

Dora Bloch: Victim of Entebbe

IN THE EARLY hours of June 28, 1976, the Air France plane
hijacked by the Popular Front for the Liberation of
Palestine arrived at Entebbe Airport. I first heard of its
arrival from a BBC broadcast about 6:00 A.M. The
report gave few details: the flight, Air France 139, had
originated in Tel Aviv; it had been hijacked soon after
takeoff from Athens; it had some three hundred
passengers on board, many of whom must have been
Israelis. I knew at once that my ministry would be closely
involved in any operations connected with hostages and
crew.

I dressed immediately and went straight from my
residence in Kampala to the ministry headquarters in
Entebbe, which is next door to State House and about
two miles from the old Entebbe Airport building. I
arrived at my office at about 8:15 A.M. At 9:00 A.M. the
President phoned. He told me enthusiastically,
"Kyemba, Palestinians have hijacked this plane from
Israel and brought it to Entebbe." He had already been in
touch with them. He told me to arrange for a doctor and a
nurse to assist with any medical treatment required.
Clearly wanting a small, sympathetic team to preserve
secrecy, he specified a particular Nubian nurse for the job
and asked me to select a doctor acceptable to the
Palestinians. I contacted an Egyptian, Dr. Ayad, and
asked him to stand by at Entebbe hospital with the nurse

for emergency duty.

At 3:00 that afternoon, Amin called me again, directing me to go with the doctor and the nurse to check on the hostages. We left immediately with an ambulance.

At the airport, after passing through a line of Ugandan soldiers, I was met by officials from the Kampala office of the Palestinian Liberation Organization. They took me into the old airport building. Since the opening of the new international airport, the old building had fallen into disrepair. It was being used only as a warehouse, mainly for storing tea to be exported to Stanstead, England. The place was an empty shell—dusty, with broken windows and peeling paint. In the embarkation hall, the rows of fixed seats were still in place, but the water system was rusted and toilet facilities were virtually nonexistent. The hostages were all huddled on the seats, some lying on piles of clothing, others talking in low voices. They were a miserable sight. They had been there almost twelve hours and had just been served some lunch—meat stew and rice, provided by the Entebbe Airport Hotel. The hijackers, in civilian clothes and armed with pistols and grenades, were standing just inside the doorways.

A Palestinian official introduced me to the leader of the hijackers—and a woman hijacker, who, I later realized, must have been the German terrorist Gabriele Kroche-Tiedemann. She was a strikingly good-looking woman, wearing a blue skirt and jacket with a pistol slung on her hip. The Palestinian told her I was the Minister of Health. She said she was very pleased to meet me. She was about to introduce herself to me by name, but changed her mind, saying simply, "I am Miss Hijacker." I said, "Well, I'm very pleased to meet you, Miss Hijacker." She told the others who I was, pointing out the white-gowned doctor and the uniformed nurse behind me. I was then introduced all around. Gabriele told the hostages that I had come to deal with their complaints. She spoke in English, while one of the women hostages translated into Hebrew through a megaphone. In another part of the hall, I heard someone else speaking in a low voice, perhaps translating into French.

I then told my medical staff to carry on, talked to the hijackers for a few minutes, and left. I was later told by the doctor and the nurse that the hostages were generally in good shape. They only had to distribute anti-malaria tablets and treat a few headaches.

The following day, Tuesday, June 29, several problems arose. Three elderly French ladies became very vociferous about their detention and insisted on being allowed to leave. One of them even urinated at the side of the hall, clearly determined to make herself as objectionable as possible until she was removed. On the doctor's recommendation, the hijackers, worried about their ability to preserve calm in such circumstances, allowed the women to be taken to the hospital in Entebbe.

Another hostage, also French, was admitted to Mulago Hospital. He was an old man with a suspected heart problem, but we found nothing seriously wrong. Amin, however, dramatized the case. He announced that the Frenchman had been treated by doctors all over the world and that his condition was only properly diagnosed and cured when he came to Uganda.

Amin ordered that as soon as the old people had been treated, they should be returned to the airport building. I pointed out that if one of them died it would make disastrous publicity. Amin took the point. Accordingly, the four old people were discharged and given over to the French Embassy (which by international law bore responsibility for all the passengers and crew of the Air France plane.)

In the airport building itself, a number of the hostages complained of backache. They had only the chairs to sit on and the floors to lie on. The doctor recommended that blankets and mattresses be brought for them. I spoke to the President about this, and told him I agreed with the doctor. Amin said he would instruct the Minister of

Tourism, who is responsible for Uganda's hotels, to implement the recommendations.

The whole operation was being supervised by Amin himself, working together with the Palestinians based in Kampala. He thought he saw a fine opportunity to humiliate the Israelis and increase his stock with the Arabs. He wanted all the glory. "Well, Kyemba," he said to me several times, "now I've got these people where I want them," and "I've got the Israelis fixed up this time." He was closely involved in drafting the Palestinians' demands, announced on Tuesday: in exchange for the hostages, fifty-three Palestinian prisoners held in various prisons around the world must be freed. The conditions would have to be met by Thursday, July 1—in two days' time—otherwise the hostages would all be killed.

The deadline was impossibly tight; there was hardly time to contact all the authorities involved, let alone get their agreement to the terms. On Thursday morning, Amin arrived at the airport building in battle fatigues and explained the situation to the hostages. The deadline was extended to Sunday, July 4, at 1:00 A.M. This date was devised to suit Amin. It would allow him time to go to Mauritius, where the OAU were holding their annual summit, and there officially hand over his chairmanship to the Prime Minister of Mauritius. He would have considered it humiliating not to do this in person, for that would make it seem that he was afraid to leave the country; he would also have an opportunity to dramatize the hold he had over Israel. He would then be able to return on Saturday, in time for the expiration of the new deadline on Sunday. It was this extension, of course, that gave the Israelis time to complete their plans for a military rescue.

Amin left on Thursday afternoon for Mauritius, ebullient as ever, certain that the Palestinian demands would be met. I am sure that he never had any intention of killing the hostages—they were far too valuable to him. But likewise, he had no contingency plans if his own scheme did not work out perfectly. It simply never occurred to him that anything could go wrong.

I was in frequenct contact with Amin over the next thirty-six hours. A report came through that many of the hostages had become sick, and that others were pretending to be sick to force their release. Amin called me up and instructed me to increase the size of the medical team at the airport. But when I told Dr. Ayad I had arranged for further medical staff to assist him, he replied that it was not necessary. Sanitary conditions had become disastrous, and many hostages had stomach troubles and headaches, but he assured me there was no need for additional assistance.

On the evening of Friday, July 2, one of the hostages, an elderly lady, Dora Bloch, who held dual British-Israeli nationality, choked on a piece of meat which had lodged deep in her throat. She was having difficulty breathing and was rushed to Mulago. It could have proved critical, but once in the hospital the piece of meat was easily removed by one of the surgeons in a minor operation. I had left town on Friday and learned of Mrs. Bloch's admission only late that evening. Early on Saturday morning, I returned to Kampala to see her.

I arrived at her ward at about 11:00 in the morning. She was in one of the VIP wards (6B) on the sixth floor, with a police guard posted outside her door. I was introduced to her by the doctor, who accompanied me into her room. She was in bed, wearing the dress she had arrived in. She had brought her handbag and her cane, which was standing in the corner.

I said, "Hello, how are you? I hope you will be well soon."

"I'm all right," she replied, "but I am worried about my son." (He was still at the airport.)

I said, "Don't worry, everything will be all right."

"I hope so," she replied, "but I am frightened of the guard—he keeps looking through the window."

I went out immediately and told the guard to stay on

his bench and not to come and look through the window. "You don't need to check on her all the time," I told him, "after all, she's very old and can't walk very well."

I walked back in and told Mrs. Bloch that I had instructed the guard to stay out of sight. She thanked me and I left.

It was only a brief conversation, but in that short time I developed a strong sympathy for Mrs. Bloch. Her gentleness and her helplessness moved me. She reminded me very much of my own mother, who was about the same age and who had recently been hospitalized. Mrs. Bloch had made a good recovery, and could have gone back to the airport that day, but feeling the way I did, I arranged instead for her to stay another night in Mulago rather than face the discomfort of the airport hall.

That afternoon, while trying to tune into a news program on the radio, I picked up Tel Aviv. They announced that President Amin had left Mauritius and was on his way home to Entebbe. It struck me as odd that the Israelis should know more about our own President's movements than the Ugandan government.

Amin arrived in the early evening and paid a visit to the 106 Israeli hostages (the others had been released by the Palestinians a short time before). He called me about 10:00 P.M. to check on the medical treatment they were receiving. I told him the only thing to worry about was the sanitation. I then mentioned Mrs. Bloch, explained why she was in Mulago, and said that she was now almost fit again. He directed me to arrange for her to be returned to the airport the next day (Sunday) before the expiration of the deadline at 1:00. I told him that I would see to it.

At about 12:30 that night, the telephone rang. It was one of Amin's mistresses calling from Kampala. She said Amin had just telephoned her from Entebbe with the news that there was fighting at the airport and that the situation was out of control. The airport had been captured, Amin had said—he did not know by whom. He stated that he was taking care of himself, and advised her to do the same. He said that he was sending a car for her, and suggested she go into hiding. But the woman could not think of anywhere to go, and wanted my advice and help. But there was little I—or indeed anyone else—could do.

I must admit that the news did not altogether surprise me. "It's the Israelis," I said to Teresa. "It must be. They've come to take the hostages." But it was only a guess. We phoned a few of our relatives and told them what little we knew, and then went back to sleep.

Amin, as I learned later, had assumed the attack was some sort of a mutiny backed by a foreign power— Kenya, perhaps, or Tanzania. He could not discover the truth, however, because as soon as the fighting started his senior officers vanished. At the time of the attack, at 11:45 P.M., many of the senior officers in charge of the airport were drinking and dancing at Lake Victoria Hotel near State House. When the Israeli commandos landed, the sudden burst of firing sent everyone fleeing from the bar and the swimming pool to their own homes. There they went into hiding, telling their families that if anyone phoned they were to say they were not available. Until it was clear who was fighting whom, no officers wanted to risk becoming involved with the wrong side.

Amin, too, went into hiding, in a driver's quarters near State House itself. He tried to telephone his staff from there, with little success. I don't blame him for fleeing. If his army mutinied, he would head the wanted list, and State House would be the first place the soldiers would look.

The battle lasted less than an hour. Within an hour and a half the Israelis had gone, taking the hostages with them. They left behind twenty-seven dead—twenty Ugandans and seven hijackers. Two hostages were also killed. Their bodies were taken by the Israelis.

Meanwhile, in Kampala, I slept through the night, except that about 3:00 A.M. I was awakened briefly by the rumbling of tanks and trucks. Then about 6:00 in the morning the phone rang. It was one of the senior officers at Entebbe, asking for ambulances to ferry the injured from Entebbe to Mulago. "It was the Israelis," he told me. "All the hostages are gone. There are lots of injured down here, and a few dead." I immediately contacted Mulago and told them to assist in whatever way they could. I left early and went directly to the hospital to supervise the admissions.

In the hospital compound, army trucks and ambulances were passing in and out, delivering the injured, while relatives crowded around, wailing. The dead had been taken to the mortuary, where attempts were being made to identify them. The seriously injured (about ten in all) were in emergency wards. Several with minor injuries were being treated and discharged. Later, a number of civilian casualties were also admitted, victims of our own humiliated troops who had taken to the streets to prove their loyalty and strength; the soldiers had simply beaten up anyone who dared laugh at them.

I then went home for a while, and returned to the hospital at 10:00 A.M. I was worried about Mrs. Bloch. Some of the injured soldiers had been moved to nearby wards and anti-Israeli feeling among Amin's troops (though not among civilians) was so intense that I feared there might be a revenge killing. I had no real idea of what to do about Mrs. Bloch; I just wanted to go and say hello, and to warn the staff not to talk to her about the events of the previous night, in case she became unduly frightened. I hoped, vaguely, that the French Embassy might get her out of the country. I considered transferring her to another hospital, but this would only have drawn attention to her; I thought of getting Amin's agreement to move her so that it could be done under proper guard, but there was a danger that he might order her execution on the spot. To my lasting regret, I did nothing. I hoped that if I left her where she was and kept quiet about her, the problem would solve itself.

When I went in, Mrs. Bloch asked me if she could wash

the dress that she had been wearing for the last couple of
days. A hospital gown—one of the few available—was
found for her, a three-quarter-length white smock with
short sleeves.

I left the ward and returned to my official residence.
About 6:00 in the evening, the hospital contacted me and
told me that an official from the British High
Commission, Peter Chandley, had asked to see Mrs.
Bloch. They asked me what they should do about him. I
knew that Amin would not agree to a member of the
British High Commission staff talking to her, but I told
the hospital to allow Chandley a quick visit. I thought it
would provide some kind of reassurance to both parties.

The details of what happened next have never been
officially revealed, but they were made available to me
within hours. When Chandley went in to see Mrs. Bloch,
she requested some European food. Chandley went back
home to prepare something for her. In the meantime,
Amin, smarting with the humiliation he had suffered at
the hands of the Israelis, took action.

In Chandley's absence, four State Research men
arrived at Mulago, driving two cars. They parked on the
up-hill side of the hospital, opposite the entrance that led
through the casualty department. Two of the men, whom
I later understood to be Major Farouk Minawa, the
effective head of the State Research Bureau, and Captain
Nasur Ondoga, Chief of Protocol to the President,
marched up to her ward. They were dressed in civilian
clothes and carried pistols. Clearly, they knew where they
were going, and knew that their victim would not put up
much of a struggle. They shouted to the staff to stand
back, ordered aside the police guard outside Mrs. Bloch's
door, threw open the door and hauled her out of bed.
Mrs. Bloch, by then, must have known of the raid, and
there could have been no doubt in her mind of the men's
intentions. They grabbed her by both arms and
frog-marched her down three flights of stairs, leaving
behind her cane, handbag, shoes and dress. Since she

could hardly walk, they must have half-dragged and half-carried her all the way. She screamed continuously.

Patients, staff and visitors crowded by the doors of the wards to see what was happening. Horrified, they watched as the two men dragged her, still screaming, through the casualty department and out of the main hospital door. All who were watching knew that Mrs. Bloch was going to her execution. They did nothing. Interference could mean death. And after all, this was not the first public kidnapping in Kampala. It had become an everyday occurrence. Mrs. Bloch was dragged into one of the waiting cars, both of which then sped out of the hospital compound. The whole thing had taken no more than five minutes from start to finish. It was then about 9:00.

Within minutes, I received, in quick succession, two calls from the hospital, telling me what had happened. I immediately called Amin. His reaction was typically bland. He just said, "Is that so? O.K. I'll see." I had no doubt that he already knew what had happened. Nobody would have come into my hospital and done such a thing except on Amin's direct orders. At that moment, I hoped that he might try to use Mrs. Bloch—the only remaining hostage—as a pawn to enforce the Palestinians' demands. But I dismissed the thought almost at once. She had been seized in public by Amin's own thugs; there was no doubt that she was going to be executed.

At 9:45 Amin telephoned me to discuss those injured in the raid and the arrangements for the burial of the dead on the following day. At the end of the conversation, he said casually, "Oh, by the way, that woman in hospital— don't worry about her—she has been killed." I felt a pang of horror, but was used by now to keeping my reactions to myself. All I said was, "Oh, dear."

I put the phone down, turned to Teresa and a visitor who was with us and let my anger out. I told them what had happened and said, "This is outrageous—that poor old lady—to take revenge on her like that—this is terrible."

The following morning, the inquiries started. The British High Commission wanted access to Mrs. Bloch. Soon after 8:00, they phoned the hospital to ask where she was. I was informed of the call, but didn't know what to say. Then, at 9:10, Amin called. He told me that if any inquiries were made about the sick hostage, I was to say that she had been returned to the airport one hour before the Israeli commandos had arrived, and that the commandos had taken her with them. The official position of the Uganda Government, he said, was that they had no knowledge of her whereabouts.

We both knew this was an outright lie, but I was in no position to refuse to comply. On the other hand, I could not simply lie so blatantly. The evidence was there for all to see in the hospital, on Mrs. Bloch's diet sheet, on the treatment register, and on the discharge record, which of course did not mention her name. I pointed this out to Amin. He just told me to fix the records.

I spent an agonized hour at the hospital, having new record sheets prepared. I had the old ones removed from the hospital and hidden, as evidence for any possible inquiry that might ensue. I also hid away Mrs. Bloch's belongings. I felt sickened by my actions. But I justified it by reflecting that everyone involved knew the truth of what had happened. The records had to be changed because Amin ordered it; it did not change the truth.

One of the most extraordinary things about this particular murder was that it was so unnecessarily brutal and public. Amin could have acted the humanitarian by helping Mrs. Bloch. The State Research people could have hidden their deed by arranging for her to be officially discharged from the hospital and then picking her up afterward. Or they could have removed her quietly through a back entrance. Instead, Amin sent two of his most notorious thugs, who no doubt revelled in the chance to display their viciousness in public. No coverup, however efficient, could conceal their crime.

It was extraordinary enough that the State Research men did not even bother to hide the evidence of their murder. It was even more astounding that Amin never acknowledged there had been a murder. Instead, he blamed the medical staff at the hospital and my ministry for spreading false rumors. "It was the doctors who were at fault," he told me, "for telling people Mrs. Bloch was still in the hospital at the time of the raid."

Mrs. Bloch's murder was soon a matter of public knowledge. Her body was dumped by the side of a road twenty miles outside Kampala, off the main road to Jinja. An attempt was made to burn the body, but the white hair was not touched and it remained conspicuously indentifiable. Word spread and people came by the hundreds to view her body. Yet the government repeatedly announced to anyone who asked that no one had any idea where Mrs. Bloch was.

Among those who saw her body was a famous Ugandan photographer called Jimmy Parma, who took some shots of the corpse. Parma, a good freelance photographer, had been allocated one of the best photographic shops at the time of the Asian exodus. He also worked for the *Voice of Uganda* newspaper. He was picked up soon afterward, near the *Voice of Uganda* offices, in full public view. His body was recovered later, riddled with bullets and lacerated by knife wounds.

A few weeks later the pressure of world opinion forced Amin to appoint an "inquiry" into the raid and the disappearance of Mrs. Bloch. The hospital staff and I, who knew most about the matter, were never questioned. The commissioners dutifully reported that, according to their findings, Mrs. Bloch had been returned to the airport and taken by the Israelis. I am the first to tell what really—and tragically—happened.

Today Mrs. Bloch's body lies in an unmarked grave in a corner of a grass field not far from Kampala. I know the exact location but it must remain a secret for fear of further ghoulish interference by Amin.

All the local villagers are convinced that the Israelis will return for her remains and I think Amin is secretly afraid that they are right. It is quite conceivable that if he knew where she was buried he would have her exhumed.

After my arrival in London I was contacted by lawyers acting for Mrs. Bloch's family. They are seeking formal redress by gathering evidence that can be used to make a case against Amin and his henchmen under international law. One day soon that evidence will be made public. When that happens, Amin will be ordered to appear in front of an international court of law. He will not of course do so, but in refusing he will again be severely embarrassed in the eyes of the world. It will be another small step toward the end of his regime. It has given me some solace to know that my revelations, and my formal evidence taken in London in July 1977, will form part of the case against him.

8

"No One Is Sacred"

AFTER THE TERRIBLE humiliation Amin had suffered at the hands of the Israelis, he desperately needed to reassert his authority. He chose to do so in the only way he really knows: by striking out at those against whom he has a grievance, however slight. In this case his victims were the Anglican Archbishop Janan Luwuum and two of my colleagues in the Cabinet. Their killing was the immediate cause of my defection.

Part of Amin's grievance against the archbishop reflected his hostility toward the Christian Church as a whole, a hostility which stemmed from his ludicrous efforts to turn Uganda into a Moslem state. His Moslemization policies had their counterpart in a number of anti-Christian acts. He attacked Christian fund-raising functions for the 1977 centenary of the Ugandan Church with insults. ("This was," he said, "doing *magendo* (business) in Church.") Missionaries were expelled (including twenty Catholic missionaries who were thrown out shortly before Amin met the Pope in late 1976). At the opening of the Catholic Martyrs' Shrine in 1975, in the presence of a papal representative, he even appeared ostentatiously dressed in the full robes of an Arab sheik.

Amin's atrocities and his antagonism to the Church had already had some effect on Christians. In 1976, for instance, he was dropped from the prayers normally offered in services on behalf of the head of state. In addition, church attendance had increased significantly. I myself attended more services than usual at this time. I have never seen such congregations. Several friends remarked to me that there seemed nothing else to do. Prayer seemed to offer the only hope of coming through our nightmare.

The insult that finally drove the Christian leaders into outspoken protest occurred on Christmas Day 1976. A military spokesman claimed on the radio that churchmen were preaching hatred instead of love in their sermons. This was a charge no Christian could believe. Broadcast on Christmas Day, it seemed a deliberate insult to the Christian majority.

In response to this insult, and wishing to object to Amin's activities in general, Archbishop Luwuum tried to see the President. He telephoned many times to arrange an appointment; each time an aide would say the President was very busy and would call back. He never did.

Amin's initial response, when it came, was typically vicious, brutal and heavy-handed. At 1:30 A.M. on the morning of February 5, 1977, a group of Amin's soldiers arrived at Luwuum's house at Namirembe Hill on the western outskirts of Kampala near the cathedral. They parked beside the fence that surrounded the compound of the imposing two-story house and climbed over the fence, bringing with them an Acholi named Ben Ongom. He had been severely beaten up to make sure that he would do as he was told.

They told Ongom to knock on the door and warn the Archbishop that the soldiers had come. The archbishop awoke, heard the voice, came downstairs and opened the door. The soldiers rushed in, pointed guns at him, and demanded, "Show us the arms!" They searched the house for two hours. Of course, nothing was found. The soldiers left shortly before dawn, after forcing the archbishop to open the compound gates for them.

Similar treatment was meted out a few days later to

Bishop Yona Okoth of Bukedi, near the Kenyan border. For the second time Ongom was forced to play the same role. Again, soldiers burst in demanding to see arms. The bishop showed them a shotgun, for which he had a license. When they asked for other arms, he said, "I look after the church; I do not look after guns." They searched, found nothing, then took him to another house of his, where they again found nothing. They arrested him anyway and took him eighty miles to Jinja, to a private house kept as a police base. There they sat him in the kitchen, made themselves breakfast and gave him a cup of tea while they made some phone calls.

After a few calls, the officer in charge informed him, "We are very sorry; we should not have arrested you. You are free to go." They also told him to keep quiet about what had happened. The bishop replied that it was impossible for a bishop to be forced from his house in the dead of night without anyone knowing. When he returned home, he called the archbishop and told him what had happened.

In response to all this, Luwuum and his bishops drew up a memorandum dated February 10, which gave the details of the searches and went on to make a wide-ranging critique of Amin's regime. It stated that people had had cars stolen at gunpoint, that the law was ignored by the government, and that people had been murdered. Church leaders, it said, had intimate knowledge of the murders because they had buried the victims and cared for the grief-stricken relatives. It pleaded for an end to these horrors, and for a meeting with Amin to resolve the differences between him and the Church. Copies of the memorandum were sent to all Cabinet ministers and several copies were later smuggled abroad; it is reprinted here as an Appendix.

When I received my copy, I was amazed at its boldness. It was not, of course, news to me. The things that the archbishop described were commonplace, but it was the first time such a statement had been made so forcefully, to such a wide range of senior officials. I am certain that from that moment on, Amin was determined to reassert his own authority by murdering the archbishop. The method he chose was to stage manage the production of faked evidence against "conspirators," the chief of whom were to be the archbishop, Erinayo Oryema and Charles Oboth-Ofumbi.

In addition to his outspoken criticism of the regime, Luwuum had another fault in Amin's eyes. He was an Acholi, and Amin believed that the Acholi, together with the Langi a traditionally pro-Obote tribe — had been responsible for the débacle at Entebbe in July 1976. "We did not do very well in the Israeli raid," he told me in early February, just before the murder of the three men, "because the Acholi and Langi officers were in contact with the Israelis."

Oryema, the Minister of Land and Water Resources, was, like the archbishop, an Acholi. He was well respected, but sometimes somewhat impolitic. He had been with Amin in the army for several years, and had been promoted through the ranks to Inspector General of the Police Force. But of late he had not been sufficiently aware of Amin's destructive unpredictability. Once, when he had been out of Kampala on an official visit to the countryside, Amin summoned him back over the radio. Oryema returned, but then tried to save his face by promising, also on the radio, that he would announce a new date for the trip. Such actions were enough to seal his fate.

Oryema was a particularly close friend of mine. We never greeted each other with "good morning" or "good afternoon." We said instead *"Lubanga tye gulu"*—God is in heaven. It is a traditional greeting between good friends, but also a pun: *gulu,* as well as meaning "heaven," is the name of the chief town of the Acholi tribe.

Oboth-Ofumbi, whom I also knew well, was the Minister of Internal Affairs. He was a Japadhola, a small tribe in the eastern part of Uganda, and had once been a particularly close friend of Amin's. Oboth-Ofumbi had been Secretary of Defense while Amin was Deputy Commander, and later Commander, of the army. Oboth-Ofumbi knew of Amin's financial mismanagement in the army; he knew of the Congo gold and ivory scandal of the 1960s; he knew of Amin's killings after the coup of 1971; he knew of the murders committed by the army and by the police, for which he had been responsible as Minister both of Defense and, later, of Internal Affairs. In addition, as Minister of Finance, he knew of Amin's financial irresponsibility. He also had a grudge against him, and Amin knew it. When Amin fired his first Cabinet in 1973, Oboth-Ofumbi was given the task of assessing abandoned Asian property, a demotion that he continued to resent long after he had been reinstated. In short, he knew too much, and was trusted too little, to be allowed to live.

On February 16, the day before the murders, I was told that on the following day there was to be a ministerial meeting at 10:00 A.M. at the Nile Hotel. I had planned to take some visitors to the Murchison Falls National Park on that day, so I arranged that they go on ahead, planning to join them later.

On the afternoon of the sixteenth I had some business to discuss with the President. I needed his opinion on a deal with an Irish pharmaceutical company, Clonmel Chemicals, whose representatives were staying in the Nile Hotel. I tried to contact Amin in Entebbe during the day, but he was already in the Nile Hotel itself, where he had offices on the second floor. I drove to Kampala, arriving at the hotel about 8:30.

I spoke to the President from the telephone at the reception desk. He told me, "I'm sorry, but I am busy with some people here with an important statement. Could we discuss this tomorrow or the day after?" I agreed, wondering in passing what the statement could be about.

Later on that evening, I discovered that the meeting set

for the next day was to be more than a minister..i
meeting; it was to include the diplomatic corps and the
church leaders as well.

The following morning, when I arrived at the Nile
Hotel, many ministers, diplomats and church leaders,
including the archbishop in his full regalia, as befitted
such a reception, were already there. Television cameras
were in position to one side. All this I had expected. But
in addition, there were a good 2,000 soldiers, brought
from various units all over the country, sitting on the
ground in a huge semicircle in the forecourt of the hotel.
In the middle of the semicircle were neat lines of weapons:
submachine guns, grenades, and rifles. They were all
brand-new East European weapons—exactly like those
used by many units of the Ugandan army, and in fact,
supplied to ministers for official protection. Clearly they
were intended for some ominous purpose.

We took our positions, along the front of the hotel,
facing the seated soldiers. I was sitting almost exactly
behind the bank of microphones set up for the speakers.
We waited tensely in the hot sun for the President to
arrive. He did not come. I learned later that he was
watching the proceedings from his offices above, striding
back and forth between the office balcony and the
television inside. At about 11:00 A.M. the proceedings
were opened by Colonel Isaac Malyamungu. He
reminded us that time and again the government had
spoken of subversion. "Here now," he said, "is the proof
of it."

There then followed a reading of statements, by
selfconfessed "conspirators," of a reported attempt to
overthrow the Amin government. The first and longest
statement was allegedly from Obote himself to his
henchmen. It was read by the former Chairman of the
Public Service Commission, Mr. Abdulla Anyuru.
Around sixty years old, and not fit, he had retired just
after the coup and was living a quiet life in his own village.
The statement was amazingly similar to the

archbishop's memorandum. It discussed how unhappy
the people were, how Amin had mismanaged the country,
how people were being harrassed, how people were being
killed. It was, in fact, a very accurate portrait of Uganda
at the time.

The statement was not, of course, from Obote. It was
read direct from blue paper which was, I saw, the
standard State House paper used for official documents.

The statement, which lasted something over an hour,
was too long for Anyuru; halfway through he almost
collapsed. I called for a chair. One was brought. He
finished the statement with Malyamungu standing beside
him to ensure that he did not miss anything or change a
word. In the last five minutes, the archbishop was
implicated. He was said to have received some arms. The
archbishop, who was sitting near me, shook his head in
denial at what was being read.

There followed two other statements; one was read by
Lieutenant Ogwang, an intelligence officer. The other
one was read by Ben Ongom who had, less than two
weeks before, been used by Amin's secret police to force
an entry into the archbishop's house. He had, in the
meantime, grown a beard. Since beards were associated
with Obote's guerrillas, he would not have grown it
voluntarily. Perhaps he had been ordered to grow it to
make him look like a guerrilla, or to conceal scars.

In their statements, the two men "admitted" having
received instructions from Obote. They also "admitted"
having received the arms displayed there in the semicircle
of soldiers. Nothing in these statements implicated the
two cabinet ministers.

After the statements had been read, Amin asked for a
show of hands from those soldiers who wanted the
"conspirators" to die. All the soldiers raised their hands,
shouting in Swahili, *"Kinja yeye! Kinja yeye!"* (Kill them!
Kill them!) At one point during the three hours of these
proceedings, I saw a young officer, Major Moses Okello,
emerge briefly from the hotel. He spoke to a group of

officers, then vanished inside once more. It was a small
detail, but a significant one in view of what was to happen
later.

At about 3:00 P.M. all the soldiers, ministers and
church leaders—but not the diplomats, who dispersed—
were told to move into the International Conference
Center that adjoined the hotel, to hear an address by
Amin. The weapons were collected and taken away. We
filed along the covered way that led from the hotel to the
Center. It took about half an hour for all two thousand of
us to be seated.

Colonel Malyamungu then stepped up to the
microphone and asked the archbishop and other
religious leaders to return to the hotel. After they had
gone, Malyamungu ordered Oryema and Oboth-Ofumbi
to leave through another door.

Those left in the hall, myself included, were, of course,
unable to see what happened to those who had been sent
out. But the following events took place in full view of the
drivers and bodyguards in the parking lots outside.
Several of them told me what happened, as did some of
the bishops.

Halfway along the covered way, the bishops were
stopped by soldiers. The archbishop was told that the
President wanted to see him alone. He vanished into the
hotel. Within a few minutes he was hustled into a car
waiting near the area where the arms had been displayed.
He was then driven off toward the State Research
headquarters at Nakasero.

Meanwhile, on the other side of the Conference
Center, the two Cabinet ministers had been arrested. The
State Research men had been waiting for them. In full
view of our bodyguards, and others outside the building,
four men took charge of each minister, shoved them into
cars, and drove off. The cars used were the same as those
used by the President's escort unit. Amin was watching
these proceedings from the balcony of his office. At one
point he shouted out that the arrested people should not

be manhandled until they were away from the crowd of drivers and bodyguards. (As part of the same "anti-Obote" operation, a few other Langi and Acholi were also arrested, both on the spot and in the countryside. Some were later released, although some—including my former boss at the Ministry of Culture, Yekosfati Engur—were killed.)

Inside the Conference Center, the assembled crowd was addressed briefly by the Minister of State for Defense and the army Chief of Staff, Major General Isaac Lumago, who repeated the conspiracy charges. The President then joined us and gave us a surprisingly brief speech of no more than half an hour in which he recapitulated his opposition to the Church. He was clearly anxious to get away.

At about 4:00 P.M. Amin invited the ministers and soldiers to a reception in the forecourt of the hotel. Having spent the day listening in horror to patent fabrications, and knowing that the whole operation was stage-managed for some ominous purpose, none of us felt inclined to celebrate. As far as I know, all the ministers and senior government officers immediately went to their cars and were driven off. The only people who went to the reception were the soldiers, who were obviously hungry and had a long journey back to their barracks ahead of them.

I did not leave immediately because I wished to clear my trip to the Murchison Falls with the President. I walked over to the Nile Hotel, and remained in the lobby for half an hour, waiting for the President; then I decided not to go on my trip since it was getting so late, and drove straight back to my family.

I drove home via Mackinnon Road. Had I taken another equally direct route to my house, along Ternan Avenue, I would have been in time to watch the faked motor accident, which was then being staged on the road between the President's Lodge of Nakasero and the Kampala International Hotel. This faked accident was intended as a coverup for the executions of the archbishop and the two ministers, which, I learned later, had just taken place at the State Research headquarters.

Later in the evening, at about 9 P.M., Vice President Mustafa Adrisi, telephoned me. He was calling, he said, on Amin's orders. "These people, Oryema and company, have died in a motor accident," he said, speaking in Swahili. Amin then added a phrase which he also used in speaking to Godfrey Lule: "God has given them their punishment." He told me where the accident had occurred and asked me to put the Mulago mortuary on the alert for the arrival of the bodies. I replaced the receiver. I could not believe that the three people had really died in a car accident. To have died accidentally? So soon after their accusation? When they had left the proceedings in two different cars? It was simply incredible. I knew instinctively they had been killed.

Assuming the "accident" had just occurred, I expected the bodies to be at the mortuary within a matter of minutes, because the scene of the event was hardly a mile from the hospital. I phoned the hospital, ordered them to prepare for the arrival of the corpses, and told them to report to me as soon as they arrived.

At about 11:30, I called the Vice President again, and asked him what was happening. I still did not have any information about the bodies. "Don't worry," he replied, "the President says they are coming." This did not seem surprising; certain that the three had been killed, I assumed Amin wanted to see the bodies, as usual, before they were delivered to the hospital.

I went to bed at about midnight. At about 5 A.M. the hospital authorities telephoned—the bodies had just been delivered to the mortuary. They had arrived in an army truck, and had been thrown out of the back onto the ground outside the mortuary. All three were dressed as they had been the previous day. The archbishop was still in his robes; one of the ministers was in his uniform; the other was in his suit. I gave instructions to lock the mortuary and to keep everyone out, dressed, and hurried over to the hospital.

The bodies lay on the floor of the mortuary. As I expected, they were bullet-riddled. They had been shot at very close range. The archbishop had been shot through the mouth and had three or four other bullets in his chest. The two ministers had been shot in the same way, but only in the chest and not through the mouth. One of them, Oryema, also had a bullet wound through the leg.

Now I knew with terrible certainty that to Amin no one and nothing was sacred.

The news of the deaths was first announced in the morning, both on the radio and in the official newspaper *Voice of Uganda*. The paper must have been informed the evening before, and the radio personnel—in their headquarters just a quarter of a mile from the scene of the "accident"—told to suppress the news until it could be released simultaneously in the newspaper.

I later pieced together the details of the "accident" from two eyewitnesses who told me what they had seen. The area was surrounded by a cordon of troops to keep away possible witnesses, but the two who spoke to me saw the whole thing from a high-rise apartment building overlooking the scene. Amin, the producer of this gruesome charade, had apparently not considered his terrain.

Two vehicles were driven into positions that suggested an accident. When the vehicles came into gentle contact, the three bodies were immediately pulled from one of them and placed in the other. Absurd though it seems, this was intended to give the impression—to a supposedly nonexistent audience—that a serious accident had taken place. The troops dispersed. Both cars drove off.

The driver of one of the cars was Major Moses Okello, whom I had seen briefly at the hotel. He later claimed, obviously on Amin's orders, that he did not remember the accident because he had been knocked out in the crash and had been in a coma for the next two days. The truth of the matter is very different. On the day after the "accident," Amin telephoned me: he wanted Moses to be examined to substantiate his claim. Of course, what he really wanted was a medical coverup. The same day, therefore, I arranged for a doctor to examine him in my presence. Moses was escorted to the hospital by several of Amin's secret police, putting on a great show of being badly injured, and struggling along with a walking stick. The doctor, a Russian named Levashov, tried to get Moses to tell the story of his motor accident and injuries. Moses had clearly been told by Amin not to say anything. He assumed that I knew the truth of the whole thing, and wanted my assistance: I have never seen a man so embarrassed. He said to me in Swahili, "Well, Mr. Minister, you know how things are. You explain it to him." I, equally embarrassed, simply said that the patient had had a motor accident, and had pains all over. The doctor asked if Moses had been x-rayed; I said I supposed he had, but that the files were not available. The doctor suggested that Moses go home, and return later with details of his injuries. This, of course, never happened. But Amin's purpose was fulfilled; Moses had been to the hospital for examination.

As for the driver of the other car, he had been briefed to act out an attempted escape and was "arrested." Later, when Amin was being interviewed by a foreign television crew about the accident, he was asked about the second driver. He replied that he, too, had been knocked unconscious. The interviewers asked where he was now. Amin turned to one of his bodyguards, who said in Swahili, *"Apana yiko apa"* (he's—not here). Clearly the driver was known to him; this was an implicit confession to the public at large that he was one of Amin's boys. After that, the official version of the story was changed. The car was described as stationary and driverless. It was clearly too outrageous, even for Amin, to insist that both drivers had been knocked unconscious and were totally ignorant of what had happened.

Pictures were also released, showing the cars that had supposedly been in the accident—a Range Rover and a Toyota. The two cars were shown in two separate pictures. The truth about them is as follows.

The Range Rover was the President's personal car. It had been registered in his own name three weeks earlier and bore the number UVW 082. It was the vehicle he used for hunting; it was fitted with a refrigerator at the back for preserving game and a sliding roof for shooting when on the move. He was very proud of it, and had been seen driving it around in town and countryside. He drives very fast (as he has done ever since the first attempts on his life), and some time he had crashed it. It was probably for this reason that he selected it for one of the "accident" photographs.

The Toyota in the other official photograph, UVS 299, was one of the State Research Bureau's fleet. It, too, had been in a crash. It had been in the State Research garage for a couple of weeks before the alleged accident.

According to official accounts, the Toyota slid sideways into the front of the Range Rover. The idea is ludicrous. The dent mark on the Toyota's side is 8′ wide; yet the front of the Range Rover is only 5′8″ wide.

Later in the morning after the murders, Amin told me that the army would provide transport for the bodies as soon as the postmortems had been done. The consultant pathologist, Dr. Kafero, did not want to do the postmortems, for he had seen the bodies. "What do you expect me to write?" he asked. (It was rumored later that Dr. Kafero was killed for his refusal. This is not true. He suffered from severe asthma and died of natural causes some weeks later.) I understood Kafero's problem, and ordered an army doctor to write up the postmortem in any way he wished. This he did. He reported that the two ministers and the archbishop had died of injuries to the ribs and to the internal organs.

I expected the army to deliver the archbishop's body to Church of Uganda representatives and the ministers' to the appropriate relatives. But Amin had no intention of releasing the bodies to these people, for he did not want them to know the real cause of death. Instead, they were driven to army headquarters and kept in one of the barracks. This completely ignored the customary feelings of Ugandans, both Christian and Moslem: normally, when somebody dies, the body is cleaned by relatives and other forms of respect are paid to it by relatives and friends. Amin knew this perfectly well, yet without telling me or any of the relatives, he ordered the army to make arrangements for the burials.

Some time during the next week, the archbishop's body was sent to his home village near Kitgum and buried in the presence of only a few military personnel and one or two relatives who happened to be at home at the time. Oryema was buried near Gulu and Oboth-Ofumbi near Tororo. No one even dared send any messages of condolence to the relatives.

When I left Uganda, toward the end of April, all three graves were still under guard by Amin's army. Amin feared, and still fears, that one day someone will exhume the bodies to see what actually happened. It is quite possible that the bodies have been tampered with—perhaps with acid—to destroy all outward marks of the shootings.

Now I knew that my further presence in Uganda would serve no useful purpose, and that sooner or later I would face the same fate: to die at the hands of Amin, with my friends unable to pay even the simplest form of respect to my body.

Like Oryema and Oboth-Ofumbi, I knew too much.

PORTRAITS OF BIG DADDY

Nattily turned out in an English three-piece suit, Amin speaks at the twelfth anniversary of independence, October 1974.

Amin officiates at a graduation ceremony at Makerere University
of which he is Chancellor. Although he has never been to
school, he has a (self-awarded) honorary doctorate from the
university and is the (self-appointed) head of the university's
Department of Political Science. Graduates who objected to
receiving their diplomas from his blood-stained hands were
forced into line by a threat to cancel their degrees.
CAMERA PRESS LTD.

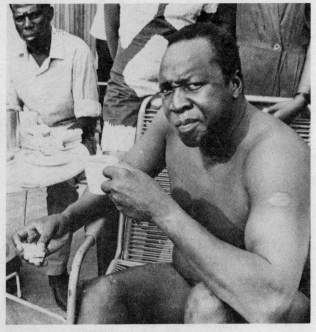

Amin taking a snack at pool-side...
CAMERA PRESS LTD.

...emerging from the sea.
KEYSTONE PRESS AGENCY LTD.

OVERLEAF: Even when listening to speeches at the UN, Amin's brooding medal-clad figure exudes a quality of menace.

Soldiers beat businessmen who have allegedly been overcharging for their products. Incidents like this, not uncommon, reflect the inability of the government to control prices by more conventional means.

ASSOCIATED PRESS LTD.

THE SEARCH FOR RESPECTABILITY

These Mercedes were especially bought to impress heads of
state of the OAU Conference in 1975. After the conference,
the cars were given to Army officers and Amin's other friends.

OVERLEAF: Amin with President Kenyatta of Kenya, where the
former has made repeated visits to try and win support and
respectability.

In the flamboyant style intended to show solidarity with the Arab cause, Amin addresses "volunteers" to fight in the 1973 Arab-Israeli War. When this picture was taken, the war was already over, and the volunteers were never used; the scene was staged purely for dramatic effect.

CAMERA PRESS LTD.

In July 1975 Amin welcomed Yasir Arafat, leader of the Palestine Liberation Organization which Amin treats as an independent nation.
KEYSTONE PRESS AGENCY LTD.

Amin, his pockets bulging as usual, arrives uninvited in Kinshasa, Zaire, and is met by Zaire's President Mobutu Sese Seko, after the invasion of Zaire from Angola. Amin had condemned Morocco for sending troops to aid Mobutu.

When Mobutu began to win, Amin decided to offer help.
(RIGHT: Amin's notoriously vicious executioner, Malyamungu).
POPPERFOTO

American journalists – left to right, AP's Brian Jeffries, NBC's Fred Briggs, and CBS's Bill McCaughlin – listen to Amin back down on a threat to hold American nationals hostage. Carter had threatened military action if he did. Amin had just been playing basketball. Standing left is Bob Astles. Beside him stand Amin's head bodyguard and two others, all Nubian.

ASSOCIATED PRESS LTD.

Amin chats with Cuban Prime Minister Fidel Castro during a summit of nonaligned countries in Geneva, September 1973. Amin has threatened to invite Cuban troops into Uganda, should the need arise.

ASSOCIATED PRESS LTD.

OVERLEAF: In September 1975, Amin, on a private visit to Italy, meets the Pope in the ceremony customarily extended to visiting heads of state. A few weeks previously Amin had expelled about 20 Catholic missionaries from Uganda. (INSET: A few minutes later it was my turn to meet His Holiness).

POPPERFOTO

At the UN Amin and Sarah meet the British UN Ambassador Ivor Richard and his wife. UN Secretary-General Kurt Waldheim looks on. Amin prizes such meetings.

PRECEDING PAGE: At the UN in October 1975, Amin listens to his own speech read by his Ambassador and former interpreter, Khalid Kinene. (INSET) Amin places the foundation stone of Uganda House in New York. Looking on is Foreign Minister Lt. Col. Juma Oris, who stands beside two of Amin's sons, Moses (LEFT) and Mwanga.

Amin, outgoing Chairman of the OAU, bids farewell to the
OAU delegates in Mauritius before returning to Entebbe where
the PLO hijackers were holding their Israeli hostages. The
Israeli commandos struck later that day.

MURDER MOST FOUL

Mrs. Dora Bloch, the hostage who was left behind after the Israeli raid, was dragged from my hospital, Mulago, and killed on Amin's orders.
POPPERFOTO

OPPOSITE: In January, 1977, Amin dances the Otole, a traditional Acholi warrior dance. It was a suitable prelude to the killing three weeks later of two of his ministers, Erinayo Oryema (in dark glasses) and Charles Oboth-Ofumbi (seen immediately behind Amin's spear). Behind Oryema's up-raised spear is Vice President Mustafa Adrisi.   J. P. LAFFONT–SYGMA

The two victims in close-up – Charles Oboth-Ofumbi and
Erinayo Oryema.
KEYSTONE PRESS AGENCY LTD.
ASSOCIATED PRESS LTD.

I knew Janan Luwuum as a brave and forthright man. He is shown here (BELOW) with Amin four days before he was killed. Amin was careful to establish a semblance of a working relationship prior to the Archbishop's murder.

POPPERFOTO

Outside the Nile Hotel on February 16, 1977, when the Archbishop was denounced. The weapons, allegedly sent in by Obote, were in fact standard issue to the Uganda army.
POPPERFOTO

ABOVE RIGHT: An army intelligence officer named Ogwang, a Langi (Obote's tribe), reads out a statement at the Nile Hotel, supposedly implicating him in a plot to overthrow Amin. Colonel Malyamungu stands to his right to ensure he misses nothing of the statement, prepared by Amin the previous evening.   **POPPERFOTO**

Through these proceedings, I was sitting, appalled, just behind the speakers. I am seen here, legs crossed, looking grim, as Vice President Mustafa Adrisi winds up the proceedings. Later that afternoon, the Archbishop and the two cabinet ministers were shot.

POPPERFOTO

Backed by his Nubian henchmen Amin "explains" to journalists how the Archbishop and the two cabinet ministers died in a car accident. On the right, Adrisi (in chair) and Colonel Malyamungu watch.

CAMERA PRESS LTD.

OPPOSITE: A facsimile of the warning letter I described in the Prologue.

PERSONAL

MR. HENRY KYEMBA
Minister for Health,
P.O. BOX 8

~~KAMPALA~~

ENTEBBE

14th Jan 77

Received 5/1/77

Dear Sir,

I have felt that I must warn you.
Recently as I was having dinner in the Speke
Hotel I over heard two men beside your own table
saying that Kyemba was next on the list, on what
list exactly I don't know.

Sir I felt it was my duty to warn you.
They entered a car UVS 335 or (336) I couldn't
really see it.

So you may take this warning and again you may
not, one of the men was mixing Luzaga and Swahili.
They also said "I hear Kyemba is coming down for
men". The other one said "Is that why they want him"
that is all I managed to hear

Yours faithfully,

Henry Kyemba (center) at the World Health Organization conference in Geneva, flanked by two other vice-presidents, Mrs. S. Obeysekera, of Sri Lanka, and Dr. E. Schultheisz, of Hungary.

9
Escape

TO REMAIN IN Uganda would be to commit suicide. I knew the facts behind the murder of Mrs. Dora Bloch. I knew the true cause of death of the archbishop and the two Cabinet ministers. I had to leave.

As it happened, I already had an official reason to leave Uganda: as the current chairman of the African Health Ministers in the World Health Organization, I had to attend the annual WHO conference in Geneva in May. This at least gave me a foundation for a plan of escape. It took two months to formulate the rest of my scheme and put it into effect. For all that time, I had to be absolutely alert for a move against me. At the time of the killing of the Archbishop, Amin was too preoccupied with foreign reactions to the atrocity to bother much about what his ministers were doing. But I took no risks. I discussed my decision with no one.

I did not even discuss it with my wives, Teresa and Elizabeth. They knew anyway, as it later turned out: Teresa, my senior wife, and Elizabeth, my junior wife, the mother of our two children, Henry (6) and Susan (5), soon drew their own correct conclusions. At first, it seemed sensible enough not to tell them my plans. I thought vaguely that I might set myself up in business in Kenya, and that I would be able to send for them almost immediately. There seemed no need to upset them. The children had a happy and secure home life in my house in

Jinja. They were surrounded by a loving family—one of
Elizabeth's sisters, a teenaged niece of mine, and servants,
as well as Teresa and their mother. We would not be apart
for long.

Thus reassured, I set about planning the details of my
escape. Since anything left behind would be snatched by
Amin, I began to give away possessions. This was not in
itself an unusual thing. I had frequent requests from
family and friends, especially in these hard times, and
often fulfilled them. Now I gave away almost anything I
could. As it happened, I took things a little too far, for my
sudden generosity sparked rumors that I was about to
vanish.

I had my property—which included a 70-acre farm as
well as the townhouse in Jinja—assessed and made plans
to bring the valuation documents out with me. It would
all be seized after my departure, but I wanted to be in a
position to reclaim the property or seek compensation if I
ever got the chance.

I wanted to make sure that I had more than one good
reason to leave the country. I also wanted to get out as
soon as possible. The WHO conference in Geneva in May
provided a good working schedule, but it was
disconcertingly far in the future. I managed to develop
two good reasons, one official, one personal, for leaving
earlier.

The official reason involved WHO. As the current
chairman of the African Health Ministers, I had been
asked, at the last Africa Region conference in September
1976, to hold consultations in Brazzaville, Addis Ababa
and Cairo on a problem facing the region. We wanted to
bring all African countries (excluding South Africa) into
a single bloc that would match the political boundaries of
the Organization of African Unity.

The proposed reorganization is a complex problem,
especially for Egypt. For one thing, it would mean closing
the WHO regional headquarters in Alexandria and
moving it to Brazzaville. My consultations had to be

completed by May for the next WHO Assembly in Geneva. Thus I could move up my departure by travelling first to the countries where I was to hold the preliminary talks.

My first plan, to go to Brazzaville in the Republic of Congo, aborted because of the murder of President Ngouabi in March. That left me with two other possibilities. One, Addis Ababa, was almost out of the question—its regime is as murderous as Amin's. I decided not to risk it. I was left with the trip to Egypt. Fortunately for me, Amin was all for it. Disturbed by the decline in the number of doctors in Uganda, he had already asked President Sadat to provide some from Cairo. He asked me to follow up on this request, in addition to my other business.

Knowing Amin's temperament, I knew that I could find myself out of office overnight, with no political reason to leave at all. Thus I formalized a personal, perfectly genuine reason to be in Geneva. I was due to have medical treatment to correct a dented septum, a small irregularity in the division between the upper nostrils, which sometimes brought on sneezing fits. In late February, I asked my Director of Medical Services to make an appointment for me with a Swiss ear, nose and throat specialist. This was confirmed on March 23, 1977. Now my departure schedule was as foolproof as I could make it. In early April, I would be in Cairo; in late April in Geneva; and some time during the three weeks of the conference itself, I would make my final move to safety.

I was now faced with the problem of planning a new life. My only thought—and it was never realized—was to return to Kenya. I could at least get a car out to Nairobi rather than leaving it for Amin's thugs. Of the two cars I owned, one—a Peugeot 504—had for a long time needed servicing in Nairobi. This was reason enough to get the permission I needed for the car to leave the country. A friend of mine drove it to Nairobi and left it there (at the same time taking the opportunity to flee the country).

The second car I kept. I needed something for the family, and it would have been suspicious to leave myself with nothing but a ministry car to use. Just before my departure I gave it to my seventy-year-old mother, who had trouble walking and needed something to get to church on Sundays. I have since learned that it was seized by Amin after my departure.

As the time of my departure approached, I tried to give every impression that I was *not* leaving the country, to counterbalance any rumors that might reach Amin. I did this in two ways. First, I mentioned to a minister, a friend of Amin's, with known connections in the State Research Bureau, that I urgently needed some land so that I could expand my farm. If the possibility of my defection ever came up in his presence, he would say: "The man is looking for land; he can't possibly be leaving for good."

Second, I bought a car in partnership with a friend. I had no intention of using it myself. The car was an Austin Princess which had belonged to the former British High Commissioner and was put on sale by the Ministry of Foreign Affairs. My friend thought it would be fun to own. We agreed to split the cost of the car—60,000 shillings (7,500 dollars), and to make it pay its way by forming a small company called "Wedding Bells" that would rent the car for weddings and other festivities. This was a perfectly sound idea, and there was no way my friend—who automatically inherited the car when I left—would know that I had any interest in the operation.

Now plans for my own escape were almost settled. I had covered my tracks, I hoped, as far as Amin was concerned. I had reasons for leaving the country. I had disposed of many of my possessions. I had safely recorded all the details of my fixed assets.

During these last weeks, I turned my attention once again to my family. I was beginning to see the significance of what I was planning. It would not, after all, be simply a matter of slipping out for a month or two and then returning to Nairobi. I would be breaking permanently

with Amin, and would have to think through the
implications for my family. Amin would not, I believed,
take revenge for a minister's defection on his two young
children and their mother. But I nevertheless decided to
take some precautions. I had Teresa pack three suitcases
of children's clothes and give them to a friend who often
traveled to Kenya. After my departure, he would ferry the
clothes across and put them in safekeeping in Nairobi.
The children were to escape, if necessary, with their
mother. Elizabeth would make her way with the children
to the undemarcated border, walk across and make
contact with a friend who lived in Kisumu, about thirty
miles into Kenya. After I left, Elizabeth made a secret trip
across the border to test these arrangements.

The arrangements for Teresa presented other problems. She was until mid-1975 Matron of Mulago Hospital, was known to Amin, and would be in danger if
she stayed behind. I devised a separate plan for her.
Officially, wives could accompany their husbands to
major functions, like the conference in Geneva, but I
could not risk asking her to accompany me to Cairo. We
therefore planned for her to come with the other three
men who were to make up the rest of the ministry
delegation, two weeks or so after my departure. But to
ensure that Teresa got out safely, we made an alternative
arrangement. If things went wrong she was to make for
the border by any means possible, go to Nairobi, and then
join me in Geneva.

There was little more to be done. I applied in the
normal way for official funds and on April 12, the day
before my departure, took out another ten thousand
shillings for personal expenses. Since I was going out
officially, I could have taken a much larger sum, but I
didn't wish to arouse suspicion.

I had one final safeguard. I had told Amin that I would
be leaving after Easter, but I never told him the actual
date of my departure in case he would try to stop me.

The last time I spoke to the President face to face was

the Thursday before the Easter weekend at a small gathering of ministers—an informal affair for drinks in the evening. I told Amin I was going shortly. He just said: "Greet President Sadat for me and wish everyone well."

Normally when I left on a long trip I telephoned Amin from my house or the airport to let him know I was off. This time I did not. On Wednesday April 13, I just picked up my bodyguard, Vincent Masiga, who, like all civilian ministerial bodyguards, was a Special Branch appointee, and went to the airport. Masiga had been with me for several years and I liked him.

In Cairo, on April 16, I began my discussions on the possibility of Egypt supplying Uganda with its badly needed doctors. The last time the Egyptians had assisted us—around the time of the expulsion of the Asians—the mission had not been all that successful. Of the thirty-five doctors the Egyptians had sent, only two now remained. I wanted a more reliable, more experienced group and was determined to make the selection more rigorous. At least twenty doctors were needed, so I asked for a list of about forty. I informed Amin of what I had done and asked him to send an interviewing team as soon as the list was drawn up. Other meetings concerned the demarcation of the WHO Africa Region, but we made little headway on this complex issue.

The following week on April 21, I went to Geneva. Meanwhile, in Kampala, the rumors had started. "Kyemba won't be back," my friends told each other. "He has given away too much." Some of them even telephoned Teresa and asked if I had gone for good. She wisely decided to get out over the border as quickly as possible, a few days ahead of her scheduled departure date.

To escape, she used Amin's own system against him. Everyone who travels outside Uganda has to get a permit signed by one of Amin's military men. She decided not to risk using the authority of my position to get a legal permit, but to buy one in a false name. The system by which such permits are obtained is well established. The men who provide regular official passes supplement their income by providing irregular ones for between 200 to 250 shillings (25 to 60 dollars each). The officials are contacted through agents, of which there are hundreds. If you don't know one, you simply ask around until you find one. You provide the cash, a photograph and a false name; back comes the permit, with some reason for the journey inserted. There is no danger, even at the border. Officials all over the country are authorized to sign these travel documents, so no one at the border checks back to see whether they are genuine. Even if they did, they would probably never discover a deception.

Leaving a note for one of the Health Ministry delegates that she had some personal matters to attend to in Nairobi and would go to Geneva from there, Teresa left by bus on April 23, ten days after my departure for Cairo. At the border she was asked if she had any identification other than her letter—a passport, for example, or a season ticket for the bus. She answered that her husband kept all such documents. She was waved through to safety, traveled on to Nairobi, and a few days later took the plane to Geneva.

By pure coincidence, she caught the same plane as the ministry delegation and arrived on April 29. Trouble started almost immediately. The three men had, of course, heard the same rumors that had caused Teresa to flee. These they passed on to Masiga, who telephoned his Kampala headquarters to say that they should inform Amin. This may seem like a disloyal action, but he had his reasons. When the Justice Minister, Godfrey Lule, defected a few weeks before, his bodyguard was blamed for not warning his Special Branch bosses and was given some rough treatment. Others had fared worse: on the same day that Erinayo Oryema was killed, his Special Branch bodyguard and driver were executed also. Masiga did not want to risk a similar fate.

When Amin heard of Masiga's report on Saturday,

April 30, he immediately ordered his troops to surround my residences. My official residence was empty; it was immediately occupied by another official. At my private residence in Jinja, the servants fled under the fence as soon as they saw the troops coming through the main gate. The soldiers arrested Elizabeth and her sister, and imprisoned them in a nearby barracks. The two women, both in their mid-thirties, were put in a bare cell with a cement floor. The only thing in the cell was a bucket to use as a toilet. There were not even any blankets. They were imprisoned there for five days. Twenty heavily armed guards were stationed at my house to guard my children, who were left alone except for my fourteen-year-old niece.

Having placed my family and home under guard, Amin telephoned our embassy in Paris and despatched Ambassador Akisoferi Ogola to Geneva, telling him what had happened and asking him to find out how the delegation was. He left Paris on Monday, May 2. While he was on his way, I was brought fully up to date by a friend well placed in official circles. At midday, via an intermediary in Nairobi, I received a message that my children were under house arrest and that some of my relatives were locked up. The ambassador arrived on Monday afternoon, somewhat surprised to see not only that I was still at the head of the delegation but that I had also been elected a Vice President of WHO. He told me about the rumors, my bodyguard's report, and Amin's telephone call.

The ambassador then telephoned Amin to tell him that I was still leading the delegation; what should he do now? The President asked where I was. The ambassador sent word for me to come to the telephone. Amin, of course, did not know that I had been tipped off about the arrest of my children. He told me that he had heard rumors that I had defected and that Masiga had started these rumors by telephoning Kampala. He pretended to be very annoyed with Masiga, and said he never wanted to hear that sort of thing again. He then added, rather strangely, that if there was any truth in the rumors he wished me to leave without embarrassing him. He was apparently worried that I might dramatize my departure. Since he had my children under guard, that was in fact the last thing I would do. Picking my words carefully and doing my best to sound as confident as I usually was with him, I told him there was clearly no truth in the rumors; if I was going to defect, I said, I wouldn't be there at all. I also told him that I would certainly not embarrass him.

It was hardly a reassuring call. It was clear to me from his tone that I was under suspicion. In normal circumstances, Amin would have given me some news of my family, or would have asked the operator to connect me to my house. When I asked him to greet my people for me, he just said casually "O.K.," which confirmed my suspicions. In fact, I discovered later that he had already put out a report that he was investigating certain irregularities in the Health Ministry, which could have been an ominous prelude to further action against me.

Two days later, on Wednesday, May 4, one of the news agency wires carried a report from Nairobi that I had defected. The agency had apparently picked up the news about my houses being surrounded, linked it to the fact that I was out of the country, and come to its own conclusions. After the day's meetings, I telephoned Amin and asked about the origin of this report. He told me he had also seen it. I said "Well, obviously, you know it is not correct. I am not in Nairobi. I am in Geneva." He said I had to deny the report publicly. I said I would. He was delighted. "You'd better blow up these imperialist propaganda journalists," he said, "reporting things like that about you."

I summoned a press conference for the same afternoon in one of the press rooms of the Palais des Nations. I told the journalists, "I am sure you can all see that I am in Geneva, and not in Nairobi. My ambassador, who is with me, can confirm to those of you who do not know me that

I am indeed the Minister of Health." Everybody laughed.

Amin saw the report of the press conference on the agency wires and immediately announced it on Uganda Radio and in the *Voice of Uganda* newspaper. Amin then rushed to Jinja barracks where Elizabeth and my sister-in-law were imprisoned and summoned them to his presence. He told them that the report about my defection was malicious, that he knew me to be a good person, and that he had given me everything I had, including the farm. He instructed them to return home, send the children back to school and resume a normal life. When the women returned home, everything was in a shambles. The children had been thoroughly frightened over the last five days, and had cried until they could cry no more. Relatives had tried to collect them, but had not been allowed to. They had brought food, but had had to hand it over the fence. At least now the family were back together again in their own home.

The next day, May 5, I learned that Amin had released the family. Now the plan which I had devised for the children, and which Elizabeth had already rehearsed, went into action. She allowed herself ten days to reestablish a semblance of normal life and thus reassure Amin that all was well; then, on May 15, she left. She did not have to take any luggage, for clothing awaited them in Nairobi. She simply took the children in a taxi the fifty miles to the Kenya border and paid off the driver two or three miles short of the border checkpoint. The three of them made their way on small paths through the grass and thorn-trees, crossing the border to the small town of Busia. It is not difficult country to walk through, but Elizabeth was nervous about bumping into anti-smuggling patrols sent out by the army. The army is vigilant about suppressing smugglers, who represent competition to their own smuggling operations. In fact, the trip to Busia went smoothly.

From Busia, Elizabeth took a taxi to Kisumu, where my friends lived. They phoned ahead to relatives in

Nairobi to warn them of my family's arrival, and then called to tell me that all was well. Elizabeth and the children then travelled the three hundred miles to Nairobi by bus.

Now, with my family out of danger, my own plans could move ahead. When I first learned of the arrest of my family, I knew that I would have to choose a destination. Uganda, as a former imperial territory, had close ties with London, which had always been in my mind as a possible haven. I now made it my choice. On May 16, I informed the British Home Office that I would be arriving shortly.

My actual departure was unconsciously assisted by Amin himself. In another phone call he asked me to send Masiga back so that he could discipline him. I knew of course that he wanted Masiga to return in order to get further information about me and my family. Since my family was now safe, that suited me perfectly. Besides, Masiga was utterly embarrassed about his role in the affair. By the time I actually left Geneva on May 17, he had gone back to Uganda.

In leaving, I fulfilled my promise to Amin not to embarrass him. There was no sensation. I did not say goodbye to anyone in the delegation. I left the Assembly Hall one evening, and got on a plane for London the next morning.

On the way, a strange incident occurred. I had to change planes in Paris, and while waiting for my connection at the Charles de Gaulle Airport, I saw one of Amin's agents who was based in Bonn. Amin has these agents in many embassies—they are normally called "two-by-two's" because they are posted in pairs to relieve and keep an eye on each other. They are given nominal posts in the embassies, but everyone knows that they are there to spy on the diplomatic staff. This two-by-two was on his way home. I recognized him but didn't know his name. He knew me, of course. Seeing me alone, he was suspicious and didn't come over to me, as he would have done normally in such a situation. Instead, he vanished at once, and—as I later learned from a source close to Amin—he telephoned one of the Paris two-by-two's to report that he had seen me.

The Paris two-by-two immediately passed the news on to Amin. He did not know where I was going, the agent said, but maybe the President would like to check to find out what was happening. Masiga, who had just arrived hotfoot in Kampala from Geneva, was put on the next plane back again.

I arrived at London's Heathrow Airport in mid-afternoon, informed the immigration officer who I was, and filled in the necessary papers. When they asked me whether I was coming as a tourist or on an extended visit I said: "I suppose somebody around here knows why I am here." It all seemed a strangely routine experience. The immigration officer retired into some rear offices and a more senior official came out and saw me through immigration. I called a hotel, took a bus into the center of London, and tried to relax.

Amin's response to my disappearance was typically vacillating. He reversed his previous statements—again—declaring in public that there were after all certain things he wanted me to explain in connection with the ministry, and that I had misappropriated 300,000 shillings ($37,000). Such accusations were by now fairly standard reaction to defections. The Ministry of Finance and the Minister of Small-Scale Industry were each accused of taking over six million shillings (some $750,000). I was flattered to be accused of taking so little.

At one point, Amin announced that I had arrived home. When people phoned my house, they were told I was on safari. Yet when the Health Ministry delegation returned to Uganda and were received by Amin, he said he had nothing against me, and claimed that he had paid for my operation (which I had not yet undergone) because, as he put it, he "wanted Ugandans to be healthy."

He sent Masiga to London after me. Masiga, however,

told the immigration authorities that he was my personal secretary, at the same time admitting he didn't know where I was. The immigration authorities telephoned the Home Office, who called to tell me of Masiga's arrival and to ask if I knew anything about him. I felt in no danger—Masiga was not a killer—but I replied "No, not a thing." They put him on the next plane out of London. Poor Masiga. It had been a tough few days.

I spent the next few days making contact with friends in London. It was soon suggested to me that I should say something about the situation in Uganda. I had for some time thought I might be able to make a detailed account of what was happening there. It would be one step toward a better life for Ugandans. Now the time was peculiarly auspicious. On June 7, the Commonwealth Conference was due to start in London. These thirty-five countries, twelve of them from Africa, would not meet in conference again until 1979.

I made my decision. I would tell all I knew about Amin. My first step was to contact the London *Sunday Times*; the result was an article published in two parts on June 5 and June 12. This led to the first forthright condemnation of Amin by the Commonwealth Conference:

"Cognizant of the accumulated evidence of sustained disregard for the sanctity of life and of massive violation of basic human rights in Uganda, it was the overwhelming view of Commonwealth leaders that these excesses were so gross as to warrant the world's concern and to evoke condemnation by the heads of government in strong and unequivocal terms. Mindful that the people of Uganda were within the fraternity of Commonwealth fellowship, heads of government looked to the day when the people of Uganda would once more fully enjoy their basic human rights which now were being so cruelly denied."

This was a major step in what I hope will become an international campaign against Amin.

10

The Eyes of the World

IN FOREIGN AFFAIRS, Amin's record is one of cynical, self-seeking vacillation. No nation now trusts him from one day to the next. Yet he survives, for he is immune to foreign opinion as long as it is not expressed in forthright terms, and as long as it does not result in a threat to his supplies of cash and goods. His dealings with other nations are guided by two breathtakingly naïve principles: the need for cash, and the need to dramatize himself. Any manipulation, any vacillation is justifiable, to Amin, if it serves these ends.

Amin got off to a good start with Britain, the first country to recognize his regime. It was a valuable friendship, for Sudan, Somalia, Guinea, several Commonwealth nations and the Eastern bloc countries reviled him. Britain had no liking for Obote—who had shown signs of wishing to make Uganda a socialist state—and was anxious to exploit his unpopularity with the Ugandans. Just prior to the coup, at the Commonwealth Conference in Singapore in 1971, Obote was among those black leaders who urged that the then British Prime Minister, Edward Heath, stop selling arms to South Africa. He even threatened to take Uganda out of the Commonwealth if supplies were not halted.

With Obote's overthrow, however, this disturbing prospect evaporated. Amin immediately began to lavish praise on the British people, on the British way of life, and on the Queen. (An affection he still professes: her portrait hangs in several of his offices). His British military background provided him with his major link to the outside world. He had been popular with the British officers under whom he had trained, and he exploited this to the full. He wore a British-style uniform, and praised the British tradition of leadership. (For some reason he was particularly taken with the Scots, and expressed a liking for bagpipes.) He even asked for British officers to come and train his army. So anxious was he for British acceptance that one of his first actions was to send a telegram to South African Prime Minister, John Vorster, saying that he wished to pay a state visit to his country. He was quite serious: he was clearly prepared to do anything—even if it meant antagonizing the black African leaders—to ingratiate himself with Britain.

The British accepted Amin at first, as the Ugandans did. Although he lacked an education, and was in no way comparable to the undoubtedly brilliant Obote, he seemed willing enough to learn from his own people and from the British. His apparent willingness to seek help prevented criticism both at home and abroad. He stated his support for private enterprise; the British at once increased their aid.

The Israelis—the other major foreign influence in Uganda at the time—were also delighted that Obote had been overthrown. Before the coup, the Israelis had been extending their influence into Southern Sudan, with Obote's backing, by helping the Southern Sudanese in their rebellion against Khartoum. But Obote had recently indicated that he wished to make peace with Khartoum and would no longer support the Israelis in Southern Sudan. Amin, on the other hand, had worked closely with Israeli officers, had continued to give secret support to the Southern Sudanese, and was given to expressions of "love" for Israel.

The initial British and Israeli acceptance of Amin did not last for long. In the case of Israel, Amin soon demonstrated his hostility beyond a doubt. The reason for his turning against Israel was raw greed. Israel would not waste its cash on Amin. Libya had cash to waste. For Amin there was no question which of the two to choose. From the time of Amin's visit to Gaddafi on February 13, 1972, Libya became the dominant influence on Uganda's economy. As a direct result of this visit to Libya, Amin opted for those policies and phrases that would be most pleasing to Gaddafi. He determined to display rabid anti-Semitism, to force the world to see Uganda as a Moslem country, and to use the pseudo-Marxist phraseology popular with Gaddafi. In March, Amin ordered the Israelis to leave within three days. In September, after the Munich Olympics massacre of Israeli athletes, he declared his joy at the slayings, adding that he admired Hitler for "burning the Israelis alive with gas in the soil of Germany." He also sent a message to UN Secretary General Kurt Waldheim urging the removal of all Israelis from the Middle East and their "repatriation" to Britain.

It has been easy enough for Amin to become anti-Israel and pro-Palestinian. But there is one major aspect of Gaddafi's thinking that Amin could not—and cannot—adopt: his professed Marxism. For one thing, Amin does not have the political education to understand what is truly meant by Marxism. For another, it is utterly alien to the way he works. The Ugandan economy that he has built up, insofar as it is a system at all, depends upon his personal gifts; it depends on his ability to own anything he wishes within Uganda, and to give it away to whomever he wishes. For this reason, Amin has carefully avoided becoming involved in the phraseology of socialist or communist economies. He has been at pains to state time and again that Uganda is neither capitalist nor communist. And he is right—he has turned the country into a robber baron's fiefdom.

Amazingly, Amin's foreign policy has worked. He has successfully manipulated the Arab countries into providing him with cash—none of which has filtered through to the Ugandans as a whole—and has prevented Arab criticism by claiming to be the head of a Moslem country.

Britain's initial acceptance of Amin evaporated when he called for the expulsion of the Asians—an act dictated by his extraordinary greed. It was an act of piracy whereby he handed over the property of one minority to another minority—his own. Despite heavy diplomatic pressure from Britain, the United States and within the UN, he went ahead with his decision. He would have taken similar action against any large rich minority in Uganda. It was of no significance to him that it would destroy any semblance of a relationship with Britain, who would be forced to absorb the thirty thousand Asians with British passports.

The reality behind his decision was, of course, never declared. He disguised his motives by claiming that all the Asians were non-Ugandans who were "milking the cow without feeding her." He was thus able to present himself as a black leader defending the rights of other blacks against foreign exploitation. He was, he said, "Ugandanizing" the country, thus suggesting that he was dispensing with a vestige of white imperialism. Amin argued on the radio that the Asians had been brought by the forces of imperialism to build the railway that was used to carry away Uganda's wealth. Nor was the argument entirely fallacious—it showed Amin's talent for taking a partial truth and turning it to his own advantage.

When Britain tried to protest the expulsion of the Asians as a brutally racist decision—which it was—they found that their arguments held no water for Africans— whites were, in many African eyes, by definition racists. Disillusioned, the British stopped all aid to Uganda in September 1972. In retaliation, Amin threw out the British High Commissioner, Richard Slater, and recalled his own ambassador from London.

The terrible thing about his specious justifications was that they worked. I travelled to a number of different countries at the time—I was then the Permanent Secretary to the Ministry of Culture. When I visited Nigeria in October 1972, I saw the enthusiasm of the Nigerian press for Amin's policy of "Ugandanization of the economy." At the time, Nigeria, like a number of other countries—Ghana, Guinea and Somalia—had, since the early 1960s, been attempting to create an indigenous economy after the withdrawal of their imperial masters. They saw events in Uganda in the light of their own recent history, to Amin's benefit. Generally, in the African press of 1973, Amin was referred to as the hero who had kicked out the foreigners for the benefit of his own people. It was not generally appreciated that his "own people" meant another small minority of Uganda's population—one that was itself a product of British imperialism.

The response to Amin's simple propaganda amazed me. Perhaps the most startling response was that of the black community in America. Hardly had the Asians left, when a number of black American groups contacted Amin. In particular, the leader of the American organization CORE (Congress of Racial Equality), Roy Innis, suggested to Amin that he recruit black Americans to fill the gaps left by the departing Asian professionals. He said black Americans felt that they had been exploited for too long by whites, that they wished to reestablish contacts with their original African homeland. They were therefore eager to help their black brothers and sisters in Africa.

Amin was completely sold on this idea. He was delighted to exploit his association with black Americans and their attacks on whites. And since they were apparently ready to regard him as a great African nationalist leader, he was also delighted to use them to improve his tarnished image in America and the world. He was anxious to move as quickly as possible and told

Innis to go ahead.

But no one in the Cabinet liked the idea. We were sweepingly disparaging. My colleagues and I had very little faith that any black Americans would be able to solve the enormous problems created by Amin. The scheme would replace one minority group with another—except that the replacements would be paid more. Too many black Americans, we thought, were interested in supporting Amin as an individual and in enjoying his hospitality, and were not seriously interested in the country and the suffering of the Ugandans. We had known some black Americans who were worse in their attitudes toward Africans than whites—who regarded themselves as superior to African blacks. Our harsh opinions were perhaps too sweeping—we had all met black Americans of undoubted integrity and idealism—but our reservations were explicit enough to persuade Amin to cancel any schemes of importing black Americans by the plane load.

The attitude of visiting black Americans generally has been the despair of responsible Ugandans. It seemed that because of their own suffering in America's past, many were prepared to believe that everything white was wrong and everything black was beautiful. This attitude was anathema to anyone who lived under Amin.

Such attitudes among black Americans, although rarer today, are carefully fostered by Amin. He has invited black Moslem ministers and many black American journalists to Uganda, as he did in February 1977, after the murder of the archbishop and the two Cabinet ministers. Such visits are actually well-staged publicity stunts. Guided tours are organized in Kampala and outside, to Acholi and Lango and other places notoriously associated in the foreign press with Amin's atrocities. The visitors are given the best Amin can offer. Lavish hospitality prevents them from seeing how ordinary people live. They are given cars to ride about in, and therefore do not meet ordinary Ugandans except in the presence of Amin's intelligence boys. Amin certainly does not send them to the source of the Nile, or the Owen Falls Dam, unless the bodies there have been removed first. They are taken to Mulago Hospital, but they do not see or hear anything of the shortages of equipment and medicines. They are not told of the mistreatment of staff by Amin's thugs.

For these visitors to accept such propaganda as evidence, and then to make statements about present-day Uganda, is as great a disservice to the country as anyone can possibly imagine.

In a way, of course, this is understandable, because it is practically impossible to gain any reliable information about events in Uganda except from exiled sources and recent refugees. No one can send an unchecked report from Kampala. Amin selects those journalists he wants to enter the country. If they do not write what he wants they will never come back. One BBC correspondent, John Osman, was arrested along with others and locked up briefly in Makindye Prison when investigating some of the atrocities there. Another BBC correspondent in Kampala, Phillip Short, whose reports were always based firmly on Amin's press releases, was thrown out after he wrote a magazine article that included official pictures of executions. Now there are no BBC correspondents in Kampala. It is certainly impossible to get a critical reporter into Uganda. Amin even put a price on the head of the London *Observer* correspondent, David Martin, after the publication of his book, *General Amin*. Indeed, there is hardly a foreign correspondent left in Kampala—no Japanese, no Americans, no West Africans, not even any East Africans. The only correspondents left represent TASS and one or two other Eastern bloc countries.

Amin has turned the country into a prison (and one without the minimum privileges of prison life: parcels of goods in short supply cannot be sent to Uganda because it is an admission of Uganda's shortages). Ugandan YMCA leaders were not allowed to attend the last YMCA conference in Argentina in July 1977—although Uganda had hosted the previous conference in 1974. Amin was afraid of what they would say. He realizes that people who leave the country can speak freely, and he does not want this. Anyone who leaves officially must have the sanction of a minister or Amin. Bishops are under orders not to attend meetings outside the country (although Moslem religious leaders may travel freely). Even those who leave on personal business are interviewed by the police or by Amin himself.

The only means of public expression in Uganda are government controlled: television, radio and the *Voice of Uganda* newspaper, (and because of the paper shortage, there are precious few copies of that; certainly, few get abroad). The other paper, the independent Catholic daily, *Munno*, was banned after its editors were killed. All foreign papers were banned in June 1974; even professional magazines are banned because they are "imperialist propaganda."

Amin can therefore be as outrageous as he likes without fear of criticism. In the June 11, 1977, issue of *Voice of Uganda,* for instance, just after President Kaunda of Zambia (along with the Secretary General, Mr. Ramphal), had criticized Amin at the Commonwealth Conference in London the following paragraph appeared in a report headlined, "Kaunda meant to please imperialists": "It is hoped that as a token of appreciation for what these two gentlemen have spoken of about Dr. Idi Amin, maybe Her Majesty the Queen will honour them with her 25 years old knickers as souvenirs to mark the Silver Jubilee of the Queen's coronation. The same award, it is hoped, will go to the British Prime Minister, Mr. Callaghan, for his role in spoiling the good name of Uganda."

Such statements are meant only for internal consumption to dramatize Amin's own image. In the same way, his telegrams to foreign leaders—many of which have now become classics—are so wild that they could never be taken seriously. He has on various occasions: cabled Nixon a speedy recovery from Watergate (at a time when Nixon was denying any involvement in the affair); told President Ford, "I love you" and in addition instructed him to hand over his government to a black leader; described Mrs. Golda Meir, going to meet Nixon, as "waving her knickers"; and told President Nyerere that he would marry him if he were a woman. He has offered Britain his good services in mediating between Westminster and the Scottish Nationalists, whom he warned against "brainwashing" by Britain. On June 3, 1977, Amin cabled Kaunda, saying "I cannot find a better descriptive term for you other than that of an imperialist puppet, microphone and bootlicker," and "I even wonder whether your sobs and tears are not like those of a frigid woman who cannot satisfy her man."

Such statements are an attempt to show himself to his own people as a powerful leader able to talk directly and unequivocally to the world's leaders. These ludicrous efforts, of course, have no influence on world events, but they do reveal the degree to which he wishes to use foreign affairs—even those in which he has no conceivable interest—to manipulate himself into a stronger position in Uganda.

This attitude is also the motive for his flying visits abroad. They are always made without warning, because he dare not give potential plotters any chances to formulate plans. In September 1975, he arrived at the UN with one day's warning. At the UN—where his speech was read by his former interpreter and current ambassador Khalid Younis Kinene—he called for the expulsion of Israel from the UN, and its extinction as a state. "Zionists have infiltrated the CIA," he said, "and turned it into a murder squad." These and other statements—which ranged across most issues under discussion at the UN—were intended to show him at home as a politician who can speak sternly to the world's leaders. (It was after this session that US ambassador Daniel Moynihan called him a "racist murderer.")

A similarly manipulative attitude has governed his treatment of foreigners in Uganda. He has ordered some Britons in Kampala to take the oath of allegiance kneeling when they sign up for national service. After the disasters caused by the deaths of Stroh, Siedle and Dora Bloch, he knows full well the value of foreign hostages. When he sentenced the English lecturer, Dennis Hills, to death for calling him a "village tyrant" in his book *The White Pumpkin,* he never had, in my opinion, any intention of killing him. He released him happily enough, once he had forced on the British the humiliation that he sought—a visit by Foreign Minister Callaghan to plead for Hills' life. He threatened all the Americans in the country with incarceration in late 1976—although he backed down hastily enough when Carter threatened military action in return.

Unfortunately, he is able to prove to himself that his tactics work. The OAU has never formally condemned him, in part probably because some of them use Amin's own tactics on a smaller scale in their own countries, and would be afraid of similar criticisms being used against them. He was even chairman of the organization in 1975-1976 (although purely because it was Uganda's turn to act as host to the conference). In addition, the OAU nations have on occasion rallied to protect him, because they have seen an attack on any black African leader as an attack on themselves. African leaders would not like to set precedents in the criticism of a country's internal affairs. They have yet to face the difficulties of making a forthright statement about human rights.

Another element in their support of him is the fact that he is extremely entertaining. At the last OAU meeting in Gabon, in July 1977—he appeared in a brilliant blue Field Marshal's uniform and proclaimed himself the conqueror of the British Empire at a time when his country was crumbling, and everyone knew it. He claimed to have won an economic war, when his country was without even salt. All the African leaders knew that he had murdered an archbishop. He received an ovation, as was widely reported in the Western press, but this was no accolade; the applause was ironic, because no African leader takes Amin seriously. I pray that African leaders will soon be able to provide him with a more fitting reception: irony is scarcely an adequate response to a mass murderer.

Amin is a thoroughly unbalancing and destructive force for Africa and for the rest of the world. He will quarrel with anybody in order to achieve any slight advantage. He never keeps his word. He knows no morality. He has broken at various times with the USSR, Israel, the United States, Britain, Zaire, Zambia, Kenya. He has quarrelled with Italy, Ghana, Egypt, the Sudan, Rwanda, and Libya (when Gaddafi seemed about to cut off his money supply). He has proved himself a liability to the Moslem cause, the Arab cause, the cause of Africa, and above all, the cause of humanity.

11

How Long?

UGANDA IS SUFFERING from a political and economic disease. It entered the country in 1971 and caused an immediate personality change—a change in which the body politic suddenly saw itself as its own enemy. The disease spread rapidly to the essential organs and through the entire body. Twitched regularly by self-destructive spasms, the country's parts began to decay into uncoordinated masses.

This disease is not unknown to political scientists. It could be named "degenerative paranoia." Such a disease leads to the disintegration of the national character and the paralysis of the body politic. It is not, I believe, fatal, but without timely outside help, Amin's tyranny could last for another few years, a prospect I find too terrible to contemplate.

To non-Africans, this state of affairs seems inconceivable. How can a country endure such torment without rising in anger? I will tell you why. First, Amin meets any public outburst against him with murderous violence, for he has absolutely no respect for human life; not even women and children are safe from his anger. He would take a genuinely peaceful demonstration—for example, against the shortages—as a personal threat and order indiscriminate killing. He has no compunction about ordering his army to bomb schoolchildren and women. For this reason, there have, as far as I know, been no demonstrations in Uganda since 1971, except for the one at Makerere University in August 1976, which was broken up with considerable ferocity.

Second, Uganda has an ideal climate and is naturally fertile. A family can live indefinitely at subsistence level. People can retire from the towns to the comparative safety of their home villages, where it is easy enough to grow food. There are plenty of vegetables, even if there is no salt to cook them with. The climate is warm the year round. There is simply not the material suffering that might prompt a desperate, spontaneous uprising.

Failing such action, the outlook is indeed grim. Ultimately Amin's system is self-defeating, but it could survive for many years. Those years will see even further suffering. Coffee, tea, cotton, minerals, sugar will slowly disappear. There will be nothing left to export from Uganda, and eventually, no means of financing the luxury imports that Amin needs to buy the loyalty of his troops.

Of course, the period of suffering must be shortened, ideally by the Ugandans themselves.

One solution is assassination. I am personally opposed to violence, but there are many people, both inside Uganda and outside, who derive little satisfaction from the hope that Amin's regime will collapse of its own accord. To them, the only possibility of ending the suffering in Uganda is to kill him at the earliest possible opportunity. Several assassination attempts have been made. But a major attempt—one that seeks to seize power as well as to kill Amin—is hard to organize. A military operation to take over the barracks and some of the main institutions—the armories, the radio station, the television station—would be difficult to plan, let alone execute. Amin has a nose for plots both real and imaginery, and is quick to strike at anyone he suspects.

Would-be plotters should take a leaf out of Amin's own book. For the coup of January 1971, he made no plans nor did he have a firm organization to support him when he took over. There was therefore nothing for Obote to fight against. Any attempts to unseat or kill Amin must depend on a small-scale commando unit, at most. In fact, a single dedicated individual might well be able to do the job alone.

What are the chances of any action—whether individual or collective—against him? Widespread opposition to Amin's rule exists in every section of society. Few people realize how weak Amin's position really is. He has manipulated his officers one after the other; many have been humiliated and then restored to favor again; virtually no one trusts him. Even his closest henchmen have been temporarily humiliated. He feels secure only when he has destroyed the power of others, yet this very action creates a bitterness that is driven underground, thus making his own position even more insecure. Amin is hated in particular by many in the army, and by everyone in the Civil Service; he is even hated by some of his Nubian supporters and fellow tribesmen. Many members of the Nubian community regard him as a liability, realizing the disrepute into which their association with him has brought them. Amin has used the Nubians, along with the Southern Sudanese, to administer his reign of terror. Any intelligent Nubian must realize that as soon as Amin goes his days could well be numbered. Unlike the Southern Sudanese, whose real homes are in the Sudan, the Nubians have nowhere to go. It could be that some Nubians would wish to reestablish themselves in the eyes of other Ugandans by killing Amin.

There is another way of hastening Amin's downfall. Britain, the United States, the Arab nations, Uganda's immediate neighbors and the USSR could—with a combination of moral outrage and practical action—totally undermine Amin's regime. Even if less immediate than an assassination or successful uprising, such action would be inexorable, and it would provide circumstances more favorable for a move against Amin within Uganda. I believe that concerted international action would end

Amin's rule within a year.

Moral condemnation is perhaps the first step. Ideally, this should come from the United Nations. But it is too much to hope that the UN could present a united front against Amin. With over forty countries maintaining some form of representation in Uganda, many governments would be loath to go to the UN and condemn Amin. Nor do I believe that the OAU as a body is capable of condemning his regime. The idea of becoming directly involved in the internal affairs of a member nation is anathema to most OAU members.

Nevertheless, many states—African, European, and North American—could take such a stand individually and collectively. Though Amin is seemingly impervious to foreign opinion, powerful expressions of disapproval would be significant—they would help undermine the image he has been at pains to build for home consumption of a leader accepted by the large international communities.

There have already been several searing attacks on him. Some African states—notably Tanzania, Zambia and Kenya—have in the past spoken out most effectively against Amin.

The Commonwealth Conference of June 1977 issued a warning to Amin of possible future action against him, by condemning his regime for its "massive violation" of human rights. For the first time, representatives of African states permitted open discussion of the internal affairs of another African country. The same month, Andrew Young, America's Ambassador to the UN, issued a blistering attack on Amin's murderous regime. After comparing Amin's policy of tribal murder with Hitler's genocide of the Jews, he went on, "I didn't want Hitler to be saved; and I don't want Idi Amin to be saved." Yet there are still black Americans who are not ashamed to support Amin. How long, I wonder, will they close their eyes to the terrible truth?

Given such a lead, other African states, followed by

Britain and America—who cannot on their own be taken seriously as opponents of black repression—could make a combined condemnation of Amin.

But moral condemnation is not enough on its own. Practical action is needed if the words are to carry any weight. Here, Britain could take the initiative.

Despite recent publicity, few people appreciate the importance to Amin of the so-called "whisky run" which operates twice weekly between England's Stanstead airport and Entebbe. These flights, each said to carry goods to the value of $70,000, keep Amin supplied with the equipment and commodities necessary to maintain his regime. None of the goods reach the ordinary people of Uganda. The imports, which go directly to the army shops, are intended for one thing only—to keep Amin's thugs happy.

Amin himself relies heavily on these shops, especially when he wants to throw a party to impress visiting officials. "Look," he'll say to his admiring guests, "Look at all this food. There are no shortages in Uganda."

To walk into one of the army shops—each battalion has its own—is like going into a small department store in London. I have been into many. Everything is there— sugar, tea, golf clubs, cassettes, children's toys, cameras, automobile accessories, television sets, clothes, shoes, bags, bicycles, whisky, brandy, gin, radios, cigarettes, and all the other items that make for a comfortable life in the West. Despite Uganda's terrible inflation, the goods are available to those with the right identification, at bargain prices. If Amin's henchmen don't need the goods, they can buy them and then resell them on the black market for many times their true value.

As long as the "whisky runs" continue, Britain's denunciation of Amin seems, at the very least, hollow. Pressure has been brought to bear on the British government by such groups as the Uganda Freedom Committee and by MP's concerned about Britain's continued trade links with Amin. But so far, despite the closure of the British embassy in Kampala in July 1976, little has been done. In June 1977, Mrs. Judith Hart, Minister of Overseas Development, instructed her ministry to freeze the supply of all goods destined for Uganda that could be described as of a potentially military nature—radio sets, Land Rovers, spare parts, etc. This decision was taken pending a Cabinet directive to close down the shuttle service between Stanstead and Entebbe. Seven weeks later, no such directive had been given. The distinction between goods "of a potentially military nature" and others is in any case academic. Everything that Amin imports helps to keep him in power.

It has been suggested in Britain—by Foreign Secretary, Dr. David Owen—that breaking trade links with Uganda would hurt the Ugandan people. This is simply not true. Apart from the black market, whose prices ordinary people cannot afford, imported goods never get past the army shops. The "whisky run" represents a major lynch-pin in Amin's regime. Only Britain has the power to remove it.

The ending of the "whisky run" could mark the beginning of a policy of economic sanction imposed by Britain and other responsible governments. It was done in the case of Rhodesia; why, I wonder has Amin been spared? The United States could impose a trade embargo. It is at present the single largest purchaser of Ugandan coffee. In addition Amin flies American planes, which are serviced in the United States. At the time of the murder of the Archbishop and the two Cabinet ministers in February 1977, the Presidential jet was in the United States being serviced, so that Amin could fly in style to the March OAU Afro-Arab meeting in Cairo. The United States has in the past taken unilateral action in its own interest. In Uganda, it has a chance to act in the interests of humanity and justice. To impose a ban on trade with Amin in the interests of humanity is surely a small thing to ask of so powerful a nation, whose concern for human rights, under President Carter's administration, gives it just cause for pride.

As for the Arab countries, their reputation in the world, is being seriously undermined by their association with, and active support of, Amin's regime. Without funds from such countries as Libya, Saudi Arabia, the United Arab Emirates, and Kuwait, Amin would find it impossible to sustain his rule. Libya, of course, is a special case; Gaddafi's close friendship with Amin ensures that no amount of international pressure can persuade the Libyans to cut back on the handouts of cash and weapons freely offered to Amin and his henchmen. But the other Arab countries should consider whether it is really worthwhile to sustain a vicious regime that brings the Arab name, and the name of Islam, into disrepute. All the Arab countries have pleaded with the international community to understand the human problems of the Palestinians—yet they turn a blind eye to the human problems in Uganda. Have not all the original reasons for supporting Amin—his anti-Israeli stance, his attempt to turn Uganda into a Moslem state—been made redundant by events? Amin has surely outlived his usefulness as far as the Arab cause is concerned.

The Eastern bloc countries, in particular the USSR, should also consider the role they have played in supporting Amin. They have provided the guns and tanks that are used to administer terror; they also supply MIGs and bombs for the Ugandan Air Force, with which Amin can threaten his neighbors. They have provided them in return, not for cash but for coffee. Amin likes the deal: he does not have to part with any foreign exchange (at least not directly; in fact, he hands over the means of acquiring foreign exchange). The Russians like it: they can sell the coffee while it is still on the high seas, and build up their own foreign exchange reserves. But they should know that the end result of their dealings with Amin is death for the people of Uganda.

Of the black African states, Kenya is in the best

position to take practical action against Amin, by cutting off Uganda's fuel supply. In 1976, after the Israeli raid on Entebbe, Kenya did this. As a result, Amin's regime virtually collapsed. The blockade was lifted ostensibly because people were suffering in the villages (they were, but not from lack of fuel).

The real reason for lifting the blockade was that it landed Kenya in serious difficulties. Kenya depends for its export trade with Zaire and Rwanda on routes through Ugandan territory. Amin can, at any time, close these routes, and so cut off supplies essential both to Kenya's economy and to the peoples of Zaire and Rwanda. In 1976, in fact, he seized fuel from Kenya that was destined for Rwanda.

But there is another route into Rwanda and Zaire, longer and more expensive, which bypasses Uganda. At the Kagera river, on the border of Tanzania and Rwanda, there is a bridge linking the two countries. It was built in 1971 to strengthen links with Tanzania as a result of Amin's threats to cut off trade links with Rwanda. If Kenya were to close its border with Uganda, items essential to the economies and peoples of Kenya, Zaire and Rwanda could still flow, especially with the support of the international community. It might cost more; but the increase could be offset by a limited amount of international aid. It might take time to establish regular supplies; but an airlift could be organized. During the Rhodesian blockade of Zambia in the late 1960s America, Canada, Britain and several other Western countries ran an airlift to keep Zambia's trade alive. It would surely not be too difficult to mount a similar exercise, again.

A further difficulty Kenya might face is an invasion from Uganda. Amin threatened such action in 1976. But I believe the danger to Kenya to be slight. Although Uganda is well supplied with Soviet weaponry, its army is ill-trained and morale is at an all-time low; Kenya can have little to fear from such an adversary.

In all these uncertainties, the only great certainty is that Amin must go. It may be argued that, in common with many other countries in Africa, a successor regime could prove to be as bad as the one it has displaced. I disagree: nothing could be as bad. Amin has a unique personality, he has allowed it expression in his own particular way, and for Ugandans, he has been uniquely destructive.

What happens after Amin goes? Firstly, with his overthrow, the Southern Sudanese will flee to the northwest, back over the border into their own country. They will not be able to survive in Uganda without Amin. They know the rules of the game. They came for the luxury goods, a good proportion of which they have funneled back to their villages. They own no fixed property, and they know how loathed they are. They are ready, at a few hours' notice, to seize their cash, weapons and few valuables, pack their cars and head for the border. (To reach the border, the Southern Sudanese will have to pass through the territory of the Acholi and Langi tribes, who have borne the brunt of Amin's atrocities. What will happen to them on the way, should word leak out that Amin has been killed or arrested, is too terrible to contemplate.)

Amin has also made his own contingency plans. When it becomes apparent that he can hold power no longer, and if he escapes arrest or assassination, he too will flee. He keeps his helicopters and his jet at the ready, fueled for take-off at a moment's notice. He has stockpiled huge amounts of foreign currency, mainly American dollars, outside the country; he has considerable amounts of hard cash readily available within Uganda. He has a residence in Libya which he uses for himself and his family from time to time. This could prove to be his final retreat.

But he does not necessarily have to flee abroad: there is another, more disturbing alternative open to him. He could carve out a mini-empire for himself in the northwest. He could handpick an army from among his

Southern Sudanese supporters; he could equip them with tanks, armored personnel carriers and a large range of Soviet weaponry. In Uganda's northwest corner at Kifaru by the Zaire and Sudan borders he has developed a ranch from which he could cross into either country with impunity.

I have visited Amin at his ranch a number of times. He has expelled the native inhabitants and cleared thousands of acres for his cattle and his property. I am certain he regards this corner of Uganda as one link in a chain of possible escapes should there be a move against him. Southern Sudan is semi-autonomous, and in either Sudan or Zaire it would be extremely difficult to pin him down. It would almost certainly involve two extradition treaties and a tripartite operation to pin him down. How long, I wonder, would it take? And how many more lives would be lost before he would have to answer for his crimes?

If Amin dies or flees, what then?

There are plenty of exiles with suggestions. But their effectiveness has been severely hampered because they are divided amongst themselves. Northerners and southerners are mutually suspicious; civilians suspect army people; and many simply fear revenge killings. Presidential hopefuls, waiting to take over from Amin in various foreign capitals—Dar-es-Salaam, London, New York, Nairobi—exploit the situation for their own ends and so, tragically, deflect interest from the major task, to rid Uganda of Amin.

In fact, it is too soon to discuss the details of any future administration. There are immense problems to be faced and only the outlines of a solution can be drawn. Tribal rivalries are still strong in Uganda, although Amin's tyranny has had the effect of uniting many former rivals in opposition to his regime. But there is no central civil authority left. The only authority is a military one. The army's role, in the first few months of new administration, would be vital. Under Amin, the army has been completely discredited, but with the departure of the Southern Sudanese and the rest of Amin's henchmen, there would be an opportunity to establish a new leadership, one that could win and keep the confidence of the country. Uganda's new leaders would be faced with the delicate task of providing a genuine caretaker administration to tide the country over until democracy could be restored.

Initially events would be on their side, for Amin's overthrow would result in a tremendous outburst of euphoria. In this atmosphere, the new administration could begin the monumental task of rebuilding Uganda from the wreckage left behind by Amin. They would have to demonstrate their good faith by producing a credible timetable for a return to democratically elected civilian government. Such an undertaking should automatically ensure that all future administration would be firmly Ugandan. There are monumental tasks, not least because so much that would need to be done in the early days of the new administration—the promises, the release of prisoners, the dissociation with the former regime—could be seen as a parallel with Amin's own actions when he seized power. But once the problems are faced and overcome, Uganda's enormous capacity to rebuild itself would speed the process of recovery. Its fine climate makes it practically self-sufficient in food. With the return of Uganda's talented professionals, there would be no shortage of manpower to get the country on its feet again. With the growth of confidence, Ugandans would once more want to invest in their country's future. Foreigners would almost certainly follow their example. Tourism, formally Uganda's fourth biggest industry, would be reestablished. Export crops would be grown again. Industry would begin to revive.

With faith in their country, there is nothing Ugandans cannot do. Once again, Uganda will become "the Pearl of Africa."

CHRONOLOGY OF EVENTS

DATE	UGANDA	IDI AMIN	HENRY KYEMBA
1894	Uganda declared British Protectorate.		
1900	Buganda Agreement (Britain-Uganda).		
1925		Born Koboko county, West Nile district.	
1939			Born Bunya county (Dec.)
1945	First African members appointed to Uganda Legislative Council.		
1946		Joins King's African Rifles as a private.	
1949		Promoted corporal.	
1951			Attends Busoga College at Mwiri (1951-56).
1952	First modern political party in Uganda formed–Uganda National Congress.		
1953	Kabaka Mutesa II deported to Britain.	Serves Kenya. Becomes Uganda's heavyweight boxing champion. Begins liaison with Malyamu Kibedi.	
1955	Kabaka readmitted to Uganda.		
1962	Uganda Peoples Congress emerges as strongest political group.		Attends Makerere University (July 1957- April 1962).

DATE	UGANDA	IDI AMIN	HENRY KYEMBA
Mar.	Self-government in Uganda. Kiwanuka becomes Prime Minister.	Murder of Turkana herdsmen in northwest Kenya. Amin held responsible.	
Apr.	General Elections. Kiwanuka defeated. Milton Obote becomes Prime Minister.		Joins Civil Service.
May			Appointed to P.M.'s office as Assistant Secretary.
Oct. 9	Uganda gains Independence.		
1963	Kabaka elected President (Oct. 9).	Promoted major.	Appointed Private Secretary. Serves Obote in this capacity until 1971 coup.
1964		Promoted colonel.	
Feb. 1966	Commission of Inquiry appointed on Congolese gold and ivory dealings.	Accused of corruption by M.P. Daudi Ocheng.	
Feb. 22	Obote orders arrest of 5 ministers; suspends 1962 Constitution.		
Feb. 23		Promoted Army Chief of Staff.	
Apr. 15	Interim Constitution approved by Parliament. Obote appointed President.		
May 23	Battle for Kabaka's Palace. Kabaka then flees to Britain.	Commands government troops in battle against Kabaka.	
Late 1966		Marriage to Malyamu formalized. Marries Kay Adroa.	
1967	Uganda declared a Republic.	Promoted brigadier. Marries Nora.	
June		Promoted major-general.	
Dec. 19, 1969	Attempt on Obote's life.	Goes into hiding.	

261

DATE	UGANDA	IDI AMIN	HENRY KYEMBA
Jan. 1970		Accused by Brigadier Okoya of desertion.	
Jan. 25		Okoya and wife shot; Amin implicated.	
Sept.	Obote acts to outflank Amin.	Sent to Cairo.	
Jan. 5, 1971			Leaves for Singapore with Obote to attend Commonwealth Conference.
Jan. 25	Obote overthrown.	Amin takes over.	
Jan. 29			Invited to return to Uganda. (Jan.-March: Prin. Private Secretary to Amin.)
Jan. 30		Promises "honest, fair and completely free elections."	Jan.-July: Secretary to the Cabinet and to the Office of the Pres.
Feb. 3	Parliament abolished. Rule by decree established.		
Feb. 6	Britain recognizes Amin. Bandmaster Oduka killed at about this time.		
Feb. 22		Accepts title of President offered him by Army. Promises military govt. will end "in much less than 5 years."	
Mar.	Makindye Prison massacre.		
Apr.	Massacre at Lira.		
May 11	Decree providing for detention without trial.		
June	Massacre at Mbarara barracks.		

July	Disappearance of Americans Stroh and Siedle. Killings at Jinja barracks.		
Aug.	Leaves for London (July 11). Dines with Heath. Lunches with Queen. Sets up Inquiry into disappearance of Stroh and Siedle.		Sent on leave late July.
Sept.	Michael Kagwa, President of Industrial Court, killed.	Visits Pope Paul in Rome.	Appointed Permanent Sec. in the Ministry of Culture & Community Dev.
Oct.		Admits "tribal conflicts" have caused numerous deaths, especially among Acholi and Langi.	
Feb. 1972		Visits Gaddafi in Tripoli; issue joint communique condemning Israel.	
Mar. 27	All Israeli personnel ordered to leave Uganda within 3 days.		
Apr.	Inquiry into disappearance of Stroh and Siedle adjourned.	Accuses Justice Jones, in charge of inquiry, of "a prejudiced mind".	
Aug. 5	All Asians holding British passports ordered to leave Uganda within 3 months.		
Aug. 16		Offers to pay compensation to relatives of Stroh and Siedle.	
Sept.	Alex Ojera, Obote's Minister of Information, Killed. British Army training mission expelled.		
Sept. 17	Invasion of Obote guerrillas from Tanzania.		

DATE	UGANDA	IDI AMIN	HENRY KYEMBA
Sept. 21	Chief Justice Benedicto Kiwanuka killed.		Rehoboam Lume Kisajja (Kyemba's brother) killed.
Sept. 24		Marries Medina.	
Sept. 30			Official visit to Nigeria.
Oct.	Frank Kalimuzo, Chancellor of Makerere University, killed. Mogadishu Agreement (Oct. 5). British envoy ordered out of Uganda (Oct. 12). Ugandan ambassador to London recalled.		
Nov.	Head count of Asians remaining in Uganda begins.		Appointed Minister of Culture & Community Development.
Dec. 28	Murder of Shabani Nkutu.		Official visit to Zambia.
Jan. 1973	Libya offers to train 300 Ugandan soldiers and airmen .	Admits (Jan. 10) 85 persons missing since coup. Blames Obote guerrillas.	
Feb.	Dan Nabudere, Chairman of East African Railways, and Minister of Education Edward Rugumayo flee.	Sends first cabinet on leave. Ugandans ordered to attend first public execution in 75 years.	
Mar.	John Barigaye, Ugandan Ambassador to Germany defects. Cabinet dismissed.	Made life member of CORE.	
May.	20 Russian doctors sent to Uganda.	Attends OAU Conference at Addis Ababa (May 20).	

264

July.	Lake Edward renamed Lake Idi Amin Dada.	Sends telegram to Nixon wishing him a speedy recovery from Watergate.
Oct.		Invites Ugandan volunteers to join Arabs in war against Israel.
Nov.	4 English language newspapers banned. British High Commissioner recalled. U.S. Embassy in Kampala closed.	Taban Amin (15) sent to Russia to study.
Dec.		Sets up "Save Britain Fund."
Feb. 1974		Appointed Minister of Health.
Mar.	Murder of Lt. Col. Michael Ondoga. Coup against Amin, led by Brigadier Charles Arube (Mar. 23). 6-hour tank battle in Kampala. Murder of Arube.	Divorces Kay, Nora and Malyamu.
Apr.	Malyamu Amin arrested.	
June	All foreign newspapers and magazines banned.	
Aug.		Kay Amin arrested. Her dismembered body found Aug.14.
Nov.		Suggests UN headquarters be transferred to Uganda. Dismisses Foreign Minister, Elizabeth Bagaya (Nov. 24). Accuses her of making love with an unknown European at Paris airport.
Jan. 1975		Announces plan to visit Britain–wants to meet Scots, Irish and Welsh.

DATE	UGANDA	IDI AMIN	HENRY KYEMBA
Apr.	Arrest of Dennis Hills.	Decides against erecting a monument to Hitler.	
June	Hills sentenced to death.		
July 10		Meets with British Foreign Minister Callaghan in Kampala.	
July 11	Hills released.		
July 17		Promoted Field Marshall by popular acclaim of his troops.	
July 28	OAU summit opens Kampala.	Elected President OAU.	
Aug. 2		Weds Sarah.	
Oct.		Visits UN. Condemns Israel.	
Nov.	Uganda breaks off diplomatic relations with Russia.		
Dec.	Uganda breaks off diplomatic relations With Zaire.	Malyamu Amin seeks refuge in London.	
June 1976		Attempt on Amin's life. Proclaimed President for life.	
July 4	Entebbe raid.		
July 5	Dora Bloch killed.		
July 27	Britain breaks off diplomatic relations with Uganda.		
Aug. 3	Demonstration at Makerere University.		
Oct.		Sends two of his sons to prison.	

Date		
Jan. 1977	Dr. Kahwa flees.	Congratulates President Carter. Hopes to "work closely" with him.
Jan. 25	Celebrations to mark 6th anniversary of coup.	Distributes 2,000 medals.
Feb. 17	Arrest and death of Archbishop Luwuum and ministers Charles Oboth-Ofumbi and Erinayo Oryema.	
Mar. 9	Intl commission to investigate deaths of Archbishop and two ministers banned from Uganda.	
Apr.		Leaves Uganda for Cairo; arrives Geneva, Teresa arrives Geneva. Elizabeth arrested.
May		Holds press conference in Geneva. Elizabeth released; Elizabeth and children escape to Kenya; arrives London.
July 4	Attends OAU summit in Libreville.	
July 19		Elizabeth and children arrive London.

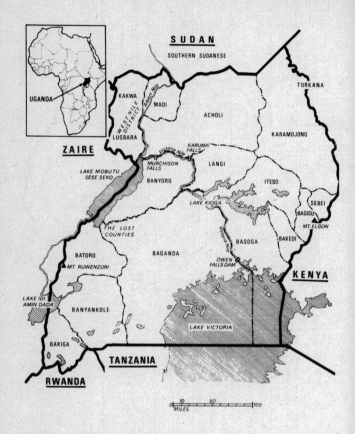

UGANDA'S TRIBES

The area occupied by the Baganda is called Buganda; that occupied by the Karamojong is called Karamoja; that occupied by the Batoro is called Toro; etc.

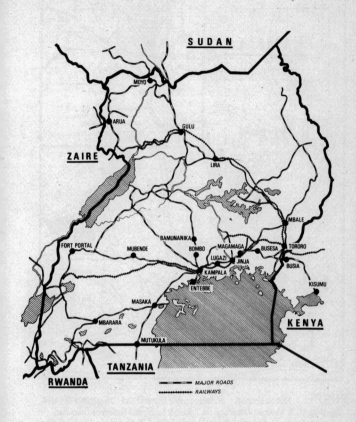

PRINCIPAL TOWNS OF UGANDA

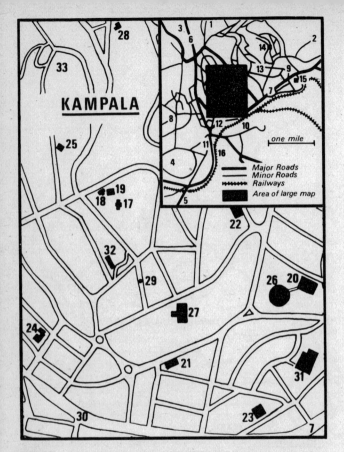

INSET: **1.** Mulago Hospital   **2.** Naguru police barracks and Headquarters of Public Safety Unit   **3.** Makerere University   **4.** Kabaka's Palace and Residence (Twekobe) **5.** Road to Entebbe   **6.** Bombo Road   **7.** Jinja Road   **8.** Namirembe Road   **9.** Place of attempted assassination of Obote, Dec 19, 1969   **10.** Place of attempted assassination of Amin, June 10, 1976   **11.** Public execution site   **12.** Entebbe Road   **13.** Former Kololo Airstrip, now an open park   **14.** Command Post (Amin's Residence)   **15.** Offices of *Voice of Uganda*   **16.** Makindye Prison

MAIN MAP: **17.** President's Lodge   **18.** Headquarters of State Research Bureau **19.** French Embassy   **20.** Nile Hotel   **21.** Speke Hotel   **22.** Ex-Israel Embassy, now occupied by P.L.O.   **23.** British High Commission (until 1976)   **24.** Central Police Station **25.** Radio Uganda, (Uganda Broadcasting Corporation)   **26.** Conference Center **27.** Kampala International Hotel (formerly Apolo Hotel)   **28.** Henry Kyemba's official residence   **29.** Place of faked accident   **30.** Kampala Road   **31.** Parliament Buildings **32.** Officers Mess (formerly Uganda Club)   **33.** Nakasero Hill

Appendix

The Letter That Led to the Archbishop's Murder

The House of Bishops of the Church of Uganda, Rwanda, Burundi and Boga-Zaire sent the following letter to President Idi Amin on February 10, 1977, following the attack by Uganda security forces on the Archbishop, Janan Luwuum, and the Bishop of Bukedi, Yona Okoth:

> Church of Uganda, Rwanda,
>   Burundi & Boga-Zaire,
> P.O. Box 14123,
> Kampala,
> Uganda.

His Excellency Al-Haji, Field Marshall Dr. Idi Amin Dada, V.C., D.S.O., M.C.,
Life President of Uganda,
The President's Office,
Kampala,
Uganda.   10th February, 1977.

Your Excellency,
    We the Archbishop and the Bishops of the Province of Uganda, Rwanda, Burundi and Boga-Zaire meeting at Namirembe on Tuesday, 8th February, 1977, humbly beg to submit our most deeply felt concern for the Church

and the welfare of the people whom we serve under your care.

In presenting this statement, we are in no way questioning the right of the Government in administering justice, to search and arrest offenders. We believe that the Government has established structures and procedures for carrying out this kind of exercise. It is these established structures and procedures that give the citizens a sense of what to expect of their Government. These structures and procedures give the police, the intelligence and the security forces a framework within which to work. When these procedures are followed in carrying out their day to day duties this gives the ordinary citizen a sense of security. It creates mutual friendship and trust between such officers and the general public irrespective of uniform. But when the police and security officers deviate from these established structures and procedures in carrying out their day to day duties, citizens become insecure, afraid and disturbed. They begin to distrust these officers.

We are deeply disturbed to learn of the incident which occurred at the Archbishop's official residence in the early hours of Saturday morning, 5th February 1977. In the history of our country such an incident in the Church has never before occurred. Security officers broke through the fence and forced their way into the Archbishop's compound. They used a man they had arrested and tortured as a decoy to entice the Archbishop to open his door to help a man seemingly in distress. Using a man under duress and torture as a source of information can lead to unnecessary suffering of innocent individuals. The Archbishop opened his door. At that point armed men who had been hiding sprung to attack cocking their rifles demanding "arms." When the Archbishop asked "What arms?", the answer was the muzzle of a rifle pressed against his stomach and immediately he was pushed forcefully into his house with the demand "Archbishop show us the arms, run into the bedroom." The full story of that incident as told by the Archbishop is appended.

First we want to register our shock and protest at this kind of treatment to the top leader of the Church of Uganda, Rwanda, Burundi and Boga-Zaire. Then we shall draw out the implications of this incident for the rest of the Bishops and all the Christians of the Church of Uganda. Your Excellency, you have said publicly on many occasions that Religious Leaders have a special place in this country and that you treat them with respect for what they stand for and represent. You have on many occasions publicly demonstrated this and we are always grateful. But what happened to the Archbishop in his house on the night we have referred to is a direct contradiction to what you yourself, Your Excellency, have said in public and to the established structures and procedures in dealing with security manners. That is why we are very disturbed, and with us the whole of the Church of Uganda. We feel that if it was necessary to search the Archbishop's house he should have been approached in broad daylight by responsible senior officers fully identified in conformity with his position in society, but to search him and his house at gunpoint deep in the night leaves us without words.

Now that the security of the Archbishop is at stake, the security of the Bishops is even more in jeopardy. Indeed we have a case in point. The night following the search of the Archbishop's house, one of us, the Bishop of Bukedi was both searched and arrested. It was only when nothing could be found at his personal and official residences that he was later released on the Sunday morning. This left the people in his diocese wondering and the wondering is spreading quickly. The Christians are asking: if this is what is happening to our Bishops then where are we? The gun whose muzzle has been pressed against the Archbishop's stomach, the gun which has been used to search the Bishop of Bukedi's houses, is a gun which is being pointed at every Christian in the Church, unless

Your Excellency can give us something new to change this situation.

The security of the ordinary Christian has been in jeopardy for quite a long time. It may be that what has happened to the Archbishop and the Bishop of Bukedi is a climax of what is consistently happening to our Christians. We have buried many who have died as a result of being shot and there are many more whose bodies have not been found, yet their disappearance is connected with the activities of some members of the Security Forces. Your Excellency, if it is required, we can give concrete evidence of what is happening because widows and orphans are members of our Church.

Furthermore, we are made sad by the increasing forces that are setting Ugandans one against another. While it is common in Uganda for members of one family to be members of different religious organizations there is an increasing feeling that one particular religious organization is being favored more than any other. So much so that in some parts of Uganda members of Islam who are in leading positions are using these positions to coerce Christians into becoming Muslims. Secondly members of the Security Forces are sons of civilians and they have civilian brothers and sisters. When they begin to use the gun in their hands to destroy instead of protecting the civilian then the relationship of mutual trust and respect is destroyed. Instead of that relationship you have suspicion, fear and hidden hatred. There is also a war against the educated which is forcing many of our people to run away from this country in spite of what the country has paid to educate them. This brain drainage of our country, the fear and the mistrust make development, progress and stability of our country almost impossible. The gun which was meant to protect Uganda as a nation, the Ugandan as a citizen and his property is increasingly being used against the Ugandan to take away his life and his property. For instance, many cars, almost daily are being taken at gunpoint and their owners killed. And most of the culprits never brought to justice. If required, we can enumerate many cases. Too much power has been given to members of State Research who arrest and kill at will innocent individuals. Therefore that which was meant to provide the Ugandan citizen with security is increasingly becoming the means of his insecurity.

We are also concerned about the developing gap between the leaders of the Christian Churches, Archbishops in particular, and Your Excellency. We had been assured by you of your ready availability to Religious Leaders whenever they had serious matters to discuss with you. You had even gone to the extent of giving His Grace, the Archbishop, the surest means of contacting you in this country wherever you may be. But a situation has developed now where you have become more and more inaccessible to the Archbishop and even when he tried to write he has not received any reply. This gap has brought a sad feeling of estrangement and alienation not only to the Archbishop and the Bishops but also it is reaching down to the ordinary citizens. While you, Your Excellency, have stated on the national radio that your government is not under any foreign influence, and that your decisions are guided by your Defence Council and Cabinet, the general trend of things in Uganda has created a feeling that the affairs of our nation are being directed by outsiders who do not have the welfare of this country and the value of the lives and properties of Ugandans at their heart. A situation like this breeds unnecessary misunderstanding and mistrust. Indeed we were shocked to hear over the radio on Christmas Day, Your Excellency saying that some Bishops had preached bloodshed. We waited anxiously to be called by Your Excellency to clarify such a serious situation, but all in vain. Your Excellency, we want to say here again that we are ready to come to you whenever there are serious matters that concern the Church and the nation, you've only got to call us. This used not to be so, Your Excellency, when you freely moved amongst us and we freely came to you.

The Archbishop is not only the Archbishop of the Church of Uganda but he is the Archbishop of the Church of Rwanda, Burundi and Boga-Zaire. So what happens to him here is also the concern of the Christians in Rwanda, the concern of the Christians in Burundi and the concern of the Christians in Zaire. In fact, it goes further than that because he is an Archbishop in the Anglican Communion which is a world wide community, so are the Bishops. An action such as this one damages the good image of our nation. It also threatens our preparations for the Centenary Celebrations. Christians everywhere have become very cautious about taking part in the fund raising activities of the Church for fear of being misrepresented and misinterpreted. The ban on sales of things donated for fund raising in aid of the Church is a case in point. This too, could have been cleared if only Your Excellency had given the Archbishop an opportunity to brief you on the matter.

In addition to the concern of the Christians in the Anglican Communion there is also the concern of the Christians of other denominations in Uganda and all over the world with whom we are in fellowship.

In conclusion, Your Excellency, we are very grateful that you have kindly given us this opportunity to express our grievances and concerns to you.

"For God and Our Country".

Signed:

The Most Rev. Janan Luwuum, *Archbishop of Uganda, Rwanda, Burundi and Boga-Zaire and Bishop of Uganda.*

The Rt. Rev. Silvanus G. Wani, *Bishop of Madi and West Nile and Dean of the Province.*

The Rt. Rev. Amos Betungura, *Bishop of East Ankole.*

The Rt. Rev. Yona Okoth, *Bishop of Bukedi.*

The Rt. Rev. Dr. Yustasi Ruhindi, *Bishop of Bunyoro-Kitara.*

The Rt. Rev. Cyprian Bamwoze, *Bishop of Busoga.*

The Rt. Rev. Brian Herd, *Bishop of Karamoja (who was on leave and did not sign)*

The Rt. Rev. Festo Kivengere, *Bishop of Kigezi.*

The Rt. Rev. Melkisedek Otim, *Bishop of Lango.*

The Rt. Rev. John Wasikye, *Bishop of Mbale.*

The Rt. Rev. Dr. Dunstan Nsubuga, *Bishop of Namirembe.*

The Rt. Rev. Dr. B.Y. Ogwal, *Bishop of Northern Uganda.*

The Rt. Rev. Y. Rwakaikara, *Bishop of Ruwenzori.*

The Rt. Rev. G. Ilukor, *Bishop of Soroti.*

The Rt. Rev. C.D. Senyonjo, *Bishop of West Buganda.*

The Rt. Rev. Y.K. Bamunoba, *Bishop of West Ankole.*

The Rt. Rev. William Rukirande, *Assistant Bishop of Kigezi.*

The Rt. Rev. R. Ringtho, *Assistant Bishop of Madi and West Nile.*

The Rt. Rev. M. Kauma, *Assistant Bishop of Namirembe.*

Distributed to:

1. His Excellency Al-Haji Field Marshall Dr. Idi Amin Dada, V.C., D.S.O., M.C. Life President of Uganda.

2. His Excellency, the Vice President of Uganda and Minister of Defence, General Mustafa Adrisi.

3. His Eminence Emmanuel, Cardinal Nsubuga, Archbishop of Kampala.

4. His Eminence Sheikh Mufti of Uganda, Muslim Supreme Council.

5. The Rt. Rev. Theodorous of Novoratis, Uganda Orthodox Church.

6. All Cabinet Ministers.

7. Secretary to the Defence Council.

8. The Acting Permanent Secretary for Religious Affairs.

9. All Bishops of the Province of the Church of Uganda, Rwanda, Burundi and Boga-Zaire.

Report of a Very Serious Incident at the Archbishop's House in the Early Hours of Saturday, 5th February 1977

At about 1:30 A.M. on Saturday morning I heard the dog barking wildly and the fence been broken down and I knew some people had come into the compound. I walked downstairs very quietly without switching any lights on and as usual I stopped at the door. I opened the curtain on the door on one side and I was able to observe one man standing straight in front of the door. He began calling "Archbishop, Archbishop, open, we have come." This man was called Ben Ongom. Because he had some cuts on his face and I knew him in the past I thought he was in some kind of danger, needing help. So I opened the door and immediately these armed men who had been hiding sprang on me cocking their rifles and shouting "Archbishop, Archbishop, show us the arms."

I replied "What arms?"

They replied, "There are arms in this house."

I said "No."

At this point their leader who was speaking in Arabic, wearing a red kaunda suit [i.e., with short sleeves and open neck, as popularized by the Zambian President] put his rifle in my stomach on the right-hand side whilst another man searched me from head to foot. He pushed me with the rifle shouting "Walk, run, show us the arms, take us to your bedroom." So we went up to our bedroom where Mary my wife was asleep. We woke her up and they began crawling underneath the bed. They opened the wardrobes climbing right up into the upper deck of the cupboard. They searched the bedroom, thoroughly looking in suitcases, boxes, etc. but finding nothing. They proceeded to search the two children's bedrooms upstairs, repeating the same exercise of searching everywhere. Fortunately the younger children slept through it but the bigger children woke up and went round with us.

After that we came downstairs, and at this point Mr.

Ben Ongom, who was handcuffed, began to say, "Archbishop, you see sometime back we brought some ammunition and divided it up with Mr. Olobo who works in the Ministry of Labor in Kampala. I kept some and Mr. Olobo kept some. Now mine has been found and certainly because of involving myself in politics I am going to die in any case for it. When we went to Olobo's home with the security people and they searched his house, they found nothing but they arrested him. I thought Mr. Olobo might have transferred his share of the arms to Dr. Lalobo's home (Medical Superintendent of Mengo Hospital) since he was also an Acholi and they seem to be related. We have been to Dr. Lalobo's home and searched the house but found nothing. The security men have arrested him. Then I suggested to the security men that Dr. Lalobo might have transferred the ammunition to the Archbishop's house. This is why we have come to you. Please help us. If the arms are not here, tell us the location of any Acholi or Langi homes on Namirembe so that they may be searched."

I told Mr. Ongom that I did not come to Namirembe for the Acholi or the Langi but I was the Archbishop of Uganda, Rwanda, Burundi and Boga-Zaire and there were no arms in my house. Our house was God's house. We pray for the President. We pray for the security forces—whatever they do. We preach the Gospel and pray for others. That is our work, not keeping arms.

All the same, the search continued. They demanded we opened the study. They searched there. We opened the Chapel. They searched there, even looking underneath the Holy Table. They searched the food stores putting their hands into sacks of sim-sim [sorghum], millet, groundnuts, trying to feel for hidden objects. We went to the guest wing. They searched through the toilets, bathrooms etc. They searched the cars parked in the compound. Finding nothing, we continued to complain that the incident was a serious one for the whole Church, since we knew nothing of any arms. I said, "What will the

Christians think about this incident when they hear about it since we shall certainly not keep quiet?" I told them I was going to talk to the President immediately.

The security men thought that since arms had been brought into the country to overthrow the Government and since Ben Ongom suggested our house, they had no alternative but to follow his suggestion. I told them they should have come in a more respectable way. Their leader, who was a Nubian, remarked that they had to come in a military way since the matter was a serious one. I told him I had done nothing wrong to warrant the treatment of a rifle being put in my stomach.

My neighbours, Bishop Kauma and the Provincial Secretary, had rung Old Kampala Police Station when they saw there were men with arms in our compound, thinking they were robbers. When the military police came these men sent them away before they entered our compound.

About 3:00 A.M. these men left. They requested that we opened the gate for them to go out, but my wife suggested they should go the way they came. I said we were Christians. We have clean hearts and as a witness we would open the gates for them. They left and entered their cars which they had parked down the road. The number plates were covered. Eventually they drove away.

Earlier on Friday evening at 7:00 P.M. I had heard from the hospital that the security men had searched Dr. Lalobo's home and that the doctor was missing. Up to now the doctor is still missing. [By the time I left, he had been released—Henry Kyemba.]

Postscript

Of the uncounted thousands who have fled Uganda in recent years, these fifty—mostly prominent people— were all known to me personally. I knew many other refugees as well. Their flight is a testimony to the revulsion and fear felt by the country at large.

For Fifty Who Fled

N. Zikusoka, *engineer, and Minister of Works.*
Dr. J. H. Gesa, *Minister of Health.*
J. Wanume Kibedi, *Minister of Foreign Affairs.*
Edward Rugumayo, *Minister of Education.*
Emmanuel Wakweya, *Minister of Finance.*
Godfrey Lule, *Minister of Justice.*
Wilson Lutara, *Minister of Commerce and Industry.*
I. K. Kabanda, *Minister/Director of Planning.*
W. W. Rwetsiba, *Minister for the East African Community*
Semei Nyanzi, *Minister of Small Scale Industries.*
Elizabeth Bagaya, *Minister of Foreign Affairs.*
Professor Banage, *Minister of Animal Resources.*
Valorin Ovonji, *Minister of Public Service.*
Asavia Wandira, *Vice Chancellor of Makerere University.*
A. M. Odonga, *Dean of the Makerere Medical School.*
John Barigye, *Ambassador to the Federal Republic of Germany.*
Grace Ibingira, *Ambassador to the UN.*
Godfrey Binaisa, Q.C., *Former Attorney General.*

A. Tiberondwa, *Director, Teacher Training College.*

Jack Ssentongo, *Secretary to the Treasury.*

John Kazzora, *lawyer.*

Chris Mboijana, *lawyer.*

Dr. Martin Aliker, *dentist.*

Chris K. Ntende, *Secretary, Internal Affairs.*

Z. H. K. Bigirwenkya, *Permanent secretary, President's Office.*

Paulo Muwanga, *Ambassador to Paris.*

Erisa Kironde, *Chairman of Uganda Electricity Board.*

A. K. Mubanda, *Secretary for Planning.*

Prof. John Kibukamusoke, *physician.*

Dr. Emuron, *radiologist.*

Dr. Besigye, *radiologist.*

Dr. John Luwuliza Kirunda, *gynecologist.*

Peter Ucanda, *Secretary to the Cabinet.*

Andrew Adimola, *permanent secretary, Education.*

Dr. John Nsibambi, *dermatologist.*

Col. Wilson Toko, *former Commander of the Air Force.*

Y. K. Lule, *former Vice Chancellor of Makerere.*

Bishop Yona Okoth, *Bukedi Diocese.*

Bishop Kivengeri, *Kigezi Diocese.*

Professor Oloya, *Agriculture, Makerere University.*

Prof. M. Kiwanuka, *History Department, Makerere University.*

Dan Okunga, *Lecturer, Education, Makerere University.*

Dr. Sinabulya, *eye specialist.*

Dr. Bisase, *dentist.*

Dr. Opio, *physician.*

Wamala, *businessman.*

Dr. Semu Nsibirwa, *gynecologist.*

Dan Nabudere, *lawyer, Chairman East African Railways.*

Dr. Wacha, *medical specialist.*

Paul Kibukamusoke, *businessman.*

Index

ACCLAIM FOR

Coraline:

"This book tells a fascinating and disturbing story that frightened me
nearly to death."   —Lemony Snicket

"This is a marvelously strange and scary book."   —Philip Pullman

"This book will send a shiver down your spine, out through your
shoes, and into a taxi to the airport. It has the delicate horror of the
finest fairy tales, and it is a masterpiece."   —Terry Pratchett

"I think this book will nudge ALICE IN WONDERLAND out of its niche
at last. It is the most splendidly original, weird, and frightening book I
have read, and yet full of things children will love."
                                                —Diana Wynne Jones

"A deliciously scary book. The magical elements are surprising and
new, and the evil that she has to fight is disturbing in ways that matter."
                                                —Orson Scott Card

"A modern ghost story with all the creepy trimmings. Well done."
                                        —The New York Times Book Review

"CORALINE is by turns creepy and funny, bittersweet and playful. A
book that can be read quickly and enjoyed deeply."
                                        —San Francisco Chronicle Book Review

"An electrifyingly creepy tale likely to haunt young readers for many
moons."   —Publishers Weekly (starred review)

"CORALINE may be Gaiman's most disciplined and fully controlled
novel to date, and it may even end up as something of a classic."
                                                            —Locus

"Chilly, finely wrought prose, a truly weird setting, and a fable that taps
into our most uncomfortable fears."
                                        —Times Educational Supplement (London)

Also by Neil Gaiman
with Illustrations by Dave McKean

THE WOLVES IN THE WALLS

THE DAY I SWAPPED MY DAD FOR 2 GOLDFISH

Coraline

Coraline

NEIL GAIMAN

WITH ILLUSTRATIONS BY DAVE McKEAN

HarperEntertainment
An Imprint of HarperCollinsPublishers

Library of Congress Cataloging-in-Publication Data
Gaiman, Neil.
Coraline / Neil Gaiman ;
with illustrations by Dave McKean.
p.   cm.
Summary: Looking for excitement, Coraline ventures
through a mysterious door into a world that is similar, yet
disturbingly different from her own, where she must challenge a gruesome entity in order to save herself, her parents, and the souls of three others.
ISBN 978-0-06-164969-1 (pbk.)
[1. Supernatural—Fiction.]   I. McKean, Dave, ill.
II. Title.
PZ7.G1273 Co 2002   [Fic]—dc21   2002018937

Typography by Hilary Zarycky
❖
First Harper Entertainment edition, 2008

I started this for Holly
I finished it for Maddy

Fairy tales are more than true: not because
they tell us that dragons exist, but because
they tell us that dragons can be beaten.
                                        —G. K. Chesterton

Coraline

I.

CORALINE DISCOVERED THE DOOR a little while after they moved into the house.

It was a very old house—it had an attic under the roof and a cellar under the ground and an overgrown garden with huge old trees in it.

Coraline's family didn't own all of the house—it was too big for that. Instead they owned part of it.

There were other people who lived in the old house.

Miss Spink and Miss Forcible lived in the flat below Coraline's, on the ground floor. They were both old and round, and they lived in their flat with a number of ageing Highland terriers who had names like Hamish and Andrew and Jock. Once upon a time Miss Spink and Miss Forcible had been actresses, as Miss Spink told Coraline the first time she met her.

"You see, Caroline," Miss Spink said, getting Coraline's name wrong, "both myself and Miss Forcible were famous actresses, in our time. We trod the boards, luvvy. Oh, don't let Hamish eat the fruitcake, or he'll be up all night with his tummy."

"It's Coraline. Not Caroline. Coraline," said Coraline.

In the flat above Coraline's, under the roof, was a crazy old man with a big mustache. He told Coraline that he was training a mouse circus. He wouldn't let anyone see it.

"One day, little Caroline, when they are all ready, everyone in the whole world will see the wonders of my mouse circus. You ask me why you cannot see it now. Is that what you asked me?"

"No," said Coraline quietly, "I asked you not to call me Caroline. It's Coraline."

"The reason you cannot see the mouse circus," said the man upstairs, "is that the mice are not yet ready and rehearsed. Also, they refuse to play the songs I have written for them. All the songs I have written for the mice to play go *oompah oompah*. But the white mice will only play *toodle oodle*, like that. I am thinking of trying them on different types of cheese."

Coraline didn't think there really was a mouse circus. She thought the old man was probably making it up.

The day after they moved in, Coraline went exploring.

She explored the garden. It was a big garden: at the very back was an old tennis court, but no one in the house played tennis and the fence around the court had holes in it and the net had mostly rotted away; there was an old rose garden, filled with stunted, flyblown rosebushes; there was a rockery that was all rocks; there was a fairy ring, made of squidgy brown toadstools which smelled dreadful if you accidentally trod on them.

There was also a well. On the first day Coraline's family moved in, Miss Spink and Miss Forcible made a point of telling Coraline how dangerous the well was, and they warned her to be sure she kept away from it. So Coraline set off to explore for it, so that she knew where it was, to keep away from it properly.

She found it on the third day, in an overgrown meadow beside the tennis court, behind a clump of trees—a low brick circle almost hidden in the high grass. The well had been covered up by wooden boards, to stop anyone falling in. There was a small knothole in one of the boards, and Coraline spent an afternoon dropping pebbles and acorns through the hole and waiting, and counting, until she heard the *plop* as they hit the water far below.

Coraline also explored for animals. She found a hedge-hog, and a snakeskin (but no snake), and a rock that looked just like a frog, and a toad that looked just like a rock.

There was also a haughty black cat, who sat on walls and tree stumps and watched her but slipped away if ever she went over to try to play with it.

That was how she spent her first two weeks in the

house—exploring the garden and the grounds.

Her mother made her come back inside for dinner and for lunch. And Coraline had to make sure she dressed up warm before she went out, for it was a very cold summer that year; but go out she did, exploring, every day until the day it rained, when Coraline had to stay inside.

"What should I do?" asked Coraline.

"Read a book," said her mother. "Watch a video. Play with your toys. Go and pester Miss Spink or Miss Forcible, or the crazy old man upstairs."

"No," said Coraline. "I don't want to do those things. I want to explore."

"I don't really mind what you do," said Coraline's mother, "as long as you don't make a mess."

Coraline went over to the window and watched the rain come down. It wasn't the kind of rain you could go out in—it was the other kind, the kind that threw itself down from the sky and splashed where it landed. It was rain that meant business, and currently its business was turning the garden into a muddy, wet soup.

Coraline had watched all the videos. She was bored with her toys, and she'd read all her books.

She turned on the television. She went from channel to channel to channel, but there was nothing on but men in suits talking about the stock market, and talk shows.

Eventually, she found something to watch: it was the last half of a natural history program about something called protective coloration. She watched animals, birds, and insects which disguised themselves as leaves or twigs or other animals to escape from things that could hurt them. She enjoyed it, but it ended too soon and was followed by a program about a cake factory.

It was time to talk to her father.

Coraline's father was home. Both of her parents worked, doing things on computers, which meant that they were home a lot of the time. Each of them had their own study.

"Hello Coraline," he said when she came in, without turning round.

"Mmph," said Coraline. "It's raining."

"Yup," said her father. "It's bucketing down."

"No," said Coraline. "It's just raining. Can I go outside?"

"What does your mother say?"

"She says you're not going out in weather like that, Coraline Jones."

"Then, no."

"But I want to carry on exploring."

"Then explore the flat," suggested her father. "Look— here's a piece of paper and a pen. Count all the doors and windows. List everything blue. Mount an expedition to discover the hot water tank. And leave me alone to work."

"Can I go into the drawing room?" The drawing room was where the Joneses kept the expensive (and uncomfortable) furniture Coraline's grandmother had left them when she died. Coraline wasn't allowed in there. Nobody went in there. It was only for best.

"If you don't make a mess. And you don't touch anything."

Coraline considered this carefully, then she took the paper and pen and went off to explore the inside of the flat.

She discovered the hot water tank (it was in a cupboard in the kitchen).

She counted everything blue (153).

She counted the windows (21).

She counted the doors (14).

Of the doors that she found, thirteen opened and closed. The other—the big, carved, brown wooden door at the far corner of the drawing room—was locked.

She said to her mother, "Where does that door go?"

"Nowhere, dear."

"It has to go somewhere."

Her mother shook her head. "Look," she told Coraline. She reached up and took a string of keys from the top of the kitchen doorframe. She sorted through them carefully, and selected the oldest, biggest, blackest, rustiest key.

They went into the drawing room. She unlocked the door with the key.

The door swung open.

Her mother was right. The door didn't go anywhere. It opened onto a brick wall.

"When this place was just one house," said Coraline's mother, "that door went somewhere. When they turned the house into flats, they simply bricked it up. The other side is the empty flat on the other side of the house, the one that's still for sale."

She shut the door and put the string of keys back on top of the kitchen doorframe.

"You didn't lock it," said Coraline.

Her mother shrugged. "Why should I lock it?" she asked. "It doesn't go anywhere."

Coraline didn't say anything.

It was nearly dark outside now, and the rain was still coming down, pattering against the windows and blurring the lights of the cars in the street outside.

Coraline's father stopped working and made them all dinner.

Coraline was disgusted. "Daddy," she said, "you've made a *recipe* again."

"It's leek and potato stew with a tarragon garnish and

melted Gruyère cheese," he admitted.

Coraline sighed. Then she went to the freezer and got out some microwave chips and a microwave minipizza.

"You know I don't like recipes," she told her father, while her dinner went around and around and the little red numbers on the microwave oven counted down to zero.

"If you tried it, maybe you'd like it," said Coraline's father, but she shook her head.

That night, Coraline lay awake in her bed. The rain had stopped, and she was almost asleep when something went *t-t-t-t-t-t*. She sat up in bed.

Something went *kreeee* . . .

. . . *aaaak*

Coraline got out of bed and looked down the hall, but saw nothing strange. She walked down the hall. From her parents' bedroom came a low snoring—that was her father—and an occasional sleeping mutter—that was her mother.

Coraline wondered if she'd dreamed it, whatever it was. Something moved.

It was little more than a shadow, and it scuttled down the darkened hall fast, like a little patch of night.

She hoped it wasn't a spider. Spiders made Coraline intensely uncomfortable.

The black shape went into the drawing room, and

Coraline followed it a little nervously.

The room was dark. The only light came from the hall, and Coraline, who was standing in the doorway, cast a huge and distorted shadow onto the drawing room carpet—she looked like a thin giant woman.

Coraline was just wondering whether or not she ought to turn on the lights when she saw the black shape edge slowly out from beneath the sofa. It paused, and then dashed silently across the carpet toward the farthest corner of the room.

There was no furniture in that corner of the room.

Coraline turned on the light.

There was nothing in the corner. Nothing but the old door that opened onto the brick wall.

She was sure that her mother had shut the door, but now it was ever so slightly open. Just a crack. Coraline went over to it and looked in. There was nothing there—just a wall, built of red bricks.

Coraline closed the old wooden door, turned out the light, and went to bed.

She dreamed of black shapes that slid from place to place, avoiding the light, until they were all gathered together under the moon. Little black shapes with little red eyes and sharp yellow teeth.

They started to sing,

We are small but we are many
We are many we are small
We were here before you rose
We will be here when you fall.

Their voices were high and whispering and slightly whiney. They made Coraline feel uncomfortable.

Then Coraline dreamed a few commercials, and after that she dreamed of nothing at all.

II.

THE NEXT DAY IT HAD stopped raining, but a thick white fog had lowered over the house.

"I'm going for a walk," said Coraline.

"Don't go too far," said her mother. "And dress up warmly."

Coraline put on her blue coat with a hood, her red scarf, and her yellow Wellington boots.

She went out.

Miss Spink was walking her dogs. "Hello, Caroline," said Miss Spink. "Rotten weather."

"Yes," said Coraline.

"I played Portia once," said Miss Spink. "Miss Forcible talks about her Ophelia, but it was my Portia they came to see. When we trod the boards."

Miss Spink was bundled up in pullovers and cardigans, so she seemed more small and circular than ever. She looked like a large, fluffy egg. She wore thick glasses that made her eyes seem huge.

"They used to send flowers to my dressing room. They *did*," she said.

"Who did?" asked Coraline.

Miss Spink looked around cautiously, looking over first one shoulder and then over the other, peering into the mists as though someone might be listening.

"*Men*," she whispered. Then she tugged the dogs to heel and waddled off back toward the house.

Coraline continued her walk.

She was three quarters of the way around the house when she saw Miss Forcible, standing at the door to the flat she shared with Miss Spink.

"Have you seen Miss Spink, Caroline?"

Coraline told her that she had, and that Miss Spink was out walking the dogs.

"I do hope she doesn't get lost—it'll bring on her shingles if she does, you'll see," said Miss Forcible. "You'd have to be an explorer to find your way around in this fog."

"I'm an explorer," said Coraline.

"Of course you are, luvvy," said Miss Forcible. "Don't get lost, now."

Coraline continued walking through the gardens in the gray mist. She always kept in sight of the house. After about ten minutes of walking she found herself back where she had started.

The hair over her eyes was limp and wet, and her face felt damp.

"Ahoy! Caroline!" called the crazy old man upstairs.

"Oh, hullo," said Coraline.

She could hardly see the old man through the mist.

He walked down the steps on the outside of the house that led up past Coraline's front door to the door of his flat. He walked down very slowly. Coraline waited at the bottom of the stairs.

"The mice do not like the mist," he told her. "It makes their whiskers droop."

"I don't like the mist much, either," admitted Coraline.

The old man leaned down, so close that the bottoms of his mustache tickled Coraline's ear. "The mice have a message for you," he whispered.

Coraline didn't know what to say.

"The message is this. *Don't go through the door.*" He paused. "Does that mean anything to you?"

"No," said Coraline.

The old man shrugged. "They are funny, the mice. They get things wrong. They got your name wrong, you know. They kept saying Coraline. Not Caroline. Not Caroline at all."

He picked up a milk bottle from the bottom of the stairs and started back up to his attic flat.

Coraline went indoors. Her mother was working in her study. Her mother's study smelled of flowers.

"What shall I do?" asked Coraline.

"When do you go back to school?" asked her mother.

"Next week," said Coraline.

"Hmph," said her mother. "I suppose I shall have to get you new school clothes. Remind me, dear, or else I'll forget," and she went back to typing things on the computer screen.

"What shall I *do*?" repeated Coraline.

"Draw something," Her mother passed her a sheet of paper and a ballpoint pen.

Coraline tried drawing the mist. After ten minutes of drawing she still had a white sheet of paper with

    M   T

            S

      I

written on it in one corner in slightly wiggly letters. She grunted and passed it to her mother.

"Mm. Very modern, dear," said Coraline's mother.

Coraline crept into the drawing room and tried to open the old door in the corner. It was locked once more. She supposed her mother must have locked it again. She shrugged.

Coraline went to see her father.

He had his back to the door as he typed. "Go away," he said cheerfully as she walked in.

"I'm bored," she said.

"Learn how to tap-dance," he suggested, without turning around.

Coraline shook her head. "Why don't you play with me?" she asked.

"Busy," he said. "Working," he added. He still hadn't turned around to look at her. "Why don't you go and bother Miss Spink and Miss Forcible?"

Coraline put on her coat and pulled up her hood and went out of the house. She went downstairs. She rang the door of Miss Spink and Miss Forcible's flat. Coraline could hear a frenzied woofing as the Scottie dogs ran out into the hall. After a while Miss Spink opened the door.

"Oh, it's you, Caroline," she said. "Angus, Hamish, Bruce, down now, luvvies. It's only Caroline. Come in, dear. Would you like a cup of tea?"

The flat smelled of furniture polish and dogs.

"Yes, please," said Coraline. Miss Spink led her into a dusty little room, which she called the parlor. On the walls were black-and-white photographs of pretty women, and theater programs in frames. Miss Forcible was sitting in one of the armchairs, knitting hard.

They poured Coraline a cup of tea in a little pink bone china cup, with a saucer. They gave her a dry Garibaldi biscuit to go with it.

Miss Forcible looked at Miss Spink, picked up her knitting, and took a deep breath. "Anyway, April. As I was saying: you still have to admit, there's life in the old dog yet."

"Miriam, dear, neither of us is as young as we were."

"Madame Arcati," replied Miss Forcible. "The nurse in *Romeo*. Lady Bracknell. Character parts. They can't retire you from the stage."

"Now, Miriam, we *agreed*," said Miss Spink. Coraline wondered if they'd forgotten she was there. They weren't making much sense; she decided they were having an argument as old and comfortable as an armchair, the kind of argument that no one ever really wins or loses but which can go on forever, if both parties are willing.

She sipped her tea.

"I'll read the leaves, if you want," said Miss Spink to Coraline.

"Sorry?" said Coraline.

"The tea leaves, dear. I'll read your future."

Coraline passed Miss Spink her cup. Miss Spink peered shortsightedly at the black tea leaves in the bottom. She pursed her lips.

"You know, Caroline," she said, after a while, "you are in terrible danger."

Miss Forcible snorted, and put down her knitting. "Don't be silly, April. Stop scaring the girl. Your eyes are going. Pass me that cup, child."

Coraline carried the cup over to Miss Forcible. Miss Forcible looked into it carefully, shook her head, and looked into it again.

"Oh dear," she said. "You were right, April. She *is* in danger."

"See, Miriam," said Miss Spink triumphantly. "My eyes are as good as they ever were. . . ."

"What am I in danger from?" asked Coraline.

Misses Spink and Forcible stared at her blankly. "It didn't say," said Miss Spink. "Tea leaves aren't reliable for that kind of thing. Not really. They're good for general, but not for specifics."

"What should I do then?" asked Coraline, who was slightly alarmed by this.

"Don't wear green in your dressing room," suggested Miss Spink.

"Or mention the Scottish play," added Miss Forcible.

Coraline wondered why so few of the adults she had met made any sense. She sometimes wondered who they thought they were talking to.

"And be very, very careful," said Miss Spink. She got up from the armchair and went over to the fireplace. On the mantelpiece was a small jar, and Miss Spink took off the top of the jar and began to pull things out of it. There was a tiny china duck, a thimble, a strange little brass coin, two paper clips and a stone with a hole in it.

She passed Coraline the stone with a hole in it.

"What's it for?" asked Coraline. The hole went all the way through the middle of the stone. She held it up to the window and looked through it.

"It might help," said Miss Spink. "They're good for bad things, sometimes."

Coraline put on her coat, said good-bye to Misses Spink and Forcible and to the dogs, and went outside.

The mist hung like blindness around the house. She walked slowly to the stairs up to her family's flat, and then stopped and looked around.

In the mist, it was a ghost-world. *In danger?* thought Coraline to herself. It sounded exciting. It didn't sound like a bad thing. Not really.

Coraline went back upstairs, her fist closed tightly around her new stone.

III.

THE NEXT DAY THE sun shone, and Coraline's mother took her into the nearest large town to buy clothes for school. They dropped her father off at the railway station. He was going into London for the day to see some people.

Coraline waved him good-bye.

They went to the department store to buy the school clothes.

Coraline saw some Day-Glo green gloves she liked a lot. Her mother refused to buy them for her, preferring instead to buy white socks, navy blue school underpants, four gray blouses, and a dark gray skirt.

"But Mum, *everybody* at school's got gray blouses and everything. *Nobody's* got green gloves. I could be the only one."

Her mother ignored her; she was talking to the shop assistant. They were talking about which kind of sweater to get for Coraline, and were agreeing that the best thing to do would be to get one that was embarrassingly large and baggy, in the hopes that one day she might grow into it.

Coraline wandered off and looked at a display of Wellington boots shaped like frogs and ducks and rabbits.

Then she wandered back.

"Coraline? Oh, there you are. Where on earth were you?"

"I was kidnapped by aliens," said Coraline. "They came down from outer space with ray guns, but I fooled them by wearing a wig and laughing in a foreign accent, and I escaped."

"Yes, dear. Now, I think you could do with some more hair clips, don't you?"

"No."

"Well, let's say half a dozen, to be on the safe side," said her mother.

Coraline didn't say anything.

In the car on the way back home, Coraline said, "What's in the empty flat?"

"I don't know. Nothing, I expect. It probably looks like our flat before we moved in. Empty rooms."

"Do you think you could get into it from our flat?"

"Not unless you can walk through bricks, dear."

"Oh."

They got home around lunchtime. The sun was shining, although the day was cold. Coraline's mother looked in the fridge and found a sad little tomato and a piece of cheese with green stuff growing on it. There was only a crust in the bread bin.

"I'd better dash down to the shops and get some fish fingers or something," said her mother. "Do you want to come?"

"No," said Coraline.

"Suit yourself," said her mother, and left. Then she came back and got her purse and car keys and went out again.

Coraline was bored.

She flipped through a book her mother was reading about native people in a distant country; how every day they would take pieces of white silk and draw on them in wax, then dip the silks in dye, then draw on them more in wax and dye them some more, then boil the wax out in hot water, and then finally, throw the now-beautiful cloths on a fire and burn them to ashes.

It seemed particularly pointless to Coraline, but she hoped that the people enjoyed it.

She was still bored, and her mother wasn't yet home.

Coraline got a chair and pushed it over to the kitchen door. She climbed onto the chair and reached up. She got down, then got a broom from the broom cupboard. She climbed back on the chair again and reached up with the broom.

Chink.

She climbed down from the chair and picked up the keys. She smiled triumphantly. Then she leaned the broom against the wall and went into the drawing room.

The family did not use the drawing room. They had inherited the furniture from Coraline's grandmother, along with a wooden coffee table, a side table, a heavy glass ash-tray, and the oil painting of a bowl of fruit. Coraline could never work out why anyone would want to paint a bowl of fruit. Other than that, the room was empty: there were no knickknacks on the mantelpiece, no statues or clocks; nothing that made it feel comfortable or lived-in.

The old black key felt colder than any of the others. She pushed it into the keyhole. It turned smoothly, with a sat-isfying *clunk*.

Coraline stopped and listened. She knew she was doing something wrong, and she was trying to listen for her mother coming back, but she heard nothing. Then Coraline put her hand on the doorknob and turned it; and, finally, she opened the door.

It opened on to a dark hallway. The bricks had gone as if they'd never been there. There was a cold, musty smell coming through the open doorway: it smelled like some-thing very old and very slow.

Coraline went through the door.

She wondered what the empty flat would be like—if

that was where the corridor led.

Coraline walked down the corridor uneasily. There was something very familiar about it.

The carpet beneath her feet was the same carpet they had in her flat. The wallpaper was the same wallpaper they had. The picture hanging in the hall was the same that they had hanging in their hallway at home.

She knew where she was: she was in her own home. She hadn't left.

She shook her head, confused.

She stared at the picture hanging on the wall: no, it wasn't exactly the same. The picture they had in their own hallway showed a boy in old-fashioned clothes staring at some bubbles. But now the expression on his face was different—he was looking at the bubbles as if he was planning to do something very nasty indeed to them. And there was something peculiar about his eyes.

Coraline stared at his eyes, trying to figure out what exactly was different.

She almost had it when somebody said, "Coraline?"

It sounded like her mother. Coraline went into the kitchen, where the voice had come from. A woman stood in the kitchen with her back to Coraline. She looked a little like Coraline's mother. Only . . .

Only her skin was white as paper.

Only she was taller and thinner.

Only her fingers were too long, and they never stopped moving, and her dark red fingernails were curved and sharp.

"Coraline?" the woman said. "Is that you?"

And then she turned around. Her eyes were big black buttons.

"Lunchtime, Coraline," said the woman.

"Who are you?" asked Coraline.

"I'm your other mother," said the woman. "Go and tell your other father that lunch is ready." She opened the door of the oven. Suddenly Coraline realized how hungry she was. It smelled wonderful. "Well, go on."

Coraline went down the hall, to where her father's study was. She opened the door. There was a man in there, sitting at the keyboard, with his back to her. "Hello," said Coraline. "I—I mean, she said to say that lunch is ready."

The man turned around.

His eyes were buttons, big and black and shiny.

"Hello Coraline," he said. "I'm starving."

He got up and went with her into the kitchen. They sat at the kitchen table, and Coraline's other mother brought them lunch. A huge, golden-brown roasted chicken, fried potatoes, tiny green peas. Coraline shoveled the food into her mouth. It tasted wonderful.

"We've been waiting for you for a long time," said Coraline's other father.

"For me?"

"Yes," said the other mother. "It wasn't the same here without you. But we knew you'd arrive one day, and then we could be a proper family. Would you like some more chicken?"

It was the best chicken that Coraline had ever eaten. Her mother sometimes made chicken, but it was always out of packets or frozen, and was very dry, and it never tasted of anything. When Coraline's father cooked chicken he bought real chicken, but he did strange things to it, like stewing it in wine, or stuffing it with prunes, or baking it in pastry, and Coraline would always refuse to touch it on principle.

She took some more chicken.

"I didn't know I had another mother," said Coraline, cautiously.

"Of course you do. Everyone does," said the other mother, her black button eyes gleaming. "After lunch I thought you might like to play in your room with the rats."

"The rats?"

"From upstairs."

Coraline had never seen a rat, except on television. She was quite looking forward to it. This was turning out to be a very interesting day after all.

After lunch her other parents did the washing up, and Coraline went down the hall to her other bedroom.

It was different from her bedroom at home. For a start it was painted in an off-putting shade of green and a peculiar shade of pink.

Coraline decided that she wouldn't want to have to sleep in there, but that the color scheme was an awful lot more interesting than her own bedroom.

There were all sorts of remarkable things in there she'd never seen before: windup angels that fluttered around the bedroom like startled sparrows; books with pictures that writhed and crawled and shimmered; little dinosaur skulls that chattered their teeth as she passed. A whole toy box filled with wonderful toys.

This is more like it, thought Coraline. She looked out of the window. Outside, the view was the same one she saw from her own bedroom: trees, fields, and beyond them, on the horizon, distant purple hills.

Something black scurried across the floor and vanished under the bed. Coraline got down on her knees and looked under the bed. Fifty little red eyes stared back at her.

"Hello," said Coraline. "Are you the rats?"

They came out from under the bed, blinking their eyes

in the light. They had short, soot-black fur, little red eyes, pink paws like tiny hands, and pink, hairless tails like long, smooth worms.

"Can you talk?" she asked.

The largest, blackest of the rats shook its head. It had an unpleasant sort of smile, Coraline thought.

"Well," asked Coraline, "what *do* you do?"

The rats formed a circle.

Then they began to climb on top of each other, carefully but swiftly, until they had formed a pyramid with the largest rat at the top.

The rats began to sing, in high, whispery voices,

We have teeth and we have tails
We have tails we have eyes
We were here before you fell
You will be here when we rise.

It wasn't a pretty song. Coraline was sure she'd heard it before, or something like it, although she was unable to remember exactly where.

Then the pyramid fell apart, and the rats scampered, fast and black, toward the door.

The other crazy old man upstairs was standing in the doorway, holding a tall black hat in his hands. The rats scampered up him, burrowing into his pockets, into his shirt, up his trouser legs, down his neck.

The largest rat climbed onto the old man's shoulders, swung up on the long gray mustache, past the big black button eyes, and onto the top of the man's head.

In seconds the only evidence that the rats were there at all were the restless lumps under the man's clothes, forever sliding from place to place across him; and there was still the largest rat, who stared down, with glittering red eyes, at Coraline from the man's head.

The old man put his hat on, and the last rat was gone.

"Hello Coraline," said the other old man upstairs. "I heard you were here. It is time for the rats to have their dinner. But you can come up with me, if you like, and watch them feed."

There was something hungry in the old man's button eyes that made Coraline feel uncomfortable. "No, thank you," she said. "I'm going outside to explore."

The old man nodded, very slowly. Coraline could hear the rats whispering to each other, although she could not tell what they were saying.

She was not certain that she wanted to know what they were saying.

Her other parents stood in the kitchen doorway as she walked down the corridor, smiling identical smiles, and waving slowly. "Have a nice time outside," said her other mother.

"We'll just wait here for you to come back," said her other father.

When Coraline got to the front door, she turned back and looked at them. They were still watching her, and waving, and smiling.

Coraline walked outside, and down the steps.

IV.

THE HOUSE LOOKED EXACTLY the same from the outside. Or almost exactly the same: around Miss Spink and Miss Forcible's door were blue and red lightbulbs that flashed on and off spelling out words, the lights chasing each other around the door. On and off, around and around. ASTOUNDING! was followed by A THEATRICAL and then TRIUMPH!!!

It was a sunny, cold day, exactly like the one she'd left.

There was a polite noise from behind her.

She turned around. Standing on the wall next to her was a large black cat, identical to the large black cat she'd seen in the grounds at home.

"Good afternoon," said the cat.

Its voice sounded like the voice at the back of Coraline's head, the voice she thought words in, but a man's voice, not a girl's.

"Hello," said Coraline. "I saw a cat like you in the garden at home. You must be the other cat."

The cat shook its head. "No," it said. "I'm not the other

anything. I'm me." It tipped its head to one side; green eyes glinted. "You people are spread all over the place. Cats, on the other hand, keep ourselves together. If you see what I mean."

"I suppose. But if you're the same cat I saw at home, how can you talk?"

Cats don't have shoulders, not like people do. But the cat shrugged, in one smooth movement that started at the tip of its tail and ended in a raised movement of its whiskers. "I can talk."

"Cats don't talk at home."

"No?" said the cat.

"No," said Coraline.

The cat leaped smoothly from the wall to the grass near Coraline's feet. It stared up at her.

"Well, you're the expert on these things," said the cat dryly. "After all, what would I know? I'm only a cat."

It began to walk away, head and tail held high and proud.

"Come back," said Coraline. "Please. I'm sorry. I really am."

The cat stopped walking, sat down, and began to wash itself thoughtfully, apparently unaware of Coraline's existence.

"We . . . we could be friends, you know," said Coraline.

"We *could* be rare specimens of an exotic breed of African dancing elephants," said the cat. "But we're not. At least," it added cattily, after darting a brief look at Coraline, "*I'm* not."

Coraline sighed.

"Please. What's your name?" Coraline asked the cat. "Look, I'm Coraline. Okay?"

The cat yawned slowly, carefully, revealing a mouth and tongue of astounding pinkness. "Cats don't have names," it said.

"No?" said Coraline.

"No," said the cat. "Now, *you* people have names. That's because you don't know who you are. We know who we are, so we don't need names."

There was something irritatingly self-centered about the cat, Coraline decided. As if it were, in its opinion, the only thing in any world or place that could possibly be of any importance.

Half of her wanted to be very rude to it; the other half of her wanted to be polite and deferential. The polite half won.

"Please, what is this place?"

The cat glanced around briefly. "It's here," said the cat.

"I can see that. Well, how did you get here?"

"Like you did. I walked," said the cat. "Like this."

Coraline watched as the cat walked slowly across the lawn. It walked behind a tree, but didn't come out the other side. Coraline went over to the tree and looked behind it. The cat was gone.

She walked back toward the house. There was another polite noise from behind her. It was the cat.

"By the by," it said. "It was sensible of you to bring protection. I'd hang on to it, if I were you."

"Protection?"

"That's what I said," said the cat. "And anyway—"

It paused, and stared intently at something that wasn't there.

Then it went down into a low crouch and moved slowly forward, two or three steps. It seemed to be stalking an invisible mouse. Abruptly, it turned tail and dashed for the woods.

It vanished among the trees.

Coraline wondered what the cat had meant.

She also wondered whether cats could all talk where she came from and just chose not to, or whether they could only talk when they were here—wherever *here* was.

She walked down the brick steps to the Misses Spink and Forcible's front door. The blue and red lights flashed on and off.

The door was open, just slightly. She knocked on it, but

her first knock made the door swing open, and Coraline went in.

She was in a dark room that smelled of dust and velvet. The door swung shut behind her, and the room was black. Coraline edged forward into a small anteroom. Her face brushed against something soft. It was cloth. She reached up her hand and pushed at the cloth. It parted.

She stood blinking on the other side of the velvet curtains, in a poorly lit theater. Far away, at the edge of the room, was a high wooden stage, empty and bare, a dim spotlight shining onto it from high above.

There were seats between Coraline and the stage. Rows and rows of seats. She heard a shuffling noise, and a light came toward her, swinging from side to side. When it was closer she saw the light was coming from a flashlight being carried in the mouth of a large black Scottie dog, its muzzle gray with age.

"Hello," said Coraline.

The dog put the flashlight down on the floor, and looked up at her. "Right. Let's see your ticket," he said gruffly.

"Ticket?"

"That's what I said. Ticket. I haven't got all day, you know. You can't watch the show without a ticket."

Coraline sighed. "I don't have a ticket," she admitted.

"Another one," said the dog gloomily. "Come in here,

bold as anything. 'Where's your ticket?' 'Haven't got one,' I don't know . . .'" It shook its head, then shrugged. "Come on, then."

He picked up the flashlight in his mouth and trotted off into the dark. Coraline followed him. When he got near the front of the stage he stopped and shone the flashlight onto an empty seat. Coraline sat down, and the dog wandered off.

As her eyes got used to the darkness she realized that the other inhabitants of the seats were also dogs.

There was a sudden hissing noise from behind the stage. Coraline decided it was the sound of a scratchy old record being put onto a record player. The hissing became the noise of trumpets, and Miss Spink and Miss Forcible came onto the stage.

Miss Spink was riding a one-wheeled bicycle and juggling balls. Miss Forcible skipped behind her, holding a basket of flowers. She scattered the flower petals across the stage as she went. They reached the front of the stage, and Miss Spink leaped nimbly off the unicycle, and the two old women bowed low.

All the dogs thumped their tails and barked enthusiastically. Coraline clapped politely.

Then they unbuttoned their fluffy round coats and opened them. But their coats weren't all that opened: their faces opened, too, like empty shells, and out of the old empty fluffy round bodies stepped two young women. They were thin, and pale, and quite pretty, and had black button eyes.

The new Miss Spink was wearing green tights, and high brown boots that went most of the way up her legs. The new Miss Forcible wore a white dress and had flowers in her long yellow hair.

Coraline pressed back against her seat.

Miss Spink went off the stage, and the noise of trumpets squealed as the gramophone needle dug its way across the record, and was pulled off.

"This is my favorite bit," whispered the little dog in the seat next to her.

The other Miss Forcible picked a knife out of a box on the corner of the stage. "Is this a dagger that I see before me?" she asked.

"Yes!" shouted all the little dogs. "It is!"

Miss Forcible curtsied, and all the dogs applauded again. Coraline didn't bother clapping this time.

Miss Spink came back on. She slapped her thigh, and all the little dogs woofed.

"And now," Miss Spink said, "Miriam and I proudly present a new and exciting addendum to our theatrical exposition. Do I see a volunteer?"

The little dog next to Coraline nudged her with its front

paw. "That's you," it hissed.

Coraline stood up, and walked up the wooden steps to the stage.

"Can I have big round of applause for the young volunteer?" asked Miss Spink. The dogs woofed and squealed and thumped their tails on the velvet seats.

"Now Coraline," said Miss Spink, "what's your name?"

"Coraline," said Coraline.

"And we don't know each other, do we?"

Coraline looked at the thin young woman with black button eyes and shook her head slowly.

"Now," said the other Miss Spink, "stand over here." She led Coraline over to a board by the side of the stage, and put a balloon on top of Coraline's head.

Miss Spink walked over to Miss Forcible. She blindfolded Miss Forcible's button eyes with a black scarf, and put the knife into her hands. Then she turned her round three or four times and pointed her at Coraline. Coraline held her breath and squeezed her fingers into two tight fists.

Miss Forcible threw the knife at the balloon. It popped loudly, and the knife stuck into the board just above Coraline's head and twanged there. Coraline breathed out.

The dogs went wild.

Miss Spink gave Coraline a very small box of chocolates

and thanked her for being such a good sport. Coraline went back to her seat.

"You were very good," said the little dog.

"Thank you," said Coraline.

Miss Forcible and Miss Spink began juggling with huge wooden clubs. Coraline opened the box of chocolates. The dog looked at them longingly.

"Would you like one?" she asked the little dog.

"Yes, please," whispered the dog. "Only not toffee ones. They make me drool."

"I thought chocolates weren't very good for dogs," she said, remembering something Miss Forcible had once told her.

"Maybe where you come from," whispered the little dog. "Here, it's all we eat."

Coraline couldn't see what the chocolates were, in the dark. She took an experimental bite of one which turned out to be coconut. Coraline didn't like coconut. She gave it to the dog.

"Thank you," said the dog.

"You're welcome," said Coraline.

Miss Forcible and Miss Spink were doing some acting. Miss Forcible was sitting on a stepladder, and Miss Spink was standing at the bottom.

"What's in a name?" asked Miss Forcible. "That which

we call a rose by any other name would smell as sweet."

"Have you got any more chocolates?" said the dog.

Coraline gave the dog another chocolate.

"I know not how to tell thee who I am," said Miss Spink to Miss Forcible.

"This bit finishes soon," whispered the dog. "Then they start folk dancing."

"How long does this go on for?" asked Coraline. "The theater?"

"All the time," said the dog. "For ever and always."

"Here," said Coraline. "Keep the chocolates."

"Thank you," said the dog. Coraline stood up.

"See you soon," said the dog.

"Bye," said Coraline. She walked out of the theater and back into the garden. She had to blink her eyes at the daylight.

Her other parents were waiting for her in the garden, standing side by side. They were smiling.

"Did you have a nice time?" asked her other mother.

"It was interesting," said Coraline.

The three of them walked back up to Coraline's other house together. Coraline's other mother stroked Coraline's hair with her long white fingers. Coraline shook her head. "Don't do that," said Coraline.

Her other mother took her hand away.

"So," said her other father. "Do you like it here?"

"I suppose," said Coraline. "It's much more interesting than at home."

They went inside.

"I'm glad you like it," said Coraline's mother. "Because we'd like to think that this is your home. You can stay here for ever and always. If you want to."

"Hmm," said Coraline. She put her hand in her pockets, and thought about it. Her hand touched the stone that the real Misses Spink and Forcible had given her the day before, the stone with the hole in it.

"If you want to stay," said her other father, "there's only one little thing we'll have to do, so you can stay here for ever and always."

They went into the kitchen. On a china plate on the kitchen table was a spool of black cotton, and a long silver needle, and, beside them, two large black buttons.

"I don't think so," said Coraline.

"Oh, but we want you to," said her other mother. "We want you to stay. And it's just a little thing."

"It won't hurt," said her other father.

Coraline knew that when grown-ups told you something wouldn't hurt it almost always did. She shook her head.

Her other mother smiled brightly and the hair on her head drifted like plants under the sea. "We only want what's best for you," she said.

She put her hand on Coraline's shoulder. Coraline backed away.

"I'm going now," said Coraline. She put her hands in her pockets. Her fingers closed around the stone with the hole in it.

Her other mother's hand scuttled off Coraline's shoulder like a frightened spider.

"If that's what you want," she said.

"Yes," said Coraline.

"We'll see you soon, though," said her other father. "When you come back."

"Um," said Coraline.

"And then we'll all be together as one big happy family," said her other mother. "For ever and always."

Coraline backed away. She turned and hurried into the drawing room and pulled open the door in the corner. There was no brick wall there now—just darkness, a night-black underground darkness that seemed as if things in it might be moving.

Coraline hesitated. She turned back. Her other mother and her other father were walking toward her, holding hands. They were looking at her with their black button eyes. Or at least she *thought* they were looking at her. She couldn't be sure.

Her other mother reached out her free hand and beckoned, gently, with one white finger. Her pale lips mouthed, "Come back soon," although she said nothing aloud.

Coraline took a deep breath and stepped into the darkness, where strange voices whispered and distant winds howled. She became certain that there was something in the dark behind her: something very old and very slow. Her heart beat so hard and so loudly she was scared it would burst out of her chest. She closed her eyes against the dark.

Eventually she bumped into something, and opened her eyes, startled. She had bumped into an armchair, in her drawing room.

The open doorway behind her was blocked by rough red bricks.

She was home.

V.

ORALINE LOCKED THE DOOR of the drawing room with the cold black key.

She went back into the kitchen and climbed onto a chair. She tried to put the bunch of keys back on top of the doorframe again. She tried four or five times before she was forced to accept that she just wasn't big enough, and she put them down on the counter next to the door.

Her mother still hadn't returned from her shopping expedition.

Coraline went to the freezer and took out the spare loaf of frozen bread in the bottom compartment. She made herself some toast, with jam and peanut butter. She drank a glass of water.

She waited for her parents to come back.

When it began to get dark, Coraline microwaved herself a frozen pizza.

Then Coraline watched television. She wondered why grown-ups gave themselves all the good programs, with all the shouting and running around in.

After a while she started yawning. Then she undressed, brushed her teeth, and put herself to bed.

In the morning she went into her parents' room, but their bed hadn't been slept in, and they weren't around. She ate canned spaghetti for breakfast.

For lunch she had a block of cooking chocolate and an apple. The apple was yellow and slightly shriveled, but it tasted sweet and good.

For tea she went down to see Misses Spink and Forcible. She had three digestive biscuits, a glass of limeade, and a cup of weak tea. The limeade was very interesting. It didn't taste anything like limes. It tasted bright green and vaguely chemical. Coraline liked it enormously. She wished they had it at home.

"How are your dear mother and father?" asked Miss Spink.

"Missing," said Coraline. "I haven't seen either of them since yesterday. I'm on my own. I think I've probably become a single child family."

"Tell your mother that we found the Glasgow Empire press clippings we were telling her about. She seemed very interested when Miriam mentioned them to her."

"She's vanished under mysterious circumstances," said Coraline, "and I believe my father has as well."

"I'm afraid we'll be out all day tomorrow, Caroline,

luvvy," said Miss Forcible. "We'll be staying over with April's niece in Royal Tunbridge Wells."

They showed Coraline a photographic album, with photographs of Miss Spink's niece in it, and then Coraline went home.

She opened her money box and walked down to the supermarket. She bought two large bottles of limeade, a chocolate cake, and a new bag of apples, and went back home and ate them for dinner.

She cleaned her teeth, and went into her father's office. She woke up his computer and wrote a story.

CORALINE'S STORY.

THERE WAS A GIRL HER NAME WAS APPLE. SHE USED TO DANCE A LOT. SHE DANCED AND DANCED UNTIL HER FEET TURND INTO SOSSAJES THE END.

She printed out the story and turned off the computer. Then she drew a picture of the little girl dancing underneath the words on the paper.

She ran herself a bath with too much bubble bath in it, and the bubbles ran over the side and went all over the floor. She dried herself, and the floor as best she could, and went to bed.

Coraline woke up in the night. She went into her parents' bedroom, but the bed was made and empty. The glowing green numbers on the digital clock glowed 3:12 A.M.

All alone, in the middle of the night, Coraline began to cry. There was no other sound in the empty flat.

She climbed into her parents' bed, and, after a while, she went to sleep.

Coraline was woken by cold paws batting her face. She opened her eyes. Big green eyes stared back at her. It was the cat.

"Hullo," said Coraline. "How did you get in?"

The cat didn't say anything. Coraline got out of bed. She was wearing a long T-shirt and pajama bottoms. "Have you come to tell me something?"

The cat yawned, which made its eyes flash green.

"Do you know where Mummy and Daddy are?"

The cat blinked at her, slowly.

"Is that a yes?"

The cat blinked again. Coraline decided that that was indeed a yes. "Will you take me to them?"

The cat stared at her. Then it walked out into the hall. She followed it. It walked the length of the corridor and stopped down at the very end, where a full-length mirror hung. The mirror had been, a long time before, the inside of a wardrobe door. It had been hanging there on the wall when they moved in, and, although Coraline's mother had spoken occasionally of replacing it with something newer, she never had.

Coraline turned on the light in the hall.

The mirror showed the corridor behind her; that was only to be expected. But reflected in the mirror were her parents. They stood awkwardly in the reflection of the hall. They seemed sad and alone. As Coraline watched, they waved to her, slowly, with limp hands. Coraline's father had his arm around her mother.

In the mirror Coraline's mother and father stared at her. Her father opened his mouth and said something, but she could hear nothing at all. Her mother breathed on the inside of the mirror glass, and quickly, before the fog faded, she wrote

HELP US

with the tip of her forefinger. The fog on the inside of the mirror faded, and so did her parents, and now the mirror reflected only the corridor, and Coraline, and the cat.

"Where are they?" Coraline asked the cat. The cat made no reply, but Coraline could imagine its voice, dry as a dead fly on a windowsill in winter, saying *Well, where do you think they are?*

"They aren't going to come back, are they?" said Coraline. "Not under their own steam."

The cat blinked at her. Coraline took it as a yes.

"Right," said Coraline. "Then I suppose there is only one thing left to do."

She walked into her father's study. She sat down at his desk. Then she picked up the telephone, and she opened the phone book and telephoned the local police station.

"Police," said a gruff male voice.

"Hello," she said. "My name is Coraline Jones."

"You're up a bit after your bedtime, aren't you, young lady?" said the policeman.

"Possibly," said Coraline, who was not going to be diverted, "but I am ringing to report a crime."

"And what sort of crime would that be?"

"Kidnapping. Grown-up-napping really. My parents have been stolen away into a world on the other side of the mirror in our hall."

"And do you know who stole them?" asked the police officer. Coraline could hear the smile in his voice, and she tried extra hard to sound like an adult might sound, to make him take her seriously.

"I think my other mother has them both in her

clutches. She may want to keep them and sew their eyes with black buttons, or she may simply have them in order to lure me back into reach of her fingers. I'm not sure."

"Ah. The nefarious clutches of her fiendish fingers, is it?" he said. "Mm. You know what I suggest, Miss Jones?"

"No," said Coraline. "What?"

"You ask your mother to make you a big old mug of hot chocolate, and then give you a great big old hug. There's nothing like hot chocolate and a hug for making the nightmares go away. And if she starts to tell you off for waking her up at this time of night, why you tell her that that's what the policeman said." He had a deep, reassuring voice.

Coraline was not reassured.

"When I see her," said Coraline, "I shall tell her that." And she put down the telephone.

The black cat, who had sat on the floor, grooming his fur, through this entire conversation now stood up and led the way into the hall.

Coraline went back into her bedroom and put on her blue dressing gown and her slippers. She looked under the sink for a flashlight, and found one, but the batteries had long since run down, and it barely glowed with the faintest straw-colored light. She put it down again and found a box of in-case-of-emergency white wax candles, and thrust one into a candlestick. She put an apple into each pocket. She picked up the ring of keys and took the old black key off the ring.

She walked into the drawing room and looked at the door. She had the feeling that the door was looking at her, which she knew was silly, and knew on a deeper level was somehow true.

She went back into her bedroom, and rummaged in the pocket of her jeans. She found the stone with the hole in it, and put it into her dressing-gown pocket.

She lit the candlewick with a match and watched it sputter and light, then she picked up the black key. It was cold in her hand. She put it into the keyhole in the door, but did not turn the key.

"When I was a little girl," said Coraline to the cat, "when we lived in our old house, a long, long time ago, my dad took me for a walk on the wasteland between our house and the shops.

"It wasn't the best place to go for a walk, really. There were all these things that people had thrown away back there—old cookers and broken dishes and dolls with no arms and no legs and empty cans and broken bottles. Mum and Dad made me promise not to go exploring back there, because there were too many sharp things, and tetanus and such.

"But I kept telling them I wanted to explore it. So one day my dad put on his big brown boots and his gloves and put my boots on me and my jeans and sweater, and we went for a walk.

"We must have walked for about twenty minutes. We went down this hill, to the bottom of a gully where a stream was, when my dad suddenly said to me, "Coraline—run away. Up the hill. Now!" He said it in a tight sort of way, urgently, so I did. I ran away up the hill. Something hurt me on the back of my arm as I ran, but I kept running.

"As I got to the top of the hill I heard somebody thundering up the hill behind me. It was my dad, charging like a rhino. When he reached me he picked me up in his arms and swept me over the edge of the hill.

"And then we stopped and we puffed and we panted, and we looked back down the gully.

"The air was alive with yellow wasps. We must have stepped on a wasps' nest in a rotten branch as we walked. And while I was running up the hill, my dad stayed and got stung, to give me time to run away. His glasses had fallen off when he ran.

"I only had the one sting on the back of my arm. He had thirty-nine stings, all over him. We counted later, in the bath."

The black cat began to wash its face and whiskers in a manner that indicated increasing impatience. Coraline reached down and stroked the back of its head and neck. The cat stood up, walked several paces until it was out of her reach, then it sat down and looked up at her again.

"So," said Coraline, "later that afternoon my dad went back again to the wasteland, to get his glasses back. He said if he left it another day he wouldn't be able to remember where they'd fallen.

"And soon he got home, wearing his glasses. He said that he wasn't scared when he was standing there and the wasps were stinging him and hurting him and he was watching me run away. Because he knew he had to give me enough time to run, or the wasps would have come after both of us."

Coraline turned the key in the door. It turned with a loud *clunk*.

The door swung open.

There was no brick wall on the other side of the door: only darkness. A cold wind blew through the passageway.

Coraline made no move to walk through the door.

"And he said that wasn't brave of him, doing that, just standing there and being stung," said Coraline to the cat. "It wasn't brave because he wasn't scared: it was the only thing he could do. But going back again to get his glasses, when he knew the wasps were there, when he was really scared. *That* was brave."

She took her first step down the dark corridor.

She could smell dust and damp and mustiness.

The cat padded along beside her.

"And why was that?" asked the cat, although it sounded barely interested.

"Because," she said, "when you're scared but you still do it anyway, *that's* brave."

The candle cast huge, strange, flickering shadows along the wall. She heard something moving in the darkness— beside her or to one side of her, she could not tell. It seemed as if it was keeping pace with her, whatever it was.

"And that's why you're going back to *her* world, then?" said the cat. "Because your father once saved you from wasps?"

"Don't be silly," said Coraline. "I'm going back for them because they are my parents. And if they noticed I was gone I'm sure they would do the same for me. You know you're talking again?"

"How fortunate I am," said the cat, "in having a traveling companion of such wisdom and intelligence." Its tone remained sarcastic, but its fur was bristling, and its brush of a tail stuck up in the air.

Coraline was going to say something, like *sorry* or *wasn't it a lot shorter walk last time?* when the candle went out as suddenly as if it had been snuffed by someone's hand.

There was a scrabbling and a pattering, and Coraline could feel her heart pounding against her ribs. She put out one hand . . . and felt something wispy, like a spider's web, brush her hands and her face.

At the end of the corridor the electric light went on, blinding after the darkness. A woman stood, silhouetted by the light, a little ahead of Coraline.

"Coraline? Darling?" she called.

"Mum!" said Coraline, and she ran forward, eager and relieved.

"Darling," said the woman. "Why did you ever run away from me?"

Coraline was too close to stop, and she felt the other mother's cold arms enfold her. She stood there, rigid and trembling as the other mother held her tightly.

"Where are my parents?" Coraline asked.

"We're here," said her other mother, in a voice so close to her real mother's that Coraline could scarcely tell them apart. "We're here. We're ready to love you and play with you and feed you and make your life interesting."

Coraline pulled back, and the other mother let her go, with reluctance.

The other father, who had been sitting on a chair in the

hallway, stood up and smiled. "Come on into the kitchen," he said. "I'll make us a midnight snack. And you'll want something to drink—hot chocolate perhaps?"

Coraline walked down the hallway until she reached the mirror at the end. There was nothing reflected in it but a young girl in her dressing gown and slippers, who looked like she had recently been crying but whose eyes were real eyes, not black buttons, and who was holding tightly to a burned-out candle in a candlestick.

She looked at the girl in the mirror and the girl in the mirror looked back at her.

I will be brave, thought Coraline. *No, I am brave.*

She put down the candlestick on the floor, then turned around. The other mother and the other father were looking at her hungrily.

"I don't need a snack," she said. "I have an apple. See?" And she took an apple from her dressing-gown pocket, then bit into it with relish and an enthusiasm that she did not really feel.

The other father looked disappointed. The other mother smiled, showing a full set of teeth, and each of the teeth was a tiny bit too long. The lights in the hallway made her black button eyes glitter and gleam.

"You don't frighten me," said Coraline, although they did frighten her, very much. "I want my parents back."

The world seemed to shimmer a little at the edges.

"Whatever would I have done with your old parents? If they have left you, Coraline, it must be because they became bored with you, or tired. Now, I will never become bored with you, and I will never abandon you. You will always be safe here with me." The other mother's wet-looking black hair drifted around her head, like the tentacles of a creature in the deep ocean.

"They weren't bored of me," said Coraline. "You're lying. You stole them."

"Silly, silly Coraline. They are fine wherever they are."

Coraline simply glared at the other mother.

"I'll prove it," said the other mother, and brushed the surface of the mirror with her long white fingers. It clouded over, as if a dragon had breathed on it, and then it cleared.

In the mirror it was daytime already. Coraline was looking at the hallway, all the way down to her front door. The door opened from the outside and Coraline's mother and father walked inside. They carried suitcases.

"That was a fine holiday," said Coraline's father.

"How nice it is, not to have Coraline any more," said her mother with a happy smile. "Now we can do all the things we always wanted to do, like go abroad, but were prevented from doing by having a little daughter."

"And," said her father, "I take great comfort in knowing that her other mother will take better care of her than we ever could."

The mirror fogged and faded and reflected the night once more.

"See?" said her other mother.

"No," said Coraline. "I don't see. And I don't believe it either."

She hoped that what she had just seen was not real, but she was not as certain as she sounded. There was a tiny doubt inside her, like a maggot in an apple core. Then she looked up and saw the expression on her other mother's face: a flash of real anger, which crossed her face like summer lightning, and Coraline was sure in her heart that what she had seen in the mirror was no more than an illusion.

Coraline sat down on the sofa and ate her apple.

"Please," said her other mother. "Don't be difficult." She walked into the drawing room and clapped her hands twice. There was a rustling noise and a black rat appeared. It stared up at her. "Bring me the key," she said.

The rat chittered, then it ran through the open door that led back to Coraline's own flat.

The rat returned, dragging the key behind it.

"Why don't you have your own key on this side?" asked Coraline.

"There is only one key. Only one door," said the other father.

"Hush," said the other mother. "You must not bother our darling Coraline's head with such trivialities." She put the key in the keyhole and twisted. The lock was stiff, but it clunked closed.

She dropped the key into her apron pocket.

Outside, the sky had begun to lighten to a luminous gray.

"If we aren't going to have a midnight snack," said the other mother, "we still need our beauty sleep. I am going back to bed, Coraline. I would strongly suggest that you do the same."

She placed her long white fingers on the shoulders of the other father, and she walked him out of the room.

Coraline walked over to the door at the far corner of the drawing room. She tugged on it, but it was tightly locked. The door of her other parents' bedroom was now closed.

She was indeed tired, but she did not want to sleep in the bedroom. She did not want to sleep under the same roof as her other mother.

The front door was not locked. Coraline walked out into the dawn and down the stone stairs. She sat down on the bottom step. It was cold.

Something furry pushed itself against her side in one

smooth, insinuating motion. Coraline jumped, then breathed a sigh of relief when she saw what it was.

"Oh. It's you," she said to the black cat.

"See?" said the cat. "It wasn't so hard recognizing me, was it? Even without names."

"Well, what if I wanted to call you?"

The cat wrinkled its nose and managed to look unimpressed. "Calling cats," it confided, "tends to be a rather overrated activity. Might as well call a whirlwind."

"What if it was dinnertime?" asked Coraline. "Wouldn't you want to be called then?"

"Of course," said the cat. "But a simple cry of 'dinner!' would do nicely. See? No need for names."

"Why does she want me?" Coraline asked the cat. "Why does she want me to stay here with her?"

"She wants something to love, I think," said the cat. "Something that isn't her. She might want something to eat as well. It's hard to tell with creatures like that."

"Do you have any advice?" asked Coraline.

The cat looked as if it were about to say something else sarcastic. Then it flicked its whiskers and said, "Challenge her. There's no guarantee she'll play fair, but her kind of thing loves games and challenges."

"What kind of thing is that?" asked Coraline.

But the cat made no answer, simply stretched luxuriantly

and walked away. Then it stopped, and turned, and said, "I'd go inside if I were you. Get some sleep. You have a long day ahead of you."

And then the cat was gone. Still, Coraline realized, it had a point. She crept back into the silent house, past the closed bedroom door inside which the other mother and the other father . . . what? she wondered. Slept? Waited? And then it came to her that, should she open the bedroom door she would find it empty, or more precisely, that it was an empty room and it would remain empty until the exact moment that she opened the door.

Somehow, that made it easier. Coraline walked into the green-and-pink parody of her own bedroom. She closed the door and hauled the toy box in front of it—it would not keep anyone out, but the noise somebody would make trying to dislodge it would wake her, she hoped.

The toys in the toy box were still mostly asleep, and they stirred and muttered as she moved their box, and then they went back to sleep. Coraline checked under her bed, looking for rats, but there was nothing there. She took off her dressing gown and slippers and climbed into bed and fell asleep with barely enough time to reflect, as she did so, on what the cat could have meant by *a challenge*.

VI.

CORALINE WAS WOKEN BY the midmorning sun, full on her face.

For a moment she felt utterly dislocated. She did not know where she was; she was not entirely sure *who* she was. It is astonishing just how much of what we are can be tied to the beds we wake up in in the morning, and it is astonishing how fragile that can be.

Sometimes Coraline would forget who she was while she was daydreaming that she was exploring the Arctic, or the Amazon rain forest, or Darkest Africa, and it was not until someone tapped her on the shoulder or said her name that Coraline would come back from a million miles away with a start, and all in a fraction of a second have to remember who she was, and what her name was, and that she was even there at all.

Now there was sun on her face, and she was Coraline Jones. Yes. And then the green and pinkness of the room she was in, and the rustling of a large painted paper butterfly as it fluttered and beat its way about the ceiling, told

her where she had woken up.

She climbed out of the bed. She could not wear her pajamas, dressing gown, and slippers during the day, she decided, even if it meant wearing the other Coraline's clothes. (Was there an other Coraline? No, she realized, there wasn't. There was just her.) There were no regular clothes in the cupboard, though. They were more like dressing-up clothes or (she thought) the kind of clothes she would love to have hanging in her own wardrobe at home: there was a raggedy witch costume; a patched scarecrow costume; a future-warrior costume with little digital lights in it that glittered and blinked; a slinky evening dress all covered in feathers and mirrors. Finally, in a drawer, she found a pair of black jeans that seemed to be made of velvet night, and a gray sweater the color of thick smoke with faint and tiny stars in the fabric which twinkled.

She pulled on the jeans and the sweater. Then she put on a pair of bright orange boots she found at the bottom of the cupboard.

She took her last apple out of the pocket of her dressing gown and then took, from the same pocket, the stone with the hole in it.

She put the stone into the pocket of her jeans, and it was as if her head had cleared a little. As if she had come out of some sort of a fog.

She went into the kitchen, but it was deserted.

Still, she was sure that there was someone in the flat. She walked down the hall until she reached her father's study, and discovered that it was occupied.

"Where's the other mother?" she asked the other father. He was sitting in the study, at a desk which looked just like her father's, but he was not doing anything at all, not even reading gardening catalogs as her own father did when he was only pretending to be working.

"Out," he told her. "Fixing the doors. There are some vermin problems." He seemed pleased to have somebody to talk to.

"The rats, you mean?"

"No, the rats are our friends. This is the other kind. Big black fellow, with his tail high."

"The cat, you mean?"

"That's the one," said her other father.

He looked less like her true father today. There was something slightly vague about his face—like bread dough that had begun to rise, smoothing out the bumps and cracks and depressions.

"Really, I mustn't talk to you when she's not here," he said. "But don't you worry. She won't be gone often. I shall demonstrate our tender hospitality to you, such that you will not even think about ever going back." He closed his mouth and folded his hands in his lap.

"So what am I to do now?" asked Coraline.

The other father pointed to his lips. *Silence.*

"If you won't even talk to me," said Coraline, "I am going exploring."

"No point," said the other father. "There isn't anywhere but here. This is all she made: the house, the grounds, and the people in the house. She made it and she waited." Then he looked embarrassed and he put one finger to his lips again, as if he had just said too much.

Coraline walked out of his study. She went into the drawing room, over to the old door, and she pulled it, rattled and shook it. No, it was locked fast, and the other mother had the key.

She looked around the room. It was so familiar—that was what made it feel so truly strange. Everything was exactly the same as she remembered: there was all her grandmother's strange-smelling furniture, there was the painting of the bowl of fruit (a bunch of grapes, two plums, a peach and an apple) hanging on the wall, there was the low wooden table with the lion's feet, and the empty fireplace which seemed to suck heat from the room.

But there was something else, something she did not remember seeing before. A ball of glass, up on the mantelpiece.

She went over to the fireplace, went up on tiptoes, and lifted it down. It was a snow globe, with two little people in it. Coraline shook it and set the snow flying, white snow that glittered as it tumbled through the water.

Then she put the snow globe back on the mantelpiece, and carried on looking for her true parents and for a way out.

She went out of the flat. Past the flashing-lights door, behind which the other Misses Spink and Forcible performed their show forever, and she set off into the woods.

Where Coraline came from, once you were through the patch of trees, you saw nothing but the meadow and the old tennis court. In this place, the woods went on farther, the trees becoming cruder and less treelike the farther you went.

Pretty soon they seemed very approximate, like the idea of trees: a grayish-brown trunk below, a greenish splodge of something that might have been leaves above.

Coraline wondered if the other mother wasn't interested in trees, or if she just hadn't bothered with this bit properly because nobody was expected to come out this far.

She kept walking.

And then the mist began.

It was not damp, like a normal fog or mist. It was not cold and it was not warm. It felt to Coraline like she was walking into nothing.

I'm an explorer, thought Coraline to herself. *And I need all the ways out of here that I can get. So I shall keep walking.*

The world she was walking through was a pale nothingness, like a blank sheet of paper or an enormous, empty white room. It had no temperature, no smell, no texture, and no taste.

It certainly isn't mist, thought Coraline, although she did not know what it was. For a moment she wondered if she might not have gone blind. But no, she could see herself, plain as day. But there was no ground beneath her feet, just a misty, milky whiteness.

"And what do you think you're doing?" said a shape to one side of her.

It took a few moments for her eyes to focus on it properly: she thought it might be some kind of lion, at first, some distance away from her; and then she thought it might be a mouse, close beside her. And then she knew what it was.

"I'm exploring," Coraline told the cat.

Its fur stood straight out from its body and its eyes were wide, while its tail was down and between its legs. It did not look a happy cat.

"Bad place," said the cat. "If you want to call it a place, which I don't. What are you doing here?"

"I'm exploring."

"Nothing to find here," said the cat. "This is just the out-side, the part of the place *she* hasn't bothered to create."

"She?"

"The one who says she's your other mother," said the cat.

"What *is* she?" asked Coraline.

The cat did not answer, just padded through the pale mist beside Coraline.

A shape began to appear in front of them, something high and towering and dark.

"You were wrong!" she told the cat. "There is something there!"

And then it took shape in the mist: a dark house, which loomed at them out of the formless whiteness.

"But that's—" said Coraline.

"The house you just left," agreed the cat. "Precisely."

"Maybe I just got turned around in the mist," said Coraline.

The cat curled the high tip of its tail into a question mark, and tipped its head to one side. "*You* might have done," it said. "*I* certainly would not. Wrong, indeed."

"But how can you walk away from something and still come back to it?"

"Easy," said the cat. "Think of somebody walking around the world. You start out walking away from something and end up coming back to it."

"Small world," said Coraline.

"It's big enough for her," said the cat. "Spiders' webs only have to be large enough to catch flies."

Coraline shivered.

"He said that she's fixing all the gates and the doors," she told the cat, "to keep you out."

"She may *try*," said the cat, unimpressed. "Oh yes. She may try." They were standing under a clump of trees now, beside the house. These trees looked much more likely. "There's ways in and ways out of places like this that even *she* doesn't know about."

"Did she make this place, then?" asked Coraline.

"Made it, found it—what's the difference?" asked the cat. "Either way, she's had it a very long time. Hang on—" And it gave a shiver and a leap and before Coraline could blink the cat was sitting with its paw holding down a big black rat. "It's not that I like rats at the best of times," said the cat, conversationally, as if nothing had happened, "but the rats in this place are all spies for her. She uses them as her eyes and hands . . ." And with that the cat let the rat go.

It ran several feet and then the cat, with one bound, was upon it, batting it hard with one sharp-clawed paw, while with the other paw it held the rat down. "I love this bit," said the cat, happily. "Want to see me do that again?"

"No," said Coraline. "Why do you do it? You're torturing it."

"Mm," said the cat. It let the rat go.

The rat stumbled, dazed, for a few steps, then it began to run. With a blow of its paw, the cat knocked the rat into the air, and caught it in its mouth.

"Stop it!" said Coraline.

The cat dropped the rat between its two front paws. "There are those," it said with a sigh, in tones as smooth as oiled silk, "who have suggested that the tendency of a cat to play with its prey is a merciful one—after all, it permits the occasional funny little running snack to escape, from time to time. How often does your dinner get to escape?"

And then it picked the rat up in its mouth and carried it off into the woods, behind a tree.

Coraline walked back into the house.

All was quiet and empty and deserted. Even her footsteps on the carpeted floor seemed loud. Dust motes hung in a beam of sunlight.

At the far end of the hall was the mirror. She could see herself walking toward the mirror, looking, reflected, a little braver than she actually felt. There was nothing else there in the mirror. Just her, in the corridor.

A hand touched her shoulder, and she looked up. The

other mother stared down at Coraline with big black button eyes.

"Coraline, my darling," she said. "I thought we could play some games together this morning, now you're back from your walk. Hopscotch? Happy Families? Monopoly?"

"You weren't in the mirror," said Coraline.

The other mother smiled. "Mirrors," she said, "are never to be trusted. Now, what game shall we play?"

Coraline shook her head. "I don't want to play with you," she said. "I want to go home and be with my real parents. I want you to let them go. To let us all go."

The other mother shook her head, very slowly. "Sharper than a serpent's tooth," she said, "is a daughter's ingratitude. Still, the proudest spirit can be broken, with love." And her long white fingers waggled and caressed the air.

"I have no plans to love you," said Coraline. "No matter what. You can't make me love you."

"Let's talk about it," said the other mother, and she turned and walked into the lounge. Coraline followed her.

The other mother sat down on the big sofa. She picked up a shopping bag from beside the sofa and took out a white, rustling, paper bag from inside it.

She extended the hand with it to Coraline. "Would you like one?" she asked politely.

Expecting it to be a toffee or a butterscotch ball, Coraline looked down. The bag was half filled with large shiny blackbeetles, crawling over each other in their efforts to get out of the bag.

"No," said Coraline. "I don't want one."

"Suit yourself," said her other mother. She carefully picked out a particularly large and black beetle, pulled off its legs (which she dropped, neatly, into a big glass ashtray on the small table beside the sofa), and popped the beetle into her mouth. She crunched it happily.

"Yum," she said, and took another.

"You're sick," said Coraline. "Sick and evil and weird."

"Is that any way to talk to your mother?" her other mother asked, with her mouth full of blackbeetles.

"You aren't my mother," said Coraline.

Her other mother ignored this. "Now, I think you are a little overexcited, Coraline. Perhaps this afternoon we could do a little embroidery together, or some watercolor painting. Then dinner, and then, if you have been good, you may play with the rats a little before bed. And I shall read you a story and tuck you in, and kiss you good night." Her long white fingers fluttered gently, like a tired butterfly, and Coraline shivered.

"No," said Coraline.

The other mother sat on the sofa. Her mouth was set in a line; her lips were pursed. She popped another blackbeetle into her mouth and then another, like someone with a bag of chocolate-covered raisins. Her big black button eyes stared into Coraline's hazel eyes. Her shiny black hair twined and twisted about her neck and shoulders, as if it were blowing in some wind that Coraline could not touch or feel.

They stared at each other for over a minute. Then the other mother said, "Manners!" She folded the white paper bag carefully so no blackbeetles could escape, and she placed it back in the shopping bag. Then she stood up, and up, and up: she seemed taller than Coraline remembered. She reached into her apron pocket and pulled out, first the black door key, which she frowned at and tossed into her shopping bag, then a tiny silver-colored key. She held it up triumphantly. "There we are," she said. "This is for you, Coraline. For your own good. Because I love you. To teach you manners. Manners makyth man, after all."

She pulled Coraline back into the hallway and advanced upon the mirror at the end of the hall. Then she pushed the tiny key into the fabric of the mirror, and she *twisted* it.

It opened like a door, revealing a dark space behind it. "You may come out when you've learned some manners," said the other mother. "And when you're ready to be a loving daughter."

She picked Coraline up and pushed her into the dim

space behind the mirror. A fragment of beetle was sticking to her lower lip, and there was no expression at all in her black button eyes.

Then she swung the mirror door closed, and left Coraline in darkness.

VII.

Somewhere inside her Coraline could feel a huge sob welling up. And then she stopped it, before it came out. She took a deep breath and let it go. She put out her hands to touch the space in which she was imprisoned. It was the size of a broom closet: tall enough to stand in or to sit in, not wide or deep enough to lie down in.

One wall was glass, and it felt cold to the touch.

She went around the tiny room a second time, running her hands over every surface that she could reach, feeling for doorknobs or switches or concealed catches—some kind of way out—and found nothing.

A spider scuttled over the back of her hand and she choked back a shriek. But apart from the spider she was alone in the closet in the pitch dark.

And then her hand touched something that felt for all the world like somebody's cheek and lips, small and cold; and a voice whispered in her ear, "Hush! And shush! Say nothing, for the beldam might be listening!"

Coraline said nothing.

She felt a cold hand touch her face, fingers running over it like the gentle beat of a moth's wings.

Another voice, hesitant and so faint Coraline wondered if she were imagining it, said, "Art thou—art thou *alive?*"

"Yes," whispered Coraline.

"Poor child," said the first voice.

"Who are you?" whispered Coraline.

"Names, names, names," said another voice, all faraway and lost. "The names are the first things to go, after the breath has gone, and the beating of the heart. We keep our memories longer than our names. I still keep pictures in my mind of my governess on some May morning, carrying my hoop and stick, and the morning sun behind her, and all the tulips bobbing in the breeze. But I have forgotten the name of my governess, and of the tulips too."

"I don't think tulips have names," said Coraline. "They're just tulips."

"Perhaps," said the voice, sadly. "But I have always thought that these tulips must have had names. They were red, and orange and red, and red and orange and yellow, like the embers in the nursery fire of a winter's evening. I remember them."

The voice sounded so sad that Coraline put out a hand to the place where the voice was coming from, and she found a cold hand, and she squeezed it tightly.

Her eyes were beginning to get used to the darkness. Now Coraline saw, or imagined she saw, three shapes, each as faint and pale as the moon in the daytime sky. They were the shapes of children about her own size. The cold hand squeezed her hand back. "Thank you," said the voice.

"Are you a girl?" asked Coraline. "Or a boy?"

There was a pause. "When I was small I wore skirts and my hair was long and curled," it said, doubtfully. "But now that you ask, it does seem to me that one day they took my skirts and gave me britches and cut my hair."

"'Tain't something we give a mind to," said the first of the voices.

"A boy, perhaps, then," continued the one whose hand she was holding. "I believe I was once a boy." And it glowed a little more brightly in the darkness of the room behind the mirror.

"What happened to you all?" asked Coraline. "How did you come here?"

"She left us here," said one of the voices. "She stole our hearts, and she stole our souls, and she took our lives away, and she left us here, and she forgot about us in the dark."

"You poor things," said Coraline. "How long have you been here?"

"So very long a time," said a voice.

"Aye. Time beyond reckoning," said another voice.

"I walked through the scullery door," said the voice of the one that thought it might be a boy, "and I found myself back in the parlor. But *she* was waiting for me. She told me she was my other mamma, but I never saw my true mamma again."

"Flee!" said the very first of the voices—another girl, Coraline fancied. "Flee, while there's still air in your lungs and blood in your veins and warmth in your heart. Flee while you still have your mind and your soul."

"I'm not running away," said Coraline. "She has my parents. I came to get them back."

"Ah, but she'll keep you here while the days turn to dust and the leaves fall and the years pass one after the next like the tick-tick-ticking of a clock."

"No," said Coraline. "She won't."

There was silence then in the room behind the mirror.

"Peradventure," said a voice in the darkness, "if you could win your mamma and your papa back from the beldam, you could also win free our souls."

"Has she taken them?" asked Coraline, shocked.

"Aye. And hidden them."

"That is why we could not leave here, when we died. She kept us, and she fed on us, until now we've nothing left of ourselves, only snakeskins and spider husks. Find our secret hearts, young mistress."

"And what will happen to you if I do?" asked Coraline. The voices said nothing.

"And what is she going to do to me?" she said.

The pale figures pulsed faintly; she could imagine that they were nothing more than afterimages, like the glow left by a bright light in your eyes, after the lights go out.

"It doth not hurt," whispered one faint voice.

"She will take your life and all you are and all you care'st for, and she will leave you with nothing but mist and fog. She'll take your joy. And one day you'll awake and your heart and your soul will have gone. A husk you'll be, a wisp you'll be, and a thing no more than a dream on waking, or a memory of something forgotten."

"Hollow," whispered the third voice. "Hollow, hollow, hollow, hollow, hollow."

"You must flee," sighed a voice faintly.

"I don't think so," said Coraline. "I tried running away, and it didn't work. She just took my parents. Can you tell me how to get out of this room?"

"If we knew then we would tell you."

"Poor things," said Coraline to herself.

She sat down. She took off her sweater and rolled it up and put it behind her head as a pillow. "She won't keep me in the dark forever," said Coraline. "She brought me here to play games. *Games and challenges*, the cat said. I'm not much of a challenge here in the dark." She tried to get comfortable, twisting and bending herself to fit the cramped space behind the mirror.

Her stomach rumbled. She ate her last apple, taking the tiniest bites, making it last as long as she could. When she had finished she was still hungry.

Then an idea struck her, and she whispered, "When she comes to let me out, why don't you three come with me?"

"We wish that we could," they sighed to her, in their barely-there voices. "But she has our hearts in her keeping. Now we belong to the dark and to the empty places. The light would shrivel us, and burn."

"Oh," said Coraline.

She closed her eyes, which made the darkness darker, and she rested her head on the rolled-up sweater, and she went to sleep. And as she fell asleep she thought she felt a ghost kiss her cheek, tenderly, and a small voice whisper into her ear, a voice so faint it was barely there at all, a gentle wispy nothing of a voice so hushed that Coraline could almost believe she was imagining it. "Look through the stone," it said to her.

And then she slept.

VIII.

THE OTHER MOTHER looked healthier than before: there was a little blush to her cheeks, and her hair was wriggling like lazy snakes on a warm day. Her black button eyes seemed as if they had been freshly polished.

She had pushed through the mirror as if she were walking through nothing more solid than water and had stared down at Coraline. Then she had opened the door with the little silver key. She picked Coraline up, just as Coraline's real mother had when Coraline was much younger, cradling the half-sleeping child as if she were a baby.

The other mother carried Coraline into the kitchen and put her down very gently upon the countertop.

Coraline struggled to wake herself up, conscious only for the moment of having been cuddled and loved, and wanting more of it, then realizing where she was and who she was with.

"There, my sweet Coraline," said her other mother. "I came and fetched you out of the cupboard. You needed to be taught a lesson, but we temper our justice with mercy here; we love the sinner and we hate the sin. Now, if you will be a good child who loves her mother, be compliant and fair-spoken, you and I shall understand each other perfectly and we shall love each other perfectly as well."

Coraline scratched the sleep grit from her eyes.

"There were other children in there," she said. "Old ones, from a long time ago."

"Were there?" said the other mother. She was bustling between the pans and the fridge, bringing out eggs and cheeses, butter and a slab of sliced pink bacon.

"Yes," said Coraline. "There were. I think you're planning to turn me into one of them. A dead shell."

Her other mother smiled gently. With one hand she cracked the eggs into a bowl; with the other she whisked them and whirled them. Then she dropped a pat of butter into a frying pan, where it hissed and fizzled and spun as she sliced thin slices of cheese. She poured the melted butter and the cheese into the egg-mixture, and whisked it some more.

"Now, I think you're being silly, dear," said the other mother. "I love you. I will always love you. Nobody sensible believes in ghosts anyway—that's because they're all such liars. Smell the lovely breakfast I'm making for you." She poured the yellow mixture into the pan. "Cheese omelette. Your favorite."

Coraline's mouth watered. "You like games," she said. "That's what I've been told."

The other mother's black eyes flashed. "Everybody likes games," was all she said.

"Yes," said Coraline. She climbed down from the counter and sat at the table.

The bacon was sizzling and spitting under the grill. It smelled wonderful.

"Wouldn't you be happier if you won me, fair and square?" asked Coraline.

"Possibly," said the other mother. She had a show of unconcernedness, but her fingers twitched and drummed and she licked her lips with her scarlet tongue. "What exactly are you offering?"

"Me," said Coraline, and she gripped her knees under the table, to stop them from shaking. "If I lose I'll stay here with you forever and I'll let you love me. I'll be a most dutiful daughter. I'll eat your food and play Happy Families. And I'll let you sew your buttons into my eyes."

Her other mother stared at her, black buttons unblinking. "That sounds very fine," she said. "And if you do not lose?"

"Then you let me go. You let everyone go—my real father and mother, the dead children, everyone you've trapped here."

The other mother took the bacon from under the grill and put it on a plate. Then she slipped the cheese omelette from the pan onto the plate, flipping it as she did so, letting it fold itself into a perfect omelette shape.

She placed the breakfast plate in front of Coraline, along with a glass of freshly squeezed orange juice and a mug of frothy hot chocolate.

"Yes," she said. "I think I like this game. But what kind of game shall it be? A riddle game? A test of knowledge or of skill?

"An exploring game," suggested Coraline. "A finding-things game."

"And what is it you think you should be finding in this hide-and-go-seek game, Coraline Jones?"

Coraline hesitated. Then, "My parents," said Coraline. "And the souls of the children behind the mirror."

The other mother smiled at this, triumphantly, and Coraline wondered if she had made the right choice. Still, it was too late to change her mind now.

"A deal," said the other mother. "Now eat up your breakfast, my sweet. Don't worry—it won't hurt you."

Coraline stared at the breakfast, hating herself for giving in so easily, but she was starving.

"How do I know you'll keep your word?" asked Coraline.

"I swear it," said the other mother. "I swear it on my own mother's grave."

"Does she have a grave?" asked Coraline.

"Oh yes," said the other mother. "I put her in there myself. And when I found her trying to crawl out, I put her back."

"Swear on something else. So I can trust you to keep your word."

"My right hand," said the other mother, holding it up. She waggled the long fingers slowly, displaying the clawlike nails. "I swear on that."

Coraline shrugged. "Okay," she said. "It's a deal." She ate the breakfast, trying not to wolf it down. She was hungrier than she had thought.

As she ate, her other mother stared at her. It was hard to read expressions into those black button eyes, but Coraline thought that her other mother looked hungry, too.

She drank the orange juice, but even though she knew she would like it she could not bring herself to taste the hot chocolate.

"Where should I start looking?" asked Coraline.

"Where you wish," said her other mother, as if she did not care at all.

Coraline looked at her, and Coraline thought hard. There was no point, she decided, in exploring the garden and the grounds: they didn't exist; they weren't real. There was no abandoned tennis court in the other mother's world, no bottomless well. All that was real was the house itself.

She looked around the kitchen. She opened the oven, peered into the freezer, poked into the salad compartment of the fridge. The other mother followed her about, looking at Coraline with a smirk always hovering at the edge of her lips.

"How big are souls anyway?" asked Coraline.

The other mother sat down at the kitchen table and leaned back against the wall, saying nothing. She picked at her teeth with a long crimson-varnished fingernail, then she tapped the finger, gently, *tap-tap-tap* against the polished black surface of her black button eyes.

"Fine," said Coraline. "Don't tell me. I don't care. It doesn't matter if you help me or not. Everyone knows that a soul is the same size as a beach ball."

She was hoping the other mother would say something like "Nonsense, they're the size of ripe onions—or suitcases—or grandfather clocks," but the other mother simply smiled, and the *tap-tap-tap*ping of her fingernail against her eye was as steady and relentless as the drip of water droplets from the faucet into the sink. And then, Coraline realized, it *was* simply the noise of the water, and she was alone in the room.

Coraline shivered. She preferred the other mother to have a location: if she were nowhere, then she could be anywhere. And, after all, it is always easier to be afraid of something you cannot see. She put her hands into her pockets and her fingers closed around the reassuring shape of the stone with the hole in it. She pulled it out of her pocket, held it in front of her as if she were holding a gun, and walked out into the hall.

There was no sound but the *tap-tap* of the water dripping into the metal sink.

She glanced at the mirror at the end of the hall. For a moment it clouded over, and it seemed to her that faces swam in the glass, indistinct and shapeless, and then the faces were gone, and there was nothing in the mirror but a girl who was small for her age holding something that glowed gently, like a green coal.

Coraline looked down at her hand, surprised: it was just a stone with a hole in it, a nondescript brown pebble. Then she looked back into the mirror where the stone glimmered like an emerald. A trail of green fire blew from the pebble in the mirror and drifted toward Coraline's bedroom.

"Hmm," said Coraline.

She walked into the bedroom. The toys fluttered excitedly as she walked in, as if they were pleased to see her, and a little tank rolled out of the toy box to greet her, its tread rolling over several other toys. It fell from the toy box onto the floor, tipping as it fell, and it lay on the carpet like a beetle on its back, grumbling and grinding its treads before Coraline picked it up and turned it over. The tank fled under the bed in embarrassment.

Coraline looked around the room.

She looked in the cupboards, and the drawers. Then she picked up one end of the toy box and tipped all the toys in it out onto the carpet, where they grumbled and stretched and wiggled awkwardly free of each other. A gray marble rolled across the floor and clicked against the wall. None of the toys looked particularly soul-like, she thought. She picked up and examined a silver charm bracelet from which hung tiny animal charms that chased each other around the perimeter of the bracelet, the fox never catching the rabbit, the bear never gaining on the fox.

Coraline opened her hand and looked at the stone with the hole in it, hoping for a clue but not finding one. Most of the toys that had been in the toy box had now crawled away to hide under the bed, and the few toys that were left (a green plastic soldier, the glass marble, a vivid pink yo-yo, and such) were the kind of things you find in the bottoms of toy boxes in the real world: forgotten objects, abandoned and unloved.

She was about to leave and look elsewhere. And then she remembered a voice in the darkness, a gentle whispering voice, and what it had told her to do. She raised the stone with a hole in it and held it in front of her right eye. She closed her left eye and looked at the room through the hole in the stone.

Through the stone, the world was gray and colorless, like a pencil drawing. Everything in it was gray—no, not quite everything: something glinted on the floor, something the color of an ember in a nursery fireplace, the color of a scarlet-and-orange tulip nodding in the May sun. Coraline reached out her left hand, scared that if she took her eye off it it would vanish, and she fumbled for the burning thing.

Her fingers closed about something smooth and cool. She snatched it up, and then lowered the stone with a hole in it from her eye and looked down. The gray glass marble from the bottom of the toy box sat, dully, in the pink palm of her hand. She raised the stone to her eye once more and looked through it at the marble. Once again the marble burned and flickered with a red fire.

A voice whispered in her mind, "Indeed, lady, it comes to me that I certainly *was* a boy, now I do think on it. Oh, but you must hurry. There are two of us still to find, and the beldam is already angry with you for uncovering me."

If I'm going to do this, thought Coraline, *I'm not going to do it in her clothes.* She changed back into her pajamas and her dressing gown and her slippers, leaving the gray sweater and the black jeans neatly folded up on the bed, the orange boots on the floor by the toy box.

She put the marble into her dressing-gown pocket and walked out into the hall.

Something stung her face and hands like sand blowing on a beach on a windy day. She covered her eyes and pushed forward.

The sand stings got worse, and it got harder and harder to walk, as if she were pushing into the wind on a particularly blustery day. It was a vicious wind, and a cold one.

She took a step backwards, the way she had come.

"Oh, keep going," whispered a ghost voice in her ear, "for the beldam is angry."

She stepped forward in the hallway, into another gust of wind, which stung her cheeks and face with invisible sand, sharp as needles, sharp as glass.

"Play fair," shouted Coraline into the wind.

There was no reply, but the wind whipped about her one more time, petulantly, and then it dropped away, and was gone. As she passed the kitchen Coraline could hear, in the sudden silence, the *drip-drip* of the water from the leaking tap or perhaps the other mother's long fingernails tapping impatiently against the table. Coraline resisted the urge to look.

In a couple of strides she reached the front door, and she walked outside.

Coraline went down the steps and around the house until she reached the other Miss Spink and Miss Forcible's flat. The lamps around the door were flickering on and off almost randomly now, spelling out no words that Coraline could understand. The door was closed. She was afraid it was locked, and she pushed on it with all her strength. First it stuck, then suddenly it gave, and, with a jerk, Coraline stumbled into the dark room beyond.

Coraline closed one hand around the stone with the hole in it and walked forward into blackness. She expected to find a curtained anteroom, but there was nothing there. The room was dark. The theater was empty. She moved ahead cautiously. Something rustled above her. She looked up into a deeper darkness, and as she did so her feet knocked against something. She reached down, picked up a flashlight, and clicked it on, sweeping the beam around the room.

The theater was derelict and abandoned. Chairs were broken on the floor, and old, dusty spiderwebs draped the walls and hung from the rotten wood and the decomposing velvet hangings.

Something rustled once again. Coraline directed her light beam upward, toward the ceiling. There were things up there, hairless, jellyish. She thought they might once have had faces, might even once have been dogs; but no dogs had wings like bats or could hang, like spiders, like bats, upside down.

The light startled the creatures, and one of them took to the air, its wings whirring heavily through the dust. Coraline ducked as it swooped close to her. It came to rest on a far wall, and it began to clamber, upside down, back to the nest of the dog-bats upon the ceiling.

Coraline raised the stone to her eye and she scanned the room through it, looking for something that glowed or glinted, a telltale sign that somewhere in this room was another hidden soul. She ran the beam of the flashlight about the room as she searched, the thick dust in the air making the light beam seem almost solid.

There was something up on the back wall behind the ruined stage. It was grayish white, twice the size of Coraline herself, and it was stuck to the back wall like a slug. Coraline took a deep breath. "I'm not afraid," she told herself. "I'm not." She did not believe herself, but she scrambled up onto the old stage, fingers sinking into the rotting wood as she pulled herself up.

As she got closer to the thing on the wall, she saw that

it was some kind of a sac, like a spider's egg case. It twitched in the light beam. Inside the sac was something that looked like a person, but a person with two heads, with twice as many arms and legs as it should have.

The creature in the sac seemed horribly unformed and unfinished, as if two plasticine people had been warmed and rolled together, squashed and pressed into one thing.

Coraline hesitated. She did not want to approach the thing. The dog-bats dropped, one by one, from the ceiling and began to circle the room, coming close to her but never touching her.

Perhaps there are no souls hidden in here, she thought. *Perhaps I can just leave and go somewhere else.* She took a last look through the hole in the stone: the abandoned theater was still a bleak gray, but now there was a brown glow, as rich and bright as polished cherrywood, coming from inside the sac. Whatever was glowing was being held in one of the hands of the thing on the wall.

Coraline walked slowly across the damp stage, trying to make as little noise as she could, afraid that, if she disturbed the thing in the sac, it would open its eyes, and see her, and then . . .

But there was nothing that she could think of as scary as having it look at her. Her heart pounded in her chest. She took another step forward.

She had never been so scared, but still she walked forward until she reached the sac. Then she pushed her hand into the sticky, clinging whiteness of the stuff on the wall. It crackled softly, like a tiny fire, as she pushed, and it clung to her skin and clothes like a spiderweb clings, like white cotton candy. She pushed her hand into it, and she reached upward until she touched a cold hand, which was, she could feel, closed around another glass marble. The creature's skin felt slippery, as if it had been covered in jelly. Coraline tugged at the marble.

At first nothing happened: it was held tight in the creature's grasp. Then, one by one, the fingers loosened their grip, and the marble slipped into her hand. She pulled her arm back through the sticky webbing, relieved that the thing's eyes had not opened. She shone the light on its faces: they resembled, she decided, the younger versions of Miss Spink and Miss Forcible, but twisted and squeezed together, like two lumps of wax that had melted and melded together into one ghastly thing.

Without warning, one of the creature's hands made a grab for Coraline's arm. Its fingernails scraped her skin, but it was too slippery to grip, and Coraline pulled away successfully. And then the eyes opened, four black buttons glinting and staring down at her, and two voices that sounded like no voice that Coraline had ever heard began to speak to her. One of them wailed and whispered, the other buzzed like a fat and angry bluebottle at a window-pane, but the voices said, as one person, *"Thief! Give it back! Stop! Thief!"*

The air became alive with dog-bats. Coraline began to back away. She realized then that, terrifying though the thing on the wall that had once been the other Misses Spink and Forcible was, it was attached to the wall by its web, encased in its cocoon. It could not follow her.

The dog-bats flapped and fluttered about her, but they did nothing to hurt Coraline. She climbed down from the stage, shone the flashlight about the old theater looking for the way out.

"Flee, Miss," wailed a girl's voice in her head. "Flee, now. You have two of us. Flee this place while your blood still flows."

Coraline dropped the marble into her pocket beside the other. She spotted the door, ran to it, and pulled on it until it opened.

IX.

O UTSIDE, THE WORLD HAD become a formless, swirling mist with no shapes or shadows behind it, while the house itself seemed to have twisted and stretched. It seemed to Coraline that it was crouching, and staring down at her, as if it were not really a house but only the idea of a house—and the person who had had the idea, she was certain, was not a good person. There was sticky web stuff clinging to her arm, and she wiped it off as best she could. The gray windows of the house slanted at strange angles.

The other mother was waiting for her, standing on the grass with her arms folded. Her black button eyes were expressionless, but her lips were pressed tightly together in a cold fury.

When she saw Coraline she reached out one long white hand, and she crooked a finger. Coraline walked toward her. The other mother said nothing.

"I got two," said Coraline. "One soul still to go."

The expression on the other mother's face did not

change. She might not have heard what Coraline said.

"Well, I just thought you'd want to know," said Coraline.

"Thank you, Coraline," said the other mother coldly, and her voice did not just come from her mouth. It came from the mist, and the fog, and the house, and the sky. She said, "You know that I love you."

And, despite herself, Coraline nodded. It was true: the other mother loved her. But she loved Coraline as a miser loves money, or a dragon loves its gold. In the other mother's button eyes, Coraline knew that she was a possession, nothing more. A tolerated pet, whose behavior was no longer amusing.

"I don't want your love," said Coraline. "I don't want anything from you."

"Not even a helping hand?" asked the other mother. "You have been doing so well, after all. I thought you might want a little hint, to help you with the rest of your treasure hunt."

"I'm doing fine on my own," said Coraline.

"Yes," said the other mother. "But if you wanted to get into the flat in the front—the empty one—to look around, you would find the door locked, and then where would you be?"

"Oh." Coraline pondered this, for a moment. Then she said, "Is there a key?"

The other mother stood there in the paper-gray fog of the flattening world. Her black hair drifted about her head, as if it had a mind and a purpose all of its own. She coughed suddenly in the back of her throat, and then she opened her mouth.

The other mother reached up her hand and removed a small, brass front-door key from her tongue.

"Here," she said. "You'll need this to get in."

She tossed the key, casually, toward Coraline, who caught it, one-handed, before she could think about whether she wanted it or not. The key was still slightly damp.

A chill wind blew about them, and Coraline shivered and looked away. When she looked back she was alone.

Uncertainly, she walked around to the front of the house and stood in front of the door to the empty flat. Like all the doors, it was painted bright green.

"She does not mean you well," whispered a ghost voice in her ear. "We do not believe that she would help you. It must be a trick."

Coraline said, "Yes, you're right, I expect." Then she put the key in the lock and turned it.

Silently, the door swung open, and silently Coraline walked inside.

The flat had walls the color of old milk. The wooden boards of the floor were uncarpeted and dusty with the marks and patterns of old carpets and rugs on them.

There was no furniture in there, only places where furniture had once been. Nothing decorated the walls; there were discolored rectangles on the walls to show where paintings or photographs had once hung. It was so silent that Coraline imagined that she could hear the motes of dust drifting through the air.

She found herself to be quite worried that something would jump out at her, so she began to whistle. She thought it might make it harder for things to jump out at her if she was whistling.

First she walked through the empty kitchen. Then she walked through an empty bathroom, containing only a cast-iron bath, and, in the bath, a dead spider the size of a small cat. The last room she looked at had, she supposed, once been a bedroom; she could imagine that the rectangular dust shadow on the floorboards had once been a bed. Then she saw something, and smiled, grimly. Set into the floorboards was a large metal ring. Coraline knelt and took the cold ring in her hands, and she tugged upward as hard as she could.

Terribly slowly, stiffly, heavily, a hinged square of floor lifted: it was a trapdoor. It lifted, and through the opening Coraline could see only darkness. She reached down, and her hand found a cold switch. She flicked it without much hope that it would work, but somewhere below her a bulb lit, and a thin yellow light came up from the hole in the floor. She could see steps, heading down, but nothing else.

Coraline put her hand into her pocket and took out the stone with the hole in it. She looked through it at the cellar but saw nothing. She put the stone back into her pocket.

Up through the hole came the smell of damp clay, and something else, an acrid tang like sour vinegar.

Coraline let herself down into the hole, looking nervously at the trapdoor. It was so heavy that if it fell she was sure she would be trapped down in the darkness forever. She put up a hand and touched it, but it stayed in position. And then she turned toward the darkness below, and she walked down the steps. Set into the wall at the bottom of the steps was another light switch, metal and rusting. She pushed it until it clicked down, and a naked bulb hanging from a wire from the low ceiling came on. It did not give up enough light even for Coraline to make out the things that had been painted onto the flaking cellar walls. The paintings seemed crude. There were eyes, she could see that, and things that might have been grapes. And other things, below them. Coraline could not be sure that they were paintings of people.

There was a pile of rubbish in one corner of the room: cardboard boxes filled with mildewed papers and decaying curtains in a heap beside them.

Coraline's slippers crunched across the cement floor. The bad smell was worse, now. She was ready to turn and leave, when she saw the foot sticking out from beneath the pile of curtains.

She took a deep breath (the smells of sour wine and moldy bread filled her head) and she pulled away the damp cloth, to reveal something more or less the size and shape of a person.

In that dim light, it took her several seconds to recognize it for what it was: the thing was pale and swollen like a grub, with thin, sticklike arms and feet. It had almost no features on its face, which had puffed and swollen like risen bread dough.

The thing had two large black buttons where its eyes should have been.

Coraline made a noise, a sound of revulsion and horror, and, as if it had heard her and awakened, the thing began to sit up. Coraline stood there, frozen. The thing turned its head until both its black button eyes were pointed straight at her. A mouth opened in the mouthless face, strands of pale stuff sticking to the lips, and a voice that no longer even faintly resembled her father's whispered, "Coraline."

"Well," said Coraline to the thing that had once been her other father, "at least you didn't jump out at me."

The creature's twiglike hands moved to its face and pushed the pale clay about, making something like a nose. It said nothing.

"I'm looking for my parents," said Coraline. "Or a stolen soul from one of the other children. Are they down here?"

"There is nothing down here," said the pale thing indistinctly. "Nothing but dust and damp and forgetting." The thing was white, and huge, and swollen. *Monstrous,* thought Coraline, *but also miserable.* She raised the stone with the hole in it to her eye and looked through it. Nothing. The pale thing was telling her the truth.

"Poor thing," she said. "I bet she made you come down here as a punishment for telling me too much."

The thing hesitated, then it nodded. Coraline wondered how she could ever have imagined that this grublike thing resembled her father.

"I'm so sorry," she said.

"She's not best pleased," said the thing that was once the other father. "Not best pleased at all. You've put her quite out of sorts. And when she gets out of sorts, she takes it out on everybody else. It's her way."

Coraline patted its hairless head. Its skin was tacky, like warm bread dough. "Poor thing," she said. "You're just a thing she made and then threw away."

The thing nodded vigorously; as it nodded, the left

button eye fell off and clattered onto the concrete floor. The thing looked around vacantly with its one eye, as if it had lost her. Finally it saw her, and, as if making a great effort, it opened its mouth once more and said in a wet, urgent voice, "Run, child. Leave this place. She wants me to hurt you, to keep you here forever, so that you can never finish the game and she will win. She is pushing me so hard to hurt you. I cannot fight her."

"You *can*," said Coraline. "Be brave."

She looked around: the thing that had once been the other father was between her and the steps up and out of the cellar. She started edging along the wall, heading toward the steps. The thing twisted bonelessly until its one eye was again facing her. It seemed to be getting bigger, now, and more awake. "Alas," it said, "I cannot."

And it lunged across the cellar toward her then, its toothless mouth opened wide.

Coraline had a single heartbeat in which to react. She could only think of two things to do. Either she could scream and try to run away, and be chased around a badly lit cellar by the huge grub thing, be chased until it caught her. Or she could do something else.

So she did something else.

As the thing reached her, Coraline put out her hand and closed it around the thing's remaining button eye, and she tugged as hard as she knew how.

For a moment nothing happened. Then the button came away and flew from her hand, clicking against the walls before it fell to the cellar floor.

The thing froze in place. It threw its pale head back blindly, and opened its mouth horribly wide, and it roared its anger and frustration. Then, all in a rush, the thing swept toward the place where Coraline had been standing.

But Coraline was not standing there any longer. She was already tiptoeing, as quietly as she could, up the steps that would take her away from the dim cellar with the crude paintings on the walls. She could not take her eyes from the floor beneath her, though, across which the pale thing flopped and writhed, hunting for her. Then, as if it was being told what to do, the creature stopped moving, and its blind head tipped to one side.

It's listening for me, thought Coraline. *I must be extra quiet.* She took another step up, and her foot slipped on the step, and the thing heard her.

Its head tipped toward her. For a moment it swayed and seemed to be gathering its wits. Then, fast as a serpent, it slithered for the steps and began to flow up them, toward her. Coraline turned and ran, wildly, up the last half dozen steps, and she pushed herself up and onto the floor of the dusty bedroom. Without pausing, she pulled the heavy trapdoor toward her, and let go of it. It crashed down with a thump just as something large banged against it. The trapdoor shook and rattled in the floor, but it stayed where it was.

Coraline took a deep breath. If there had been any furniture in that flat, even a chair, she would have pulled it onto the trapdoor, but there was nothing.

She walked out of that flat as fast as she could, without actually ever running, and she locked the front door behind her. She left the door key under the mat. Then she walked down onto the drive.

She had half expected that the other mother would be standing there waiting for Coraline to come out, but the world was silent and empty.

Coraline wanted to go home.

She hugged herself, and told herself that she was brave, and she almost believed herself, and then she walked around to the side of the house, in the gray mist that wasn't a mist, and she made for the stairs, to go up.

X.

CORALINE WALKED UP THE stairs outside the building to the topmost flat, where, in her world, the crazy old man upstairs lived. She had gone up there once with her real mother, when her mother was collecting for charity. They had stood in the open doorway, waiting for the crazy old man with the big mustache to find the envelope that Coraline's mother had left, and the flat had smelled of strange foods and pipe tobacco and odd, sharp, cheesy-smelling things Coraline could not name. She had not wanted to go any farther inside than that.

"I'm an explorer," said Coraline out loud, but her words sounded muffled and dead on the misty air. She had made it out of the cellar, hadn't she?

And she had. But if there was one thing that Coraline was certain of, it was that this flat would be worse.

She reached the top of the house. The topmost flat had once been the attic of the house, but that was long ago.

She knocked on the green-painted door. It swung open, and she walked in.

We have eyes and we have nerveses
We have tails we have teeth
You'll all get what you deserveses
When we rise from underneath.

whispered a dozen or more tiny voices, in that dark flat with the roof so low where it met the walls that Coraline could almost reach up and touch it.

Red eyes stared at her. Little pink feet scurried away as she came close. Darker shadows slipped through the shadows at the edges of things.

It smelled much worse in here than in the real crazy old man upstairs's flat. That smelled of food (unpleasant food, to Coraline's mind, but she knew that was a matter of taste: she did not like spices, herbs, or exotic things). This place smelled as if all the exotic foods in the world had been left out to go rotten.

"Little girl," said a rustling voice in a far room.

"Yes," said Coraline. *I'm not frightened*, she told herself, and as she thought it she knew that it was true. There was nothing here that frightened her. These things—even the thing in the cellar—were illusions, things made by the other mother in a ghastly parody of the real people and real things on the other end of the corridor. She could not truly make anything, decided Coraline. She could only twist and copy and distort things that already existed.

And then Coraline found herself wondering why the other mother would have placed a snowglobe on the drawing-room mantelpiece; for the mantelpiece, in Coraline's world, was quite bare.

As soon as she had asked herself the question, she realized that there was actually an answer.

Then the voice came again, and her train of thought was interrupted.

"Come here, little girl. I know what you want, little girl." It was a rustling voice, scratchy and dry. It made Coraline think of some kind of enormous dead insect. Which was silly, she knew. How could a dead thing, especially a dead insect, have a voice?

She walked through several rooms with low, slanting ceilings until she came to the final room. It was a bedroom, and the other crazy old man upstairs sat at the far end of the room, in the near darkness, bundled up in his coat and hat. As Coraline entered he began to talk. "Nothing's changed, little girl," he said, his voice sounding like the noise dry leaves make as they rustle across a pavement. "And what if you do everything you swore you would? What then? Nothing's changed. You'll go home. You'll be bored. You'll be ignored. No one will listen to you, not really listen to you. You're too clever and too quiet for them to understand. They don't even get your name right.

"Stay here with us," said the voice from the figure at the end of the room. "We will listen to you and play with you and laugh with you. Your other mother will build whole worlds for you to explore, and tear them down every night when you are done. Every day will be better and brighter than the one that went before. Remember the toy box? How much better would a world be built just like that, and all for you?"

"And will there be gray, wet days where I just don't know what to do and there's nothing to read or to watch and nowhere to go and the day drags on forever?" asked Coraline.

From the shadows, the man said, "Never."

"And will there be awful meals, with food made from recipes, with garlic and tarragon and broad beans in?" asked Coraline.

"Every meal will be a thing of joy," whispered the voice from under the old man's hat. "Nothing will pass your lips that does not entirely delight you."

"And could I have Day-Glo green gloves to wear, and yellow Wellington boots in the shape of frogs?" asked Coraline.

"Frogs, ducks, rhinos, octopuses—whatever you desire.

The world will be built new for you every morning. If you stay here, you can have whatever you want."

Coraline sighed. "You really don't understand, do you?" she said. "I don't *want* whatever I want. Nobody does. Not really. What kind of fun would it be if I just got everything I ever wanted? Just like that, and it didn't *mean* anything. What then?"

"I don't understand," said the whispery voice.

"Of course you don't understand," she said, raising the stone with the hole in it to her eye. "You're just a bad copy she made of the crazy old man upstairs."

"Not even that anymore," said the dead, whispery voice. There was a glow coming from the raincoat of the man, at about chest height. Through the hole in the stone the glow twinkled and shone blue-white as any star. She wished she had a stick or something to poke him with: she had no wish to get any closer to the shadowy man at the end of the room.

Coraline took a step closer to the man, and he fell apart. Black rats leapt from the sleeves and from under the coat and hat, a score or more of them, red eyes shining in the dark. They chittered and they fled. The coat fluttered and fell heavily to the floor. The hat rolled into one corner of the room.

Coraline reached out one hand and pulled the coat

open. It was empty, although it was greasy to the touch. There was no sign of the final glass marble in it. She scanned the room, squinting through the hole in the stone, and caught sight of something that twinkled and burned like a star at floor level by the doorway. It was being carried in the forepaws of the largest black rat. As she looked, it slipped away.

The other rats watched her from the corners of the rooms as she ran after it.

Now, rats can run faster than people, especially over short distances. But a large black rat holding a marble in its two front paws is no match for a determined girl (even if she is small for her age) moving at a run. Smaller black rats ran back and forth across her path, trying to distract her, but she ignored them all, keeping her eyes fixed on the one with the marble, who was heading straight out of the flat, toward the front door.

They reached the steps on the outside of the building.

Coraline had time to observe that the house itself was continuing to change, becoming less distinct and flattening out, even as she raced down the stairs. It reminded her of a photograph of a house, now, not the thing itself. Then she was simply racing pell-mell down the steps in pursuit of the rat, with no room in her mind for anything else, certain she was gaining on it. She was running fast—too fast, she discovered, as she came to the bottom of one flight of stairs, and her foot skidded and twisted and she went crashing onto the concrete landing.

Her left knee was scraped and skinned, and the palm of one hand she had thrown out to stop herself was a mess of scraped skin and grit. It hurt a little, and it would, she knew, soon hurt much more. She picked the grit out of her palm and climbed to her feet and, as fast as she could, knowing that she had lost and it was already too late, she went down to the final landing at the ground level.

She looked around for the rat, but it was gone, and the marble with it.

Her hand stung where the skin had been scraped, and there was blood trickling down her ripped pajama leg from her knee. It was as bad as the summer that her mother had taken the training wheels off Coraline's bicycle; but then, back then, in with all the cuts and scrapes (her knees had had scabs on top of scabs) she had had a feeling of achievement. She was learning something, doing something she had not known how to do. Now she felt nothing but cold loss. She had failed the ghost children. She had failed her parents. She had failed herself, failed everything.

She closed her eyes and wished that the earth would swallow her up.

There was a cough.

She opened her eyes and saw the rat. It was lying on the brick path at the bottom of the stairs with a surprised look on its face—which was now several inches away from the rest of it. Its whiskers were stiff, its eyes were wide open, its teeth visible and yellow and sharp. A collar of wet blood glistened at its neck.

Beside the decapitated rat, a smug expression on its face, was the black cat. It rested one paw on the gray glass marble.

"I think I once mentioned," said the cat, "that I don't like rats at the best of times. It looked like you needed this one, however. I hope you don't mind my getting involved."

"I think," said Coraline, trying to catch her breath, "I think you may—have said—something of the sort."

The cat lifted its paw from the marble, which rolled toward Coraline. She picked it up. In her mind a final voice whispered to her, urgently.

"She has lied to you. She will never give you up, now she has you. She will no more give any of us up than change her nature." The hairs on the back of Coraline's neck prickled, and Coraline knew that the girl's voice told the truth. She put the marble in her dressing-gown pocket with the others.

She had all three marbles, now.

All she needed to do was to find her parents.

And, Coraline realized with surprise, that bit was easy. She knew exactly where her parents were. If she had stopped to think, she might have known where they were all along. The other mother could not create. She could only transform, and twist, and change.

The mantelpiece in the drawing room back home was quite empty. But knowing that, she knew something else as well.

"The other mother. She plans to break her promise. She won't let us go," said Coraline.

"I wouldn't put it past her," admitted the cat. "Like I said, there's no guarantee she'll play fair." And then he raised his head. "Hullo . . . did you see that?"

"What?"

"Look behind you," said the cat.

The house had flattened out even more. It no longer looked like a photograph—more like a drawing, a crude, charcoal scribble of a house drawn on gray paper.

"Whatever's happening," said Coraline, "thank you for helping with the rat. I suppose I'm almost there, aren't I? So you go off into the mist or wherever you go, and I'll, well, I hope I get to see you at home. If she lets me go home."

The cat's fur was on end, and its tail was bristling like a chimney sweep's brush.

"What's wrong?" asked Coraline.

"They've gone," said the cat. "They aren't there anymore. The ways in and out of this place. They just went flat."

"Is that bad?"

The cat lowered its tail, swishing it from side to side angrily. It made a low growling noise in the back of its throat. It walked in a circle, until it was facing away from Coraline, and then it began to walk backwards, stiffly, one step at a time, until it was pushing up against Coraline's leg. She put down a hand to stroke it, and could feel how hard its heart was beating. It was trembling like a dead leaf in a storm.

"You'll be fine," said Coraline. "Everything's going to be fine. I'll take you home."

The cat said nothing.

"Come on, cat," said Coraline. She took a step back toward the steps, but the cat stayed where it was, looking miserable and, oddly, much smaller.

"If the only way out is past her," said Coraline, "then that's the way we're going to go." She went back to the cat, bent down, and picked it up. The cat did not resist. It simply trembled. She supported its bottom with one hand, rested its front legs on her shoulders. The cat was heavy but not too heavy to carry. It licked at the palm of her hand, where the blood from the scrape was welling up.

Coraline walked up the stairs one step at a time, heading back to her own flat. She was aware of the marbles clicking in her pocket, aware of the stone with a hole in it, aware of the cat pressing itself against her.

She got to her front door—now just a small child's scrawl of a door—and she pushed her hand against it, half expecting that her hand would rip through it, revealing nothing behind it but blackness and a scattering of stars.

But the door swung open, and Coraline went through.

XI.

ONCE INSIDE, IN HER FLAT, or rather, in the flat that was not hers, Coraline was pleased to see that it had not transformed into the empty drawing that the rest of the house seemed to have become. It had depth, and shadows, and someone who stood in the shadows waiting for Coraline to return.

"So you're back," said the other mother. She did not sound pleased. "And you brought vermin with you."

"No," said Coraline. "I brought a friend." She could feel the cat stiffening under her hands, as if it were anxious to be away. Coraline wanted to hold on to it like a teddy bear, for reassurance, but she knew that cats hate to be squeezed, and she suspected that frightened cats were liable to bite and scratch if provoked in any way, even if they were on your side.

"You know I love you," said the other mother flatly.

"You have a very funny way of showing it," said Coraline. She walked down the hallway, then turned into the drawing room, steady step by steady step, pretending that she could not feel the other mother's blank black eyes on her back. Her grandmother's formal furniture was still there, and the painting on the wall of the strange fruit (but now the fruit in the painting had been eaten, and all that remained in the bowl was the browning core of an apple, several plum and peach stones, and the stem of what had formerly been a bunch of grapes). The lion-pawed table raked the carpet with its clawed wooden feet, as if it were impatient for something. At the end of the room, in the corner, stood the wooden door, which had once, in another place, opened onto a plain brick wall. Coraline tried not to stare at it. The window showed nothing but mist.

This was it, Coraline knew. The moment of truth. The unraveling time.

The other mother had followed her in. Now she stood in the center of the room, between Coraline and the mantelpiece, and looked down at Coraline with black button eyes. It was funny, Coraline thought. The other mother did not look anything at all like her own mother. She wondered how she had ever been deceived into imagining a resemblance. The other mother was huge—her head almost brushed the ceiling—and very pale, the color of a spider's belly. Her hair writhed and twined about her head, and her teeth were sharp as knives. . . .

"Well?" said the other mother sharply. "Where are they?"

Coraline leaned against an armchair, adjusted the cat with her left hand, put her right hand into her pocket, and pulled out the three glass marbles. They were a frosted gray, and they clinked together in the palm of her hand. The other mother reached her white fingers for them, but Coraline slipped them back into her pocket. She knew it was true, then. The other mother had no intention of letting her go or of keeping her word. It had been an entertainment, and nothing more. "Hold on," she said. "We aren't finished yet, are we?"

The other mother looked daggers, but she smiled sweetly. "No," she said. "I suppose not. After all, you still need to find your parents, don't you?"

"Yes," said Coraline. *I must not look at the mantelpiece,* she thought. *I must not even think about it.*

"Well?" said the other mother. "Produce them. Would you like to look in the cellar again? I have some other interesting things hidden down there, you know."

"No," said Coraline. "I know where my parents are." The cat was heavy in her arms. She moved it forward, unhooking its claws from her shoulder as she did so.

"Where?"

"It stands to reason," said Coraline. "I've looked

- 129 -

everywhere you'd hide them. They aren't in the house."

The other mother stood very still, giving nothing away, lips tightly closed. She might have been a wax statue. Even her hair had stopped moving.

"So," Coraline continued, both hands wrapped firmly around the black cat. "I know where they have to be. You've hidden them in the passageway between the houses, haven't you? They are behind that door." She nodded her head toward the door in the corner.

The other mother remained statue still, but a hint of a smile crept back onto her face. "Oh, they are, are they?"

"Why don't you open it?" said Coraline. "They'll be there, all right."

It was her only way home, she knew. But it all depended on the other mother's needing to gloat, needing not only to win but to show that she had won.

The other mother reached her hand slowly into her apron pocket and produced the black iron key. The cat stirred uncomfortably in Coraline's arms, as if it wanted to get down. *Just stay there for a few moments longer,* she thought at it, wondering if it could hear her. *I'll get us both home. I said I would. I promise.* She felt the cat relax ever so slightly in her arms.

The other mother walked over to the door and pushed the key into the lock.

She turned the key.

Coraline heard the mechanism *clunk* heavily. She was already starting, as quietly as she could, step by step, to back away toward the mantelpiece.

The other mother pushed down on the door handle and pulled open the door, revealing a corridor behind it, dark and empty. "There," she said, waving her hands at the corridor. The expression of delight on her face was a very bad thing to see. "You're wrong! You *don't* know where your parents are, do you? They aren't there." She turned and looked at Coraline. "Now," she said, "you're going to stay here for ever and always."

"No," said Coraline. "I'm not." And, hard as she could, she threw the black cat toward the other mother. It yowled and landed on the other mother's head, claws flailing, teeth bared, fierce and angry. Fur on end, it looked half again as big as it was in real life.

Without waiting to see what would happen, Coraline reached up to the mantelpiece and closed her hand around the snow globe, pushing it deep into the pocket of her dressing gown.

The cat made a deep, ululating yowl and sank its teeth into the other mother's cheek. She was flailing at it. Blood ran from the cuts on her white face—not red blood but a deep, tarry black stuff. Coraline ran for the door.

She pulled the key out of the lock.

"Leave her! Come on!" she shouted to the cat. It hissed, and swiped its scalpel-sharp claws at the other mother's face in one wild rake which left black ooze trickling from several gashes on the other mother's nose. Then it sprang down toward Coraline. "Quickly!" she said. The cat ran toward her, and they both stepped into the dark corridor.

It was colder in the corridor, like stepping down into a cellar on a warm day. The cat hesitated for a moment; then, seeing the other mother was coming toward them, it ran to Coraline and stopped by her legs.

Coraline began to pull the door closed.

It was heavier than she imagined a door could be, and pulling it closed was like trying to close a door against a high wind. And then she felt something from the other side starting to pull against her.

Shut! she thought. Then she said, out loud, "Come on, *please.*" And she felt the door begin to move, to pull closed, to give against the phantom wind.

Suddenly she was aware of other people in the corridor with her. She could not turn her head to look at them, but she knew them without having to look. "Help me, please," she said. "All of you."

The other people in the corridor—three children, two adults—were somehow too insubstantial to touch the door.

But their hands closed about hers, as she pulled on the big iron door handle, and suddenly she felt strong.

"Never let up, Miss! Hold strong! Hold strong!" whispered a voice in her mind.

"Pull, girl, pull!" whispered another.

And then a voice that sounded like her mother's—her own mother, her real, wonderful, maddening, infuriating, glorious mother—just said, "Well done, Coraline," and that was enough.

The door started to slip closed, easily as anything.

"No!" screamed a voice from beyond the door, and it no longer sounded even faintly human.

Something snatched at Coraline, reaching through the closing gap between the door and the doorpost. Coraline jerked her head out of the way, but the door began to open once more.

"We're going to go home," said Coraline. "We are. Help me." She ducked the snatching fingers.

They moved through her, then: ghost hands lent her strength that she no longer possessed. There was a final moment of resistance, as if something were caught in the door, and then, with a crash, the wooden door banged closed.

Something dropped from Coraline's head height to the floor. It landed with a sort of a scuttling thump.

"Come on!" said the cat. "This is not a good place to be in. Quickly."

Coraline turned her back on the door and began to run, as fast as was practical, through the dark corridor, running her hand along the wall to make sure she didn't bump into anything or get turned around in the darkness.

It was an uphill run, and it seemed to her that it went on for a longer distance than anything could possibly go. The wall she was touching felt warm and yielding now, and, she realized, it felt as if it were covered in a fine downy fur. It moved, as if it were taking a breath. She snatched her hand away from it.

Winds howled in the dark.

She was scared she would bump into something, and she put out her hand for the wall once more. This time what she touched felt hot and wet, as if she had put her hand in somebody's mouth, and she pulled it back with a small wail.

Her eyes had adjusted to the dark. She could half see, as faintly glowing patches ahead of her, two adults, three children. She could hear the cat, too, padding in the dark in front of her.

And there was something else, which suddenly scuttled between her feet, nearly sending Coraline flying. She caught herself before she went down, using her own momentum to keep moving. She knew that if she fell in that corridor she might never get up again. Whatever that corridor was was older by far than the other mother. It was deep, and slow, and it knew that she was there. . . .

Then daylight appeared, and she ran toward it, puffing and wheezing. "Almost there," she called encouragingly, but in the light she discovered that the wraiths had gone, and she was alone. She did not have time to wonder what had happened to them. Panting for breath, she staggered through the door, and slammed it behind her with the loudest, most satisfying bang you can imagine.

Coraline locked the door with the key, and put the key back into her pocket.

The black cat was huddled in the farthest corner of the room, the pink tip of its tongue showing, its eyes wide. Coraline went over to it and crouched down beside it.

"I'm sorry," she said. "I'm sorry I threw you at her. But it was the only way to distract her enough to get us all out. She would never have kept her word, would she?"

The cat looked up at her, then rested its head on her hand, licking her fingers with its sandpapery tongue. It began to purr.

"Then we're friends?" said Coraline.

She sat down on one of her grandmother's uncomfort-able armchairs, and the cat sprang up into her lap and made itself comfortable. The light that came through the picture window was daylight, real golden late-afternoon daylight, not a white mist light. The sky was a robin's-egg blue, and Coraline could see trees and, beyond the trees, green hills, which faded on the horizon into purples and grays. The sky had never seemed so *sky,* the world had never seemed so *world*.

Coraline stared at the leaves on the trees and at the patterns of light and shadow on the cracked bark of the trunk of the beech tree outside the window. Then she looked down at her lap, at the way that the rich sunlight brushed every hair on the cat's head, turning each white whisker to gold.

Nothing, she thought, had ever been so *interesting*.

And, caught up in the interestingness of the world, Coraline barely noticed that she had wriggled down and curled catlike on her grandmother's uncomfortable armchair, nor did she notice when she fell into a deep and dreamless sleep.

XII.

Her mother shook her gently awake.

"Coraline?" she said. "Darling, what a funny place to fall asleep. And really, this room is only for best. We looked all over the house for you."

Coraline stretched and blinked. "I'm sorry," she said. "I fell asleep."

"I can see that," said her mother. "And wherever did the cat come from? He was waiting by the front door when I came in. Shot out like a bullet as I opened it."

"Probably had things to do," said Coraline. Then she hugged her mother so tightly that her arms began to ache. Her mother hugged Coraline back.

"Dinner in fifteen minutes," said her mother. "Don't forget to wash your hands. And just *look* at those pajama bottoms. What did you do to your poor knee?"

"I tripped," said Coraline. She went into the bathroom, and she washed her hands and cleaned her bloody knee. She put ointment on her cuts and scrapes.

She went into her bedroom—her real bedroom, her true

bedroom. She pushed her hands into the pockets of her dressing gown, and she pulled out three marbles, a stone with a hole in it, the black key, and an empty snow globe.

She shook the snow globe and watched the glittery snow swirl through the water to fill the empty world. She put it down and watched the snow fall, covering the place where the little couple had once stood.

Coraline took a piece of string from her toy box, and she strung the black key on the string. Then she knotted the string and hung it around her neck.

"There," she said. She put on some clothes and hid the key under her T-shirt. It was cold against her skin. The stone went into her pocket.

Coraline walked down the hallway to her father's study. He had his back to her, but she knew, just on seeing him, that his eyes, when he turned around, would be her father's kind gray eyes, and she crept over and kissed him on the back of his balding head.

"Hullo, Coraline," he said. Then he looked around and smiled at her. "What was that for?"

"Nothing," said Coraline. "I just miss you sometimes. That's all."

"Oh good," he said. He put the computer to sleep, stood up, and then, for no reason at all, he picked Coraline up, which he had not done for such a long time, not since he had started pointing out to her she was much too old to be carried, and he carried her into the kitchen.

Dinner that night was pizza, and even though it was homemade by her father (so the crust was alternately thick and doughy and raw, or too thin and burnt), and even though he had put slices of green pepper on it, along with little meatballs and, of all things, pineapple chunks, Coraline ate the entire slice she had been given.

Well, she ate everything except for the pineapple chunks.

And soon enough it was bedtime.

Coraline kept the key around her neck, but she put the gray marbles beneath her pillow; and in bed that night, Coraline dreamed a dream.

She was at a picnic, under an old oak tree, in a green meadow. The sun was high in the sky and while there were distant, fluffy white clouds on the horizon, the sky above her head was a deep, untroubled blue.

There was a white linen cloth laid on the grass, with bowls piled high with food—she could see salads and sand-wiches, nuts and fruit, jugs of lemonade and water and thick chocolate milk. Coraline sat on one side of the table-cloth while three other children took a side each. They were dressed in the oddest clothes.

The smallest of them, sitting on Coraline's left, was a boy

with red velvet knee britches and a frilly white shirt. His face was dirty, and he was piling his plate high with boiled new potatoes and with what looked like cold, whole, cooked, trout. "This is the finest of pic-nics, lady," he said to her.

"Yes," said Coraline. "I think it is. I wonder who organized it."

"Why, I rather think you did, Miss," said a tall girl, sitting opposite Coraline. She wore a brown, rather shapeless dress, and had a brown bonnet on her head which tied beneath her chin. "And we are more grateful for it and for all than ever words can say." She was eating slices of bread and jam, deftly cutting the bread from a large golden-brown loaf with a huge knife, then spooning on the purple jam with a wooden spoon. She had jam all around her mouth.

"Aye. This is the finest food I have eaten in centuries," said the girl on Coraline's right. She was a very pale child, dressed in what seemed to be spider's webs, with a circle of glittering silver set in her blonde hair. Coraline could have sworn that the girl had two wings—like dusty silver butterfly wings, not bird wings—coming out of her back. The girl's plate was piled high with pretty flowers. She smiled at Coraline, as if it had been a very long time since she had smiled and she had almost, but not quite, forgotten how.

Coraline found herself liking this girl immensely.

And then, in the way of dreams, the picnic was done and they were playing in the meadow, running and shouting and tossing a glittering ball from one to another. Coraline knew it was a dream then, because none of them ever got tired or winded or out of breath. She wasn't even sweating. They just laughed and ran in a game that was partly tag, partly piggy-in-the-middle, and partly just a magnificent romp.

Three of them ran along the ground, while the pale girl fluttered a little over their heads, swooping down on butterfly wings to grab the ball and swing up again into the sky before she tossed the ball to one of the other children.

And then, without a word about it being spoken, the game was done, and the four of them went back to the picnic cloth, where the lunch dishes had been cleared away, and there were four bowls waiting for them, three of ice cream, one of honeysuckle flowers piled high.

They ate with relish.

"Thank you for coming to my party," said Coraline. "If it is mine."

"The pleasure is ours, Coraline Jones," said the winged girl, nibbling another honeysuckle blossom. "If there were but something we could do for you, to thank you and to reward you."

"Aye," said the boy with the red velvet britches and the

dirty face. He put out his hand and held Coraline's hand with his own. It was warm now.

"It's a very fine thing you did for us, Miss," said the tall girl. She now had a smear of chocolate ice cream all around her lips.

"I'm just pleased it's all over," said Coraline.

Was it her imagination, or did a shadow cross the faces of the other children at the picnic?

The winged girl, the circlet in her hair glittering like a star, rested her fingers for a moment on the back of Coraline's hand. "It is over and done with for *us*," she said. "This is our staging post. From here, we three will set out for uncharted lands, and what comes after no one alive can say. . . ." She stopped talking.

"There's a *but*, isn't there?" said Coraline. "I can feel it. Like a rain cloud."

The boy on her left tried to smile bravely, but his lower lip began to tremble and he bit it with his upper teeth and said nothing. The girl in the brown bonnet shifted uncomfortably and said, "Yes, Miss."

"But I got you three back," said Coraline. "I got Mum and Dad back. I shut the door. I locked it. What more was I meant to do?"

The boy squeezed Coraline's hand with his. She found herself remembering when it had been she, trying to reassure him, when he was little more than a cold memory in the darkness.

"Well, can't you give me a clue?" asked Coraline. "Isn't there *something* you can tell me?"

"The beldam swore by her good right hand," said the tall girl, "but she lied."

"M-my governess," said the boy, "used to say that nobody is ever given more to shoulder than he or she can bear." He shrugged as he said this, as if he had not yet made his own mind up whether or not it was true.

"We wish you luck," said the winged girl. "Good fortune and wisdom and courage—although you have already shown that you have all three of these blessings, and in abundance."

"She hates you," blurted out the boy. "She hasn't lost anything for so long. Be wise. Be brave. Be tricky."

"But it's not *fair*," said Coraline, in her dream, angrily. "It's just not *fair*. It should be over."

The boy with the dirty face stood up and hugged Coraline tightly. "Take comfort in this," he whispered. "Th'art alive. Thou livest."

And in her dream Coraline saw that the sun had set and the stars were twinkling in the darkening sky.

Coraline stood in the meadow, and she watched as the three children (two of them walking, one flying) went away from her across the grass, silver in the light of the huge moon.

The three of them came to a small wooden bridge over a stream. They stopped there and turned and waved, and Coraline waved back.

And what came after was darkness.

Coraline woke in the early hours of the morning, convinced she had heard something moving, but unsure what it was.

She waited.

Something made a rustling noise outside her bedroom door. She wondered if it was a rat. The door rattled. Coraline clambered out of bed.

"Go away," said Coraline sharply. "Go away or you'll be sorry."

There was a pause, then the whatever it was scuttled away down the hall. There was something odd and irregular about its footsteps, if they *were* footsteps. Coraline found herself wondering if it was perhaps a rat with an extra leg. . . .

"It isn't over, is it?" she said to herself.

Then she opened the bedroom door. The gray, predawn light showed her the whole of the corridor, completely deserted.

She went toward the front door, sparing a hasty glance back at the wardrobe-door mirror hanging on the wall at the other end of the hallway, seeing nothing but her own pale face staring back at her, looking sleepy and serious. Gentle, reassuring snores came from her parents' room, but the door was closed. All the doors off the corridor were closed. Whatever the scuttling thing was, it had to be here somewhere.

Coraline opened the front door and looked at the gray sky. She wondered how long it would be until the sun came up, wondered whether her dream had been a true thing while knowing in her heart that it had been. Something she had taken to be part of the shadows under the hall couch detached itself from beneath the couch and made a mad, scrabbling rush on its long white legs, heading for the front door.

Coraline's mouth dropped open in horror and she stepped out of the way as the thing clicked and scuttled past her and out of the house, running crablike on its too-many tapping, clicking, scurrying feet.

She knew what it was, and she knew what it was after. She had seen it too many times in the last few days, reaching and clutching and snatching and popping blackbeetles obediently into the other mother's mouth. Five-footed, crimson-nailed, the color of bone.

It was the other mother's right hand.

It wanted the black key.

XIII.

CORALINE'S PARENTS NEVER SEEMED to remember anything about their time in the snow globe. At least, they never said anything about it, and Coraline never mentioned it to them.

Sometimes she wondered whether they had ever noticed that they had lost two days in the real world, and came to the eventual conclusion that they had not. Then again, there are some people who keep track of every day and every hour, and there are people who don't, and Coraline's parents were solidly in the second camp.

Coraline had placed the marbles beneath her pillow before she went to sleep that first night home in her own room once more. She went back to bed after she saw the other mother's hand, although there was not much time left for sleeping, and she rested her head back on that pillow.

Something scrunched gently as she did.

She sat up, and lifted the pillow. The fragments of the glass marbles that she saw looked like the remains of eggshells one finds beneath trees in springtime: like empty, broken robin's eggs, or even more delicate—wren's eggs, perhaps.

Whatever had been inside the glass spheres had gone. Coraline thought of the three children waving good-bye to her in the moonlight, waving before they crossed that silver stream.

She gathered up the eggshell-thin fragments with care and placed them in a small blue box which had once held a bracelet that her grandmother had given her when she was a little girl. The bracelet was long lost, but the box remained.

Miss Spink and Miss Forcible came back from visiting Miss Spink's niece, and Coraline went down to their flat for tea. It was a Monday. On Wednesday Coraline would go back to school: a whole new school year would begin.

Miss Forcible insisted on reading Coraline's tea leaves.

"Well, looks like everything's mostly shipshape and Bristol fashion, luvvy," said Miss Forcible.

"Sorry?" said Coraline.

"Everything is coming up roses," said Miss Forcible. "Well, almost everything. I'm not sure what *that* is." She pointed to a clump of tea leaves sticking to the side of the cup.

Miss Spink tutted and reached for the cup. "Honestly,

Miriam. Give it over here. Let me see. . . ."

She blinked through her thick spectacles. "Oh dear. No, I have no idea what that signifies. It looks almost like a hand."

Coraline looked. The clump of leaves did look a little like a hand, reaching for something.

Hamish the Scottie dog was hiding under Miss Forcible's chair, and he wouldn't come out.

"I think he was in some sort of fight," said Miss Spink. "He has a deep gash in his side, poor dear. We'll take him to the vet later this afternoon. I wish I knew what could have done it."

Something, Coraline knew, would have to be done.

That final week of the holidays, the weather was magnificent, as if the summer itself were trying to make up for the miserable weather they had been having by giving them some bright and glorious days before it ended.

The crazy old man upstairs called down to Coraline when he saw her coming out of Miss Spink and Miss Forcible's flat.

"Hey! Hi! You! Caroline!" he shouted over the railing.

"It's Coraline," she said. "How are the mice?"

"Something has frightened them," said the old man, scratching his mustache. "I think maybe there is a weasel in the house. Something is about. I heard it in the night. In my country we would have put down a trap for it, maybe put down a little meat or hamburger, and when the creature comes to feast, then—bam!—it would be caught and never bother us more. The mice are so scared they will not even pick up their little musical instruments."

"I don't think it wants meat," said Coraline. She put her hand up and touched the black key that hung about her neck. Then she went inside.

She bathed herself, and kept the key around her neck the whole time she was in the bath. She never took it off anymore.

Something scratched at her bedroom window after she went to bed. Coraline was almost asleep, but she slipped out of her bed and pulled open the curtains. A white hand with crimson fingernails leapt from the window ledge onto a drainpipe and was immediately out of sight. There were deep gouges in the glass on the other side of the window.

Coraline slept uneasily that night, waking from time to time to plot and plan and ponder, then falling back into sleep, never quite certain where her pondering ended and the dream began, one ear always open for the sound of something scratching at her windowpane or at her bedroom door.

In the morning Coraline said to her mother, "I'm going

to have a picnic with my dolls today. Can I borrow a sheet—an old one, one you don't need any longer—as a tablecloth?"

"I don't think we have one of those," said her mother. She opened the kitchen drawer that held the napkins and the tablecloths, and she prodded about in it. "Hold on. Will this do?"

It was a folded-up disposable paper tablecloth covered with red flowers, left over from some picnic they had been on several years before.

"That's perfect," said Coraline.

"I didn't think you played with your dolls anymore," said Mrs. Jones.

"I don't," admitted Coraline. "They're protective coloration."

"Well, be back in time for lunch," said her mother. "Have a good time."

Coraline filled a cardboard box with dolls and with several plastic doll's teacups. She filled a jug with water.

Then she went outside. She walked down to the road, just as if she were going to the shops. Before she reached the supermarket she cut across a fence into some wasteland and along an old drive, then crawled under a hedge. She had to go under the hedge in two journeys in order not to spill the water from the jug.

It was a long, roundabout looping journey, but at the end of it Coraline was satisfied that she had not been followed.

She came out behind the dilapidated old tennis court. She crossed over it, to the meadow where the long grass swayed. She found the planks on the edge of the meadow. They were astonishingly heavy—almost too heavy for a girl to lift, even using all her strength, but she managed. She didn't have any choice. She pulled the planks out of the way, one by one, grunting and sweating with the effort, revealing a deep, round, brick-lined hole in the ground. It smelled of damp and the dark. The bricks were greenish, and slippery.

She spread out the tablecloth and laid it, carefully, over the top of the well. She put a plastic doll's cup every foot or so, at the edge of the well, and she weighed each cup down with water from the jug.

She put a doll in the grass beside each cup, making it look as much like a doll's tea party as she could. Then she retraced her steps, back under the hedge, along the dusty yellow drive, around the back of the shops, back to her house.

She reached up and took the key from around her neck. She dangled it from the string, as if the key were just something she liked to play with. Then she knocked on the door of Miss Spink and Miss Forcible's flat.

Miss Spink opened the door.

"Hello dear," she said.

"I don't want to come in," said Coraline. "I just wanted to find out how Hamish was doing."

Miss Spink sighed. "The vet says that Hamish is a brave little soldier," she said. "Luckily, the cut doesn't seem to be infected. We cannot imagine what could have done it. The vet says some animal, he thinks, but has no idea what. Mister Bobo says he thinks it might have been a weasel."

"Mister Bobo?"

"The man in the top flat. Mister Bobo. Fine old circus family, I believe. Romanian or Slovenian or Livonian, or one of those countries. Bless me, I can never remember them anymore."

It had never occurred to Coraline that the crazy old man upstairs actually had a name, she realized. If she'd known his name was Mr. Bobo she would have said it every chance she got. How often do you get to say a name like "Mr. Bobo" aloud?

"Oh," said Coraline to Miss Spink. "Mister Bobo. Right. Well," she said, a little louder, "I'm going to go and play with my dolls now, over by the old tennis court, round the back."

"That's nice, dear," said Miss Spink. Then she added

confidentially, "Make sure you keep an eye out for the old well. Mister Lovat, who was here before your time, said that he thought it might go down for half a mile or more."

Coraline hoped that the hand had not heard this last, and she changed the subject. "This key?" said Coraline loudly. "Oh, it's just some old key from our house. It's part of my game. That's why I'm carrying it around with me on this piece of string. Well, good-bye now."

"What an extraordinary child," said Miss Spink to herself as she closed the door.

Coraline ambled across the meadow toward the old tennis court, dangling and swinging the black key on its piece of string as she walked.

Several times she thought she saw something the color of bone in the undergrowth. It was keeping pace with her, about thirty feet away.

She tried to whistle, but nothing happened, so she sang out loud instead, a song her father had made up for her when she was a little baby and which had always made her laugh. It went,

Oh—my twitchy witchy girl
I think you are so nice,
I give you bowls of porridge
And I give you bowls of ice

Cream.
I give you lots of kisses,
And I give you lots of hugs,
But I never give you sandwiches
With bugs
In.

That was what she sang as she sauntered through the woods, and her voice hardly trembled at all.

The dolls' tea party was where she had left it. She was relieved that it was not a windy day, for everything was still in its place, every water-filled plastic cup weighed down the paper tablecloth as it was meant to. She breathed a sigh of relief.

Now was the hardest part.

"Hello dolls," she said brightly. "It's teatime!"

She walked close to the paper tablecloth. "I brought the lucky key," she told the dolls, "to make sure we have a good picnic."

And then, as carefully as she could, she leaned over and, gently, placed the key on the tablecloth. She was still holding on to the string. She held her breath, hoping that the cups of water at the edges of the well would weigh the cloth down, letting it take the weight of the key without collapsing into the well.

The key sat in the middle of the paper picnic cloth. Coraline let go of the string, and took a step back. Now it was all up to the hand.

She turned to her dolls.

"Who would like a piece of cherry cake?" she asked. "Jemima? Pinky? Primrose?" and she served each doll a slice of invisible cake on an invisible plate, chattering happily as she did so.

From the corner of her eye she saw something bone white scamper from one tree trunk to another, closer and closer. She forced herself not to look at it.

"Jemima!" said Coraline. "What a bad girl you are! You've dropped your cake! Now I'll have to go over and get you a whole new slice!" And she walked around the tea party until she was on the other side of it to the hand. She pretended to clean up spilled cake, and to get Jemima another piece.

And then, in a skittering, chittering rush, it came. The hand, running high on its fingertips, scrabbled through the tall grass and up onto a tree stump. It stood there for a moment, like a crab tasting the air, and then it made one triumphant, nail-clacking leap onto the center of the paper tablecloth.

Time slowed for Coraline. The white fingers closed around the black key. . . .

And then the weight and the momentum of the hand sent the plastic dolls' cups flying, and the paper tablecloth, the key, and the other mother's right hand went tumbling down into the darkness of the well.

Coraline counted slowly under her breath. She got up to forty before she heard a muffled splash coming from a long way below.

Someone had once told her that if you look up at the sky from the bottom of a mine shaft, even in the brightest daylight, you see a night sky and stars. Coraline wondered if the hand could see stars from where it was.

She hauled the heavy planks back onto the well, covering it as carefully as she could. She didn't want anything to fall in. She didn't want anything ever to get out.

Then she put her dolls and the cups back in the cardboard box she had carried them out in. Something caught her eye while she was doing this, and she straightened up in time to see the black cat stalking toward her, its tail held high and curling at the tip like a question mark. It was the first time she had seen the cat in several days, since they had returned together from the other mother's place.

The cat walked over to her and jumped up onto the planks that covered the well. Then, slowly, it winked one eye at her.

It sprang down into the long grass in front of her, and

rolled over onto its back, wiggling about ecstatically.

Coraline scratched and tickled the soft fur on its belly, and the cat purred contentedly. When it had had enough it rolled over onto its front once more and walked back toward the tennis court, like a tiny patch of midnight in the midday sun.

Coraline went back to the house.

Mr. Bobo was waiting for her in the driveway. He clapped her on the shoulder.

"The mice tell me that all is good," he said. "They say that you are our savior, Caroline."

"It's Coraline, Mister Bobo," said Coraline. "Not Caroline. *Coraline*."

"Coraline," said Mr. Bobo, repeating her name to himself with wonderment and respect. "Very good, Coraline. The mice say that I must tell you that as soon as they are ready to perform in public, you will come up and watch them as the first audience of all. They will play *tumpty umpty* and *toodle oodle*, and they will dance, and do a thousand tricks. That *is* what is they say."

"I would like that very much," said Coraline. "When they're ready."

She knocked at Miss Spink and Miss Forcible's door. Miss Spink let her in and Coraline went into their parlor. She put her box of dolls down on the floor. Then she put her hand into her pocket and pulled out the stone with the hole in it.

"Here you go," she said. "I don't need it anymore. I'm very grateful. I think it may have saved my life, and saved some other people's death."

She gave them both tight hugs, although her arms barely stretched around Miss Spink, and Miss Forcible smelled like the raw garlic she had been cutting. Then Coraline picked up her box of dolls and went out.

"What an extraordinary child," said Miss Spink. No one had hugged her like that since she had retired from the theater.

That night Coraline lay in bed, all bathed, teeth cleaned, with her eyes open, staring up at the ceiling.

It was warm enough that, now that the hand was gone, she had opened her bedroom window wide. She had insisted to her father that the curtains not be entirely closed.

Her new school clothes were laid out carefully on her chair for her to put on when she woke.

Normally, on the night before the first day of term, Coraline was apprehensive and nervous. But, she realized, there was nothing left about school that could scare her anymore.

She fancied she could hear sweet music on the night air:

the kind of music that can only be played on the tiniest silver trombones and trumpets and bassoons, on piccolos and tubas so delicate and small that their keys could only be pressed by the tiny pink fingers of white mice.

Coraline imagined that she was back again in her dream, with the two girls and the boy under the oak tree in the meadow, and she smiled.

As the first stars came out Coraline finally allowed herself to drift into sleep, while the gentle upstairs music of the mouse circus spilled out onto the warm evening air, telling the world that the summer was almost done.

From Visionary Director
Henry Selick
& Best Selling author
Neil Gaiman
Coming Soon To Theaters Everywhere
In Never-Been-Done-Before, eye-Popping 3-D
Coraline
Screenplay by Henry Selick
LAIKA
FOCUS FEATURES
©2008 Focus Features. All Rights Reserved.